JUST KIDS

FROM THE

BRONX

JUST KIDS

FROM THE

BRONX

TELLING IT THE WAY IT WAS

An Oral History

Arlene Alda

Henry Holt and Company
New York

Henry Holt and Company, LLC
Publishers since 1866
175 Fifth Avenue
New York, New York 10010
www.henryholt.com

Henry Holt® and 🏛® are registered trademarks
of Henry Holt and Company, LLC.

Library of Congress Cataloging-in-Publication Data

Alda, Arlene, 1933–
  Just kids from the Bronx : telling it the way it was : an oral history / Arlene Alda.—
First edition.
        pages cm
    ISBN 978-1-62779-095-6 (hardback)—ISBN 978-1-62779-096-3 (electronic
book)   1. Bronx (New York, N.Y.)—Biography.   2. New York (N.Y.)—
Biography.   3. Successful people—New York (State)—New York—Biography.
4. Oral history—New York (State)—New York.   5. Children—New York (State)—
New York—Social life and customs.   6. Bronx (New York, N.Y.)—Social life and
customs.   7. New York (N.Y.)—Social life and customs.
I. Title.
    F128.68.B8A49 2015
    974.7'275—dc23   2014022247

Henry Holt books are available for special promotions and premiums.
For details contact: Director, Special Markets.

First Edition 2015

Photo page 82 David Corio/Michael Ochs Archives/Getty Images
Map by Laura Hartman Maestro, born in the Bronx
Designed by Meryl Sussman Levavi

Printed in the United States of America

3   5   7   9   10   8   6   4   2

To the young writers and scientists and artists
and musicians and actors and educators and
doctors and lawyers and nurses and sports
figures and business people and politicians
who are the future of the Bronx . . .

and to the memory of my parents who
had the good sense to move to the
Bronx in the first place.

THE KIDS

PART TWO | I SAY IT'S THE TEACHERS . . . DESTINY

"Stories have to be told or they die, and when they die, we can't remember who we are or why we're here."

—Sue Monk Kidd, *The Secret Life of Bees*

FOREWORD

A FEW SUMMERS AGO, MY HUSBAND, ALAN, AND I WERE AT A friend's house on Long Island, having predinner snacks and drinks, when I heard the words ". . . in the Bronx," said by Millard ("Mickey") Drexler, whom I'd met for the first time minutes before.

"Are you from the Bronx?" I asked.

"I'm from the Northeast. Barnes and Arnow Avenues," Mickey answered.

"You're kidding. Which building?"

"The Mayflower," he said.

"That's unbelievable! That's my building."

We tried to figure out why we hadn't met when we were kids. The Mayflower has ninety-six apartments. That's a lot of people, but the age difference (I'm eleven years older) was probably the biggest factor. When I was in high school Mickey was a toddler. That age gap disappeared completely when we talked nonstop like long-lost friends at dinnertime, deciding that it would be fun to go back to the Mayflower together.

So a few months later we went, new buddies revisiting our old building. Alan, Mickey's cousin, and a few of Mickey's longtime friends from the neighborhood came with us. It had been well over fifty years since either Mickey or I had lived in the Mayflower and thirty years since I had last visited. Would Mickey be able to see his old apartment? (No. No one answered the doorbell when he rang.) What did the Mayflower look like now, seen with our grown-up sensibilities? (On the outside, the same as ever. A six-story, tan and brown brick building, taking up half a city block.)

Mickey, chairman and CEO of J.Crew, led the way inside, the rest of us following. The lobby looked stark—a big contrast to my upscale Manhattan apartment building, with its lobby furniture, area rugs, and walls hung with art. The simple Mayflower interior served as a pointed reminder of the unexpected turns my life had taken. Still, I felt totally at home seeing the familiar, worn terrazzo stairways and floor of the old building, which triggered vivid childhood memories. *Energetic girl on a rainy day, running and jumping in the hallways. Bouncing a ball. Noises echoing. Typical working-class Bronx Jewish first-generation kid. Me.* I clearly saw and heard myself as that ten-year-old girl again, tossing my beloved Spaldeen ball.

Mickey and I began comparing notes about our families and our oh-too-small apartments. I was fascinated by his stories—of his aunt Frances and how she became his renegade role model; of how, when he attended the Bronx High School of Science, he first started getting knowledge of lives different from his own. Lives where some kids even had their own bedrooms and where the family expectation was that the children, without a doubt, would go to college. Standing with Mickey, a picture of confidence and success, in our shopworn surroundings, both of us excited about comparing stories about our pasts, started me wondering about other interesting and accomplished people from the Bronx. What were *their* stories? What were *their* childhoods like? Who influenced them? How did they find a place for themselves in the larger world, the one beyond their own Bronx neighborhoods?

The idea for *Just Kids from the Bronx* was beginning to hatch.

I started out cautiously by interviewing only friends. Mickey was among the first "kids" I talked with. Two longtime pals of mine, the producers Martin Bregman and David Yarnell, were also delighted to be included in my project. Regis Philbin, both a friend and a wonderful storyteller who lives down the hall from me in our Manhattan building, eagerly said, "I'll be happy to talk to you. I had a great childhood in the Bronx." The enthusiasm they all showed for the project, along with the comic adventures described in those initial interviews, launched this book. Friends then recommended friends, and acquaintances mentioned names they had recognized but didn't know personally—"Did you talk to So-and so?" I knew my growing helter-skelter list of names excluded many who were worthy and interesting, which meant this book was not to be a comprehensive history of all the great people of the Bronx. But happily, this informally gathered group hinted at the actual changing demographic of the borough over the years, which went from being predominantly Jewish, Italian, and Irish in the earlier part of the twentieth century to the current majority populations of African Americans and Hispanics, all of them sharing some pride in the borough that helped raise them. When I talked with Joel Arthur Rosenthal (JAR), the only living jewelry designer to have a retrospective of his work at New York's Metropolitan Museum of Art, he said, "I'm glad that you're doing a book about the Bronx. I'm sick and tired of hearing about Brooklyn."

I EDITED THE conversational interviews, taking care to preserve each person's own wording. I arranged the material chronologically, so the differences and similarities in each person's life, along with the changes in the Bronx itself, would be more apparent. As the volume of candid, personal stories grew, I found I was deeply touched and gratified by the trust these wonderful Bronxites had in me, basically a stranger to most of them.

I became riveted as the three graffiti artists of Tats Cru told of their exploits in the 1970s and '80s, and what it meant to them to have people see their art on the outside of the number 6 train, rolling from the Bronx all the way through Manhattan, into Brooklyn, and then back again to the Bronx. I was transported by Al Pacino's lyric description of the sounds of the world on his roof in the 1940s: "And at night—at night, there was this cacophony of voices, especially in the late spring to late summer. You would hear the different accents. We had them all. There were Italians, Jews, Irish, Polish, German. It was like a Eugene O'Neill play."

I laughed, with total surprise, when David Yarnell told me about his risky exploits in the '40s, secretly growing marijuana in Bronx Park. Teenagers did things like that then? And then there was the eight-year-old Ken Davidson, in the '50s, playing with his young band of buddies in the rocky, empty lot next to their apartment house, setting fires—literally playing with fire, despite his mother's warning, "You could burn your eyes out."

I was moved and informed by Neil deGrasse Tyson's descriptions of his experiences with racism when he was an innocent and unsuspecting preteen. Similarly, I was appalled by the not so subtle racism that Joyce Hansen encountered in high school when her college guidance counselor said college was for smart kids and therefore not for her.

And who knew that the Bronx River was home to an important population of giant snapping turtles? For Erik Zeidler, born in 1991 and still living in the Bronx today, exploring the Bronx River "was like opening presents when you're not sure what the present will be, whether it's going to be something you really want or nothing. Seeing and finding these giant turtles in the river is a present I'll never forget."

Hearing Erik talk about the turtles in the Bronx River reminded me that there is more parkland in the Bronx—25 percent of the place—than in any other borough of New York City. I was lucky enough to grow up about seven blocks away from

Bronx Park, where the Bronx River flows, and which is also home to the world-class Bronx Zoo and the New York Botanical Garden. I was naively happy then and am humbly grateful now that, although I lived in a more or less urban community, I could explore the park, which first sparked my abiding love of flowers.

SOMETIMES OUT-OF-TOWN FRIENDS ask, "The Bronx. Exactly where is it?"

"You know," I say, "the Bronx is up, the Battery's down, like in the Comden and Green lyrics."

The Bronx is the northernmost of New York City's five boroughs. It was incorporated into the city at large in 1898, and it is the only borough on the mainland. The other four boroughs are either islands or attached to Long Island.

The Bronx got its name from one of its first settlers, a seventeenth-century Scandinavian named Jonas Bronck, whose lineage has been traced to Sweden and Denmark. He arrived in New Netherland in 1639, farmed some six hundred acres in what is now the Mott Haven section, and his tract was known as Bronck's Land. The river ran south of Bronck's Land and, with a change in the spelling, the river and eventually the whole borough were named after him.

The separate Bronx villages that arose long after Jonas Bronck's life and times evolved into neighborhoods . . . communities that were like hometowns. And as in other hometowns across the country, the dwellers knew most everyone and most everyone knew them. Though the people whose stories I listened to for this book came from many different neighborhoods and grew up in different decades, all of them came from places where parents and neighbors, schools and teachers, stores and storekeepers, houses of worship and clergy were important parts of their lives.

By the time I finished editing the more than sixty interviews, from ninety-two-year-old Carl Reiner's to twenty-three-year-old Erik Zeidler's, I was delighted to see an additional narrative emerging, one of changing decades and disparate times linking arms with one another. Children of Jewish, Italian, and Irish immigrants giving way to children of African American, Puerto Rican, and Dominican newcomers, and I felt moved and connected to them all.

During World War Two, Avery Corman played stickball in the streets, using the simple treasures of a Spaldeen ball and a broom handle for a bat. Even though I was a girl, and girls didn't play stickball then, those were my years of carefree playing in the streets too. Years later, similar games continued with even poorer kids creating their ball out of recyclables. As hip-hop's Grandmaster Melle Mel, born Melvin Glover, told it, "We'd take a milk container and a soda bottle and wrap the soda bottle in newspaper and stuff the soda bottle inside the milk container and shape it like a football." Yes! I could imagine doing that as well, if I had to.

For more than a hundred years the Bronx has been associated with the Yankees, the Bronx Bombers. And across the generations so many Bronx kids, me included, cheered them on, with many of the boys dreaming of playing pro ball. Bobby Bonilla, who spoke of his "indescribable love" for his supportive father, was able to realize his baseball-player dreams. And Michael Kay, fueled by an intense love of the Yankees and by his own resourcefulness, figured out early on how to get involved. "I was practical and rational, even as a nine-year-old," he told me. *"If I'm gonna be part of the Yankees, I'm gonna be that broadcaster!* So I'd interview my friends with a tape recorder." Michael Kay himself hit a metaphorical home run when he grew up to become a sports journalist and Yankees broadcaster.

THE BRONX STORYTELLERS in this book have found their niches in the fields of religion, law, education, entertainment, business, finance, science, medicine, government, politics, sports, acting, music, drawing, photography, architecture, graphic design, journalism, cartooning, writing, and dancing. Both in spirit and in fact, with their contributions to the larger community, they exemplify possibility. I am so grateful for what started out as a lark, just a fun trip back to the Mayflower. It led to one of the richest experiences of my life: the meeting of the people in and the making of *Just Kids from the Bronx: Telling It the Way It Was, An Oral History.*

ARLENE ALDA

JUST KIDS

FROM THE

BRONX

PART ONE

FRESH AIR...
A LUCKY BREAK

I knew that I wanted to be someone.... I wanted to be revered by the family ... not only by my immediate one, but my extended family as well.... They all were so excited when I finished medical school that they had this large party for me. I still have the pictures. Actually, it spawned many other doctors in the family whose fathers said to them, "Forget about being a wallpaper hanger. If Mickey could do it, then you could do it!"

—MICHAEL ("MICKEY") BRESCIA, M.D.

A. M. ("ABE") ROSENTHAL

Pulitzer Prize–winning correspondent and longtime
executive editor of the New York Times

(1922–2006)

FOR SEVEN YEARS I LIVED WITH MY FIVE SISTERS AND OUR PAR-
ents, Sarah and Harry, among flowers and trees, dancing foun-
tains, wilderness paths, birds singing in their ecstasy, and such
stupendous quantities of a particular treasure as to send my mother
into paroxysms of acquisition greed.

"Fresh air!" she would announce. And then from her lips came
the command that rang through every apartment in the Bronx
neighborhood every day: "Go grab some fresh air! Out! Fresh air!"

As other American pioneers and gamblers kept moving west,

the Jews of New York kept moving north toward fresh air. For Harry and his Pirate Queen the road led from the tenements of the Lower East Side in Manhattan to Decatur Avenue in the Bronx, where young warriors waited in ambush to pounce on the new kids and eventually declare peace. The adult pioneers worked six days a week and every hour of overtime they could get. They saved every penny with pleasure, looking down from the peak above the sea to the pass above the fruited plain-Mosholu Parkway station, far north, only a few miles south of the New York suburbs boundary line.

Beyond the station, as far as a housepainter's eye could see, stretched Van Cortlandt Park. The ride on the subway was usually an hour or more each way. Coming home, fresh air awaited, ready to be consumed in large gulps, a reservoir never dry. And during the day, breathing the paint or the lint, a workingman knew that at least at home the wife and the children were breathing that fresh air, all day long.

The pioneers stood and gazed at their children and then went to the bank with their deposit books every few months.

Paradise was known as the Amalgamated, for the Amalgamated Clothing Workers union, which built good housing for its members. Members of other unions were eligible to buy apartments too. Papa's credentials were his card in the housepainters' union and the bankbook of his life savings.

By the time we moved into our apartment Sarah and Harry had been on the waiting list for about two years.

They both knew Harry would make a living as long as he could climb a painter's ladder or crawl out a window to a scaffold. With overtime here and there he could come up with the eighty dollars a month to meet the maintenance charges. They never again might have such a chance, a great park across the street, four bedrooms, living room, nice big kitchen, and "double exposures," which gave the apartment cross ventilation from the breezes of park-fresh air whenever you raised a window sash.

Harry and Sarah went to the savings bank, took out one thousand dollars, almost all the money they had saved. They took the cash to the office of the union cooperative and put it on the table. They were gambling that money, and every dollar they would be able to put together from Harry's work, for God knows how many years. They figured that with good luck some months Harry would make enough to pay off some of the cooperative's loan for the rest of the apartment, in addition to the maintenance. In the months he was short, the building management would almost always wait another month.

We lived in those co-op buildings the first years of the thirties, when the only thing thriving in America was hard times. The eight complexes consisted of half a dozen six-story apartment buildings, each built around a courtyard that blossomed in the spring and flowered almost until the snow provided inexhaustible hills of snowball and snowman. Just across the street was our forest, Van Cortlandt Park, which not only sent out sweet perfumed fresh air for generations of workers' children twenty-four hours a day but also provided a golfing link. Golfers, who were not experts, hit balls into the hands of boys waiting to scoop them up and run to return them for a nickel apiece.

Twenty-five years later, when I was an American correspondent in Eastern Europe, I saw Polish workers and their wives in a shabby seaside resort on the Baltic going for a walk in the nearby forest or marching for hours along the narrow beach, up and down, up and down. They went back to the little boardinghouses for meals and rushed outside as soon as they could for what else? Fresh air. Then they sat in wooden chairs to put their faces into the pallid sunshine. That week on the Polish Baltic I was a boy again and the workers were my parents.

In 1967 I was appointed an assistant managing editor of the *New York Times* and immediately set off for Europe to share the magic moment in journalistic history with the foreign staff of the paper.

The first stop was London, where Anthony Lewis, then the

bureau chief and a brilliant correspondent of lucidity and range, gave a dinner party for me at the Garrick Club. During the cocktail hour there was one of those sudden drops in the noise level and the voice of a British member of the staff could be heard clear and true as a royal trumpet: "Tell me, Abe, do you think there will ever be a Jewish managing editor of the *New York Times?*"

Everybody froze, glass in hand, a living tableau. I turned slowly, martini still half raised, heard myself say, "Well, I sure as hell hope so." There were a few titters, and somebody decided it was time for dinner.

Sure enough, justice triumphed, and a couple of years later I was back in London, this time to celebrate with the crowned heads of Europe my appointment as managing editor.

The morning after my arrival, I picked up a copy of the *Times* of London outside my hotel room door—Claridge's—saw "Up from the Slums of the Bronx to the Editor's Chair, Page 3" on the front page. I knew they were singing my song and turned the page.

I saw it at once: a long story from the Washington correspondent of the *Times*, a kind of strange-customs-in-faraway-places piece in which the writer tried to explain to the British public exactly how it had come about that a poor boy from a slum in an exotic part of New York seldom visited by tourists, who attended a free college with the social prestige of a herring, whose parents were born in Russia and who also happened to be, well, Jewish, actually became managing editor of the most important, powerful, and prestigious newspaper in the United States.

It was written with a sense of kindly wonderment, as if explaining the customs of Ugandan tribesmen to the British audience.

There was a certain poignancy in the piece, discernible perhaps to only two people: the author and me. The writer was Louis Heren, who had been the correspondent in India of the *Times* of London during my years there. He had told me often that though he stood high in the regard of the proprietors of the *Times* of

London, he and they knew he could never become its editor. He was born a Roman Catholic and had compounded that initial error by attending the wrong schools.

I sent Louis Heren a message of thanks, also informing him that the Pirate Queen would have been furious if she knew that Mosholu Parkway* would ever be described as a slum.

∽

Note: This excerpt from Abe Rosenthal's unpublished memoir is printed here with permission from Shirley Lord Rosenthal. It is the only contribution in this book, aside from my own, not derived from a live interview.

---

*The Mosholu Parkway area was considered to be one of the more beautiful sections of the Bronx, a section where trafficked roads were, and still are, bordered by wide expanses of parkland. Mosholu Parkway has the Grand Concourse and Van Cortlandt Park to the west and Bronx Park, the New York Botanical Gardens, and the Bronx Zoo to the east.

CARL REINER

Award-winning actor, writer, director,
producer, and comedian

(1922–)

My father wasn't a joiner, so we were never synagogue members. When I turned thirteen, he persuaded a rabbi to rent him a synagogue in a poor neighborhood for a Thursday morning bar mitzvah for me. My only training for the event had been with another rabbi who, for a few months, was willing to teach me what I needed to know. My father, my mother, my older brother Charlie, and a group of strangers, old Jews with beards and prayer shawls, were the only ones who attended when the time arrived.

And it wasn't like today, where kids write their own speeches. My father wrote the speech for me, in both flowery language and beautiful handwriting. "Worthy Assembly. You've afforded me a great honor this day, when you have come to this temple of God to take part in and celebrate on the day I have become a bar mitzvah." It went on in the same manner, ending with "May God be with you in my endeavor to be a good member of society and a good Jew. Amen." This speech was actually the same one my father had written for my brother Charlie, who had said it at his bar mitzvah a few years earlier.

Over seventy years go by when a granddaughter of our old neighbors the Fishmans contacts me out of the blue with something she thinks I'll be interested in. It turns out to be her family's copy of that same speech in my father's own handwriting. My father had written it out for the bar mitzvah of Murray Fishman, her father, who was a year younger than I was. So that speech was delivered at three different bar mitzvahs at three different times.

I was thirteen and officially a Jewish man in the eyes of the elders, but my friends, who were older and maybe more religious than I, had already taken part in a minyan, a group of ten adult male Jews who get together for prayers. There have to be a minimum of ten or the prayers won't be valid. If I saw men in our neighborhood with prayer shawls, I quickly crossed the street. I always dodged being part of a minyan, especially since I had learned only what I needed to learn for my bar mitzvah by rote. I knew no Hebrew. I couldn't read the prayers.

But one day I was with my friends walking down our street when we were all called in for a minyan. Since I was part of the group I couldn't escape. I had no choice. When everyone else started praying, I didn't know what to do, so I prayed too—but in Hebrew double-talk. My guilt lasted many years, because at the time I thought that I was preventing the prayers of nine faithful Jews from reaching God because of my gibberish.

MY INTEREST IN performing was sparked early on by my mother's family. Her brother had been in Irving Berlin's show *Yip Yip*

Yaphank. He played the spoons and he sang. And my mother's sister, Adele, was just a funny woman who made us laugh. We also went to movies and listened to comedy shows on the radio. I guess that people are born with a talent for comedy, but if you're in a household that accepts humor as a potent force then you also develop it.

I could make kids laugh when I was very young and I liked doing it. When I was in first grade at P.S. 57 I was the teacher's pet. At Christmas they asked, "Can anyone do anything entertaining?" One kid got up and tap danced, and I could stand, put one leg behind my head, and hop around on the other. It was one of those things I found out I could do, because I had a short torso and long legs. I did that in our classroom, and then the teacher took me to two other classrooms to do it. That was my first touring in show business right there.

In third grade, I played the Headsman in the play *Six Who Pass While the Lentils Boil*. I was the guy who chopped people's heads off. We performed the play for an audience and all I remember is that my mother sat next to the principal, who said to her, "That boy is the best one." He said that because I was loud. I was the loudest one and he could hear me.

At Evander Childs High School, Mr. Raskin, who was the music teacher there, needed singers. So my friend Milton points to me and says, "He sings." I could sing loud and I had a big operatic voice but no ear and no timing. However, I could sing like Caruso if somebody conducted me. Raskin says, "Let me hear you sing." And he gives me a few notes to sing. I hit one note. "You're in!" "In what?" "In the chorus."

Then I was paired with a wonderful girl coloratura, Ruth, and we rehearsed a duet, "Yo Soy el Pato," which is "I Am the Duck" in English. In rehearsals I sang it really well. This was for our big outing—to be onstage at Julia Richman High School in Manhattan for a Spanish festival.

So we're there and Ruth starts to sing, and I'm supposed to walk behind her onstage. While I'm doing that, I can't help myself. I'm doing it duck style. I'm flopping after her and the audience is roaring with laughter. The more they roared, the more I'd both walk like a duck and jump like a duck. That was my first and only theatrical performance in high school, but by then I was bitten.

A few years ago *The New Yorker* magazine was going to do a piece on my old neighborhood, and I wanted to show them where I lived. Our apartment building was on Belmont Avenue, with a second building backed up to it, on the corner of 179th Street. But when we arrived, I was shocked to see that there was nothing there. Both buildings had been razed. So I went to the open lot, picked out two bricks, and sent one to my brother in Atlanta with a note that said, "Memories of our old homestead." Across the way were two short apartment buildings, two stories, like for three families each. They hadn't been torn down because they were historic, even though they were older and much more decrepit. One of those buildings was where I prayed in Hebrew double-talk for the minyan.

MARTIN BREGMAN

Film producer, including the Academy Award–winning
Dog Day Afternoon
(1926–)

IN THE BASEMENT OF OUR APARTMENT BUILDING THERE WAS WHAT
we called the club room. Maybe the room was ten by ten, with an
old couch, a chair, and a bench. After school, when we were about
fifteen or sixteen, we'd go down to the basement. What did we do
there? Smoke. We crowded into this room and lit our cigarettes.
We smoked until you couldn't see. You could not see. You couldn't
breathe. *Hey Solly, how're you doin' over there? I can't see you.*

At about that same age I had my first serious date. She was Italian and I was Jewish. In those days it wasn't so easy for an Italian

girl to bring a Jewish boy to meet her parents, so she wasn't so sure about bringing me home. But finally she brought me home for dinner. We were supposed to go to the movies afterward. Her mother and father were pure Italian. You know, very, very strict and domineering. The father looked like he was connected.

I was dressed magnificently. A tie. A shirt. A jacket. I was fine. And during dinner I was trying to be charming. The mother took out a cigarette. She was looking for a match or something, and I, charmingly, reached into my front pocket and pulled out a pack. I was pure sophistication. I'm talking. I'm fumbling with opening it, without ever looking at the pack, while the father looks at me. This is his daughter. Italian. *Pure.* This is a mob guy too, or at least he looked like one to me. And as I'm talking I'm opening this packet of condoms. In those days, everybody my age carried them—just in case. You never knew when lightning would come down and strike you and you'd get lucky. And I feel the stare as he's looking at me. The mother's looking at me. The girlfriend-to-be is looking at me and I'm pulling out this condom. I wasn't looking, but I felt it. I was mortified.

We didn't go to the movies that night. The girl got sick and I got sicker. I never saw her again.

During those years, I was also looking for extra money and fun, so I hooked up with a kid I went to school with who said, "You wanna go into business? Let's buy a car and then we can deliver some liquor." So we bought a car, an early 1930-something Ford. The liquor we delivered was homemade, made in a still in the Bronx. We'd load the whole back of the car up with booze and then drive it like we were delivering bottles of milk. We worked for a "man." We had no idea that we were doing something illegal.

We delivered the booze to the clubs on Fifty-Second Street and in Greenwich Village. There was one guy in the Village who looked like he was straight out of central casting. He was a huge man who liked me. After about two years, he said, "Whad'ya doin' this for? You gonna deliver this shit for the rest of your life?" Then he says, "What would ya like to do? What would ya like to be?" And I said, "I'd like to get into the entertainment business." He picked up the phone and in a week—I couldn't believe it—I started working for a booking agent in the Borscht Belt. My job was to drive people up to the mountains, and that's how I got my start in the entertainment business.

LEON FLEISHER

*Pianist, conductor, recipient of the 2007
Kennedy Center Honors award*

(1928–)

FOR SOME REASON MUSIC HAD A CERTAIN IMPORTANCE TO MY mother. She saw that music seemed to be not only a path to a better life but also that it was part of the human soul to which one should aspire. I can't remember a time in our apartment when there wasn't this little upright piano.

My older brother, Raymond, was given piano lessons but was not particularly interested. In those days, music teachers and doctors both made house visits. Whenever the teacher came to give Ray a lesson I was absolutely fascinated. I would curl up on the couch in the corner and just watch and listen. When the lesson was over, Ray would go out to the school yard and play with his friends. I would go over to the piano and repeat everything that had been done in the lesson; and apparently did it with much greater enthusiasm and alacrity than he did. I must've been four or four and a half. It turned out that Ray was very happy to let me take over his lessons so that he could spend more time in the school yard.

I enjoyed it. It was great fun. I think that it was one of those extraordinarily lucid moments when a mother's vision for a child actually coincided with the talent of the child. I had two choices. First choice was to become the first Jewish president of the United States. Second choice, become a famous musician. As I said, it was one of those rare serendipitous occasions where the dream and the reality seemed to coincide.

There came periods of time when I became bored with practicing because you have to develop certain neuromuscular responses which come about only as a result of a certain amount of repetition. I became master of being able to practice something and read a book at the same time. The only problem was hiding the book when my mother came by. I learned how to do that by slipping the book under one leg when I heard her footsteps.

I had just turned ten in 1938 when my mother and I, in effect, abandoned my father and brother in San Francisco, where my brother and I were born. My mother and I left for Lake Como, Italy, where Artur Schnabel, this world-famous, incredible teacher, taught. Schnabel had accepted me as a student. He had also discovered Lake Como long before George Clooney. It's a paradise on earth. Beautiful lakes surrounded by mountains.

I went some four months in the summer to work with him. War clouds were gathering, and Schnabel was making plans to leave Lake Como. He was going to move to New York, and if I wanted to continue working with him it made sense that my family move to New York too. So we came back from Lake Como in September. We lived on West Seventy-Ninth Street in a brownstone while looking for another, larger apartment. My father and brother joined us in New York, and I think it was toward the end of 1938 that we found an apartment at 1325 Grand Concourse in the Bronx. Our apartment faced south, the side street, which had two sides lined with cars but certainly enough room to have a rather constricted game of stickball, which was a kind of nonstop affair.

When I wasn't practicing, or doing my homework, I might be down there playing stickball. It's a great game. One of our great players was called Sluggo. The pink Spaldeen was hit onto the Grand Concourse itself by him. I forget the name of the street to the west of us, but Sluggo could hit that ball a country mile in the heart of the Bronx.

Around 1939 or '40 there was this lovely, ample-bosomed blonde girl who was my older brother's girlfriend. Her name was Natalie. She lived across the little side street on which we played stickball. The room that held my piano, my studio, if you will, faced her windows. We were up on the fifth floor, and Natalie was across the street on the second floor. There were a number of times in the summer when Ray, my brother, threw open the window, sat on the sill with his leg up, and Natalie would be like Juliet, except she was below, not above, at her window. The two would gaze and gesture to one another. It was quite a distance from the fifth floor to the second floor across the street, and, you know, with kids in between playing stickball, it wasn't quite the situation where they could converse. So they developed a kind of sign language.

One afternoon, Ray must've been in the throes of some great wave of passion. He sat me down, literally grabbed me by the arm, and put me on the piano bench. He knew that I could play the piano version of Tchaikovsky's *Romeo and Juliet*. He pointed to the music and said, "Play!" Then he went and sat on the sill while I played as loudly as I could, with the appropriate feeling. I played this love music while my brother sat on the sill making these great swooping gestures as if he were sending the music out the window down across the street to Natalie's window. I was twelve or thirteen and Ray was close to eighteen at the time. I felt like Cyrano de Bergerac. A musical Cyrano de Bergerac.

LAWRENCE SAPER

*Entrepreneur, inventor of patient-monitoring equipment
and cardiac-assist devices*

(1928–)

THE CANDY STORE, AS WAS USUAL IN THE NEIGHBORHOODS, WAS
on the corner. It was a simple business, one that was easy for someone with very little money to start. Our neighborhood candy store,
Nathan's, along with its candy, newspapers, comic books, and soda
fountain, had a public phone in a booth, on the right near the door-
way. Most people before the war didn't have phones, so the public
phone was an important one.

When the phone rang, whichever kid was there first took pri-
ority. And I was usually there first. You could only take part if you

were tall enough to reach the phone. I'd pick up the phone and say, "Who do you want to talk to?"

"Well, Mr. So-and-so."

"What's the address? What apartment?"

Another kid waiting to answer the phone would have to say, "The next one's mine." So the phone would ring, and let's say it was for Mr. Schwartz on Franklin Avenue. You'd put the phone down—and it was common knowledge that if the phone was down it was in use and you didn't hang up—and run up the street to get Mr. Schwartz. If you were lucky, he would be reasonably close by, or if you weren't so lucky, he'd be a long block away. Invariably, for some reason, and I have no explanation why this was, the person you went to was always if not on the top floor, then close enough to that to make it exhausting. Usually there weren't apartment buzzers in the downstairs entryways so you had to run up to the floor where the person lived. I knew that if the apartment number was a 6 I had a five-story run, or if it was a 5 a four-story run, and so on. Once in a while, I got lucky and I only had to run up two flights of stairs.

When you rang their doorbell, the person would say, "Who's there?"

"Telephone."

"For who?"

I don't remember a woman actually ever being called, and I don't remember ever getting a tip from a woman. The call was usually for what we called "the man of the house." Sometimes I'd be lucky and could yell up the stairwell, "Phone call!" I'd then wait and follow that person back to the candy store, so nobody would misinterpret that it was somebody else's call. It was mine.

It wasn't mandatory, but there was a certain amount of moral pressure for the person to give you a tip for getting them. It was very rare that anybody stiffed you, you know, didn't give you a tip. Two pennies was a weak tip. A nickel was a good tip. And a dime? I mean, you had struck gold. A dime was rare but it was still possible.

With pennies or a nickel you could get candy, but for a dime you could get a milkshake, or a malted—similar to a milkshake but with some malt powder thrown in—or an ice cream soda. But the malted was the best. It wasn't measured, but you knew that you were going to get two glasses. That's how large it was. That was the imperative. Two glasses full of a thick, frothy cold drink. Anybody who used a straw was out of luck because it was too thick to sip through a straw.

MARY HIGGINS CLARK

Author of worldwide bestselling suspense novels

(1929–)

PEOPLE JUST DON'T GET IT. I SIMPLY SAY THAT THERE ARE ONLY three places that have a "the" in front of their name: the Vatican, the Hague, and the Bronx, and that so much talent has come out of the Bronx. It's also so beautiful. Not only is Fordham University there, but there's also Mosholu Parkway, Pelham Parkway, and the Botanical Garden, for heaven's sake.

There were also people in my own neighborhood who became well known. There was Jake LaMotta—the "Raging Bull"—the prizefighter, who lived down the block from me. I didn't know it then, but Judith Rossner, who wrote *Looking for Mr. Goodbar*, also lived four blocks from me. And then there was a major counterfeiter who lived down the street from us. We always wondered why his son had such a snappy roadster. We found out he was on the "Ten Most Wanted" list.

When we first moved to our neighborhood, in the Pelham Parkway section, it was rural more than suburban. There was Angelina's farm on Williamsbridge Road. She would come by and say, "God bless your momma. God bless your poppa. We got lotsa fresh vegetables today."

We lived in what they call a semidivided house with a wall down the middle of two houses so it looked like one big Tudor house. I was in the neighborhood recently and I tell you our block is still lovely. These were city lots, twenty-five feet by a hundred feet, so you had a front yard and a long backyard.

When we were kids, the cars were parked in the back, so we all played in the streets. There were hardly any cars in the streets then and there were always kids on the block to play with. Every house had kids. You knew you could play stickball or jump rope in the streets, or the game where you say, "Move one step forward." I think it was called Red Light. When there was snow, we would walk four blocks over to what we called suicide hill. It was all a field then. The Jacobi Medical Center and the Einstein College of Medicine are there now. Our mother used to say, "Watch out for Johnny"—my younger brother—"and be home before dark." And we would run to be home before dark. We had lots of freedom and independence. And we explored. The neighborhoods were safe. Once you were of school age you were allowed to go out and play with the other kids.

My father died of a heart attack when I was eleven. The circumstances were shocking. He'd never been sick. Never. I was a daddy's girl. We were very, very close. The only time he came home early from work—he owned a pub, a bar and grill—was the night that he died. He would usually rush back to work after a five o'clock dinner. Since he was the owner, he had to be there. He wasn't feeling well that one night so he went upstairs. He must've been having a heart attack then, but we didn't know it. He died in his sleep, and I've missed him all my life.

I tell you, my poor mother lost our house for lack of just a few hundred dollars. After my father died, she hung on to it for almost four years, renting the rooms, but that didn't bring in enough money. She couldn't hold on to the house anymore. People said to take Joseph—the oldest of the three children—out of school and let him work. My mother said, "Education is more important than any house." After we moved, my mother would go to visit good friends still living on the block. She'd come back with her eyes glistening, saying how beautifully the roses had grown.

When my husband Warren died, I was so sorry to realize that my young daughters were going to experience the same kind of loss. I took the two littlest girls to the funeral parlor because I thought that's the only way I could get them to understand that their daddy wasn't coming back. He had been in and out of the hospital and I knew that Patty, who was five at the time, would be standing at the window waiting for him. I thought, I can't have this. I knew that they were just too young to cope. At the casket I explained that Daddy was now in Heaven and that he wasn't coming back. Two weeks later while in bed with me, Patty said, "When Daddy was home, he was in his pajamas. When did he change into his clothes?"

My aunt was working at the Shelton Hotel in Manhattan when I was fifteen. I got a part-time job from four to seven p.m. afternoons and weekends. It was one of those switchboards, "Hotel Shelton, good afternoon." And then you would connect the person who was asked for in room 502, for instance. I loved it because I loved to listen in. There was a Ginger Bates, a permanent resident of the hotel who was also the "lady of the house." She got a lot of phone calls from her many admirers. It was never salacious. It was more like, "I wonder if you'd be free on such-and-such a date." One time she said to the caller, "Don't say another word. That damned operator is listening in." And I said, into the phone, "I am not!" Then I just disconnected her. A minute later the chief operator asked, "Who had Ginger Bates on the phone?" I managed not to get caught.

The Irish have a gift of storytelling. Nobody ever came back from the store with milk without having a story to tell. Then there's the gift of laughter, the sense of humor, and of course I've always loved that quotation from Yeats: "Being Irish, he had an abiding sense of tragedy which sustained him through temporary periods of joy." I have that framed on my desk. I absolutely love it.

My mother encouraged my writing from the time I was little. She said that I was going to be a successful writer one day. The funny part is that when I had my first short story sale for fifteen hundred dollars to the *Saturday Evening Post*, to her that was the epitome of success. "Put it in the bank," she cautioned. Of course, I already had a list of all the things I was going to do with that same fifteen hundred. Shocked, she said, "But Mary, you've used your idea!"

JULES FEIFFER

Cartoonist, illustrator, and writer

(1929–)

My sister Mimi was a big shot in high school. She got good grades, she was articulate, and she was also a dogmatic Stalinist. She was a Communist and she was going to convert me. She got me to join a youth organization, American Youth for Democracy. AYD. It was a Communist front, which in those days, to the world at large, was presented as progressive. What is now called progressive had nothing to do with what used to be a "red" word. As a matter of fact, when they formed a political party, they called it the Progressive Party and got as many people from the outside as possible. They ran Henry Wallace for president in 1948.

If you were on the left at all, you supported Wallace for president. Do you remember the comedian Milt Kamen? Milt was a friend of mine. In his act he talked about his boyhood in Brooklyn, and he said, "When I was a kid in the Depression, my Jewish neighborhood was a very political one. There was the Communist Party, there was the Socialist Party, there was a Socialist Workers Party, there was a Socialist Labor Party, and there was the American Labor Party. I had to be twenty-one and move to Manhattan before I even heard of the Democratic and Republican parties." And that's pretty much the way it was for us too.

But my sister's Communist friends were infinitely more interesting and smarter and wittier than my friends, and I liked them better. My friends were these would-be thugs who I adjusted to because that's who we were hanging around with. Like every kid, I had an assortment of friends who I thought of as best friends and better friends and first best friend and second best friend, but none of them had my interests. I mean, they all knew that I was going to be a cartoonist or wanted to be a cartoonist. They didn't read but I did. They weren't political and I was. The way that gays were closeted in those days as a young man or woman—I was a "closet Jules." I hid out. I didn't even know what a Jules was at that time, but I knew that I wasn't like them. At one point, three or four of us were walking around Parkchester, which was a neighborhood I enjoyed walking in because it was middle class and upper middle class. It was about a fifteen-minute walk from where we lived on Stratford Avenue. There was a beautiful sunset. I commented on the sunset and I was called a fag. I learned what I could say and what I couldn't say, and I accepted all of that.

I was also an abject physical coward in every possible way. Therefore most of my real life was lived inward in my imagination. Radio was a close personal friend. Movies were close personal friends. Fred Astaire became a role model, and to this day I follow his lead. He took something that was impossibly hard and made it look effortless. And that's my goal as an artist. To make it look as if you're not doing anything. I use that image both as a cartoonist and as a writer. To leave no footprints. About ten years after *Carnal Knowledge* came out, I saw a screening of it somewhere and halfway through the movie when I saw Jack Nicholson and Art Garfunkel, I thought, they're making up their lines. They're improvising. And I was very pleased that that's how it felt. It didn't feel as if those lines had been written.

I used to be able to remember my dreams. I always loved this. I would dream that I was in a movie theater and I would walk in, in the middle of whatever the movie was. I'd see the movie to the end and then it would start again. Then it comes to where I had come in, in the dream I say, "Oh, this is where I came in," and then I'd wake up.

I was always terrified of leaving the neighborhood or leaving home because I had then, and have now, no sense of direction. It isn't as if I have a bad sense of direction. I have *none*. Even in New York, if I get out of the subway I can walk half a block and not know where I am, right in the middle of Manhattan. So I got lost all the time when I was a kid. And in those days I would be terrified because I didn't know where I was and would be embarrassed if I had to ask people how to get to Stratford Avenue, where I lived. I wouldn't go to Manhattan until I was in my late teens because I was terrified of getting lost. To this day I get lost all the time.

While I was terrified of getting on a subway going to a theater in Manhattan, somehow or other the Bronx seemed safer. So I saw *Death of a Salesman* at the Windsor Theater near Fordham Road and fell in love with plays. I saw theater for the first time at the Windsor and would take two trolleys to get there, as I recall. And I loved that. I saw Ethel Barrymore at the Windsor. I still remember the actor who played Willy Loman. Duncan Baldwin.

At school, I essentially wasn't good at anything except bullshitting. I was the Jewish wiseguy. I was funny! As a "closet Jules," I understood what I could get away with and what I couldn't. And what I couldn't get away with was talking seriously about any serious ideas because that was always suspect. But being funny was great and I was a funny guy. I made people laugh. I amused them. So I knew how to do that. And I knew how to draw cartoons and people liked that. I loved that because it was really where I wanted to be. Al Capp who did *Li'l Abner* and Milton Caniff who did *Terry and the Pirates*, I mean, I had real heroes. And I learned my craft by studying the work of these guys in the daily newspapers.

But I did have one friend in the Bronx, Irwin, who read books, who liked to talk, who liked opera. He was on his way to being an intellectual and because we were teenagers, you know, we had hard-ons all the time. And his luck went amok because he came from an Orthodox Jewish family and he happened to fall in love with an Italian Catholic girl. It broke the whole family up. It wasn't because of her but because of the upset in the family. When he got out of college, he married a Jewish girl but changed his name. He never had contact with his parents again. All because he was so angry and so upset that they tried to sit on him, which they did.

Years later, after I had become known, I was on a radio show being interviewed on one of those call-in shows. A woman got on the phone and said, "Jules, this is Irwin's mother. Do you know where he is?" Just like that. On the air! Well, I said, "If you give the person who takes the phone calls your number, I will call you as soon as I get off the air and we'll talk."

So then I called her and we had a painful talk. I told her what little I knew. I'd seen Irwin a few times after school but had lost touch. Then later I heard that he had died of a heart attack because his daughter, who worked for Tom Brokaw when he had the evening news, contacted me. But she had no contact with her grandparents. She didn't know anyone in her father's family. That's why I'm so fond of religion. The day after my bar mitzvah was the last day I went to synagogue.

My father was a Polish Jew. My mother was also a Polish Jew, but after first settling in New York her family moved to Richmond,

Virginia. She grew up as a southern girl. She didn't have a southern accent and didn't have a Jewish accent. She sounded, as I used to say, like Walter Cronkite, quintessentially American. And because in our Jewish neighborhood you had either a New York accent or an Eastern European accent, she was Eleanor Roosevelt. She was treated as the lady on the hill because she sounded superior to everybody and also felt that she was superior.

She had always wanted to be, and was, a fashion designer. She kept the family afloat during the Depression while my father got occasional jobs. Essentially she would go door to door to those in the rag trade on Seventh Avenue and sell sketches for three dollars a sketch. She was very adept at that and kept us going somehow. Over the years, in criticism of my father, she would say, "He's a good man, but . . ."

My mother was very seductive with other people and with her own children in terms of being charming—and then Hitler. All my friends and all my sister's friends would fall in love with my mother. She would seduce them socially.

I don't know the following for sure, but she didn't believe in sex. I think she got married because her family made her. It's what I've surmised. If my mother had her druthers, she would have been a single woman with a career as an artist or an illustrator and wouldn't have had sex at all, although if she did it might have been with a woman. I don't think she was attracted to men. And I don't think for a second that she was attracted to my father. But my mother came from a poor Jewish family and she wasn't going to defy anybody. One of the things that terrified her was when her Communist daughter and her radical son defied—no, went into the business of defiance. That scared the hell out of her.

Because of her art background, the fact that I wanted to be a cartoonist was fine with her. When she was growing up, some of the cartoonists, like those in *The New Yorker*, had great reputations. The newspaper strip cartoonists had great reputations too. Some of them went on the vaudeville circuit and she loved show business. She used to quote me stories about Moss Hart and what a down-and-out kid he was in the Bronx but how he promised his mother that when he got to be rich and famous he would buy her a mink coat. My mother expected that of me. And I promised that I would buy her a mink coat.

Mike Nichols was telling me that when he was casting *The Graduate* he had Redford in to interview, because Redford was so brilliant in *Barefoot in the Park*. Mike was talking to him about the role of Benjamin in the movie, saying, "You know what it is when you're that age and you want to get the girl and you're not sure you can get the girl and you're not sure of anything." Redford had no idea what he was talking about. Because he was Robert Redford. There are those kids who grow up to have the good fortune of being Robert Redford, knowing that they'll always be Robert Redford, or O. J. Simpson before he became an accused killer. I think the reason he found himself in that position is that from the time he's a kid, he's a star. No one ever says no to him. He was handsome. He was the best athlete in the world and he was charming. There was nothing he couldn't have.

We who weren't the best looking, we who weren't the biggest, we who wouldn't automatically have women fall all over us had to find our own way of figuring out how to deal with rejection, failure, high-level schmuckery. How to deal with the casual insults of others and the not so casual. I used to say in my twenties, and I felt it was true, I'm gonna have to get famous in order to get girls. Because I'm essentially shy, I don't know how to start a conversation. If I sit on a plane, and this is still true, if I sit on a plane next to a stranger, unless he or she talks we can ride around the world and not a word will be said.

Fame really meant a lot. When people talk about the downside of fame, I don't know what they're talking about because it's only been good for me.

The reason I'm a cartoonist is because I was good at it. If I could throw and catch a ball, maybe I would've been an athlete. But I couldn't throw or catch a ball easily. I gravitated to the thing that I felt I had a chance to be successful at. You want to break into some circle of acceptance with people who'll buy your story and pay attention to you. It was about being paid attention to. I wanted to go out in the street and get attention when I was a kid so I would draw cartoons on the sidewalk. I got some attention because I could do that and the others couldn't. I could draw Dick Tracy and Popeye. They couldn't. That's how I survived. That's how I didn't get beat up. I was little. I was underweight. I wasn't the masculine macho kid. I would've been thought of as sissy or a pansy. But no, I was an artist. I was an artist and they let me live. That was a lesson I learned at a very early age. If you draw a lot they'll let you live.

DAVID YARNELL

*Independent producer of television programs
and documentaries*

(1929–)

"THE BRONX? NO THONX!" A POEM BY OGDEN NASH, IS ONE I cynically recited for a good part of my life, but I've changed my mind. I have great memories, in spite of the awful rush-hour rides on the loud and squeaky 241st Street IRT subway line.

There were the fragrant, sweet smells from the Saperstein and Snowflake bakeries. No Parisian patisserie produced a more luscious éclair than those two Jewish corners of heaven, especially when you bit into the outer shell and the inside custard released in all its glory. There were the delicatessens with their pickle barrels, the Italian grocery stores, lilacs growing wild in empty lots—yes, lilacs! And in my restless teens I found the tiny Ascot Theater showing foreign films, a trip into an exotic world of other places, other languages, with subtitles in English. These experiences gave me a heady feeling of sophistication since I was the self-proclaimed number one expert in the Bronx on the work of the French actor Louis Jouvet.

However, I knew that I wanted to get out of the Bronx when I actually lived there. In my mind there were definitely better places, like Greenwich Village in Manhattan. When I was a teenager, I would take the subway to Manhattan and go to jazz clubs. I wanted some action. The Bronx didn't do it for me, except for the summer that I was sixteen, when I led a double life, kind of like Dr. Jekyll and Mr. Hyde.

There was the Pelham Parkway gang near where I lived. These were the Bronx High School of Science and Stuyvesant High School overachievers. They were the smart Jewish kids, studying to be professionals. Then there was the Tremont Avenue gang. Tough street kids. Knew how to hustle. They lived farther south on the White Plains Road line of the subway. I went back and forth between them.

That summer I was looking for something exciting and maybe even a bit dangerous. I had a cousin. He was a real daring, wild, great-looking guy. He was into jazz, dressing sharp—and smoking pot. Prompted by him and our friends in the Tremont Avenue gang, my friend Eugene and I decided that we would make some money by growing marijuana and then selling it.

We staked out a plot of land fifteen feet by ten feet about three hundred feet inside Bronx Park, surrounded and isolated by bushes and trees. We planted the seeds in early spring, and they were watered by nature and a nearby drinking fountain. We would dash to our crop as soon as we got home from school, thrilled to see that the plants were really growing. We weren't totally successful as farmers. One of three plants survived. But we harvested and started the curing process. The buds of the plants were placed in quart pickle jars, then placed under my bed, carefully relocated on Fridays, cleaning day, to avoid discovery by my mother.

The courier for the pot was Max, a Brooklyn College student, who drove a hack in the summer—a taxi service carrying New York City residents to the various Catskill Mountain hotels. I had met Max the previous year when he provided this service to my family on our annual trek to the mountains. His brother, a jazz trumpeter, opened the door to our customer base. These were the jazz musicians who were ready to improve their performance by smoking pot-weed-maryjane. All of this was a heady adventure that thrilled and scared the hell out of us.

With the drop-off of our product to the Nevele country club and Klein's Hillside, we had a profit of $270 for the both of us to split. That was a lot in those days. Not bad for a summer's work, but our adventure came with much more fear than I wanted. And when it was all over I was much relieved. I went back to Christopher Columbus High School and hit the books.

MILTON GLASER

Artist and graphic designer, creator of the I ♥ NY logo

(1929–)

My mother never ate with the rest of the family. My father, who had this dry-cleaning store, would come home from work at about a quarter after eight at night. My sister, who at that point was still in grade school, would come home early and have something to eat. Everybody ate by themselves. Every once in a while two would eat at the same time, but my mother was never seen eating. During the day, she was taking food from somewhere. It was very strange. My mother also cooked spaghetti in a very specific way. She would boil it for an hour until it had gotten gelatinous and lost its identity. She'd toss Velveeta cheese in before the water had boiled off. Then she would demold it from the pot because it had been reduced to a kind of pudding. It was like the Dome of St. Peter's. And after that she'd slice it and fry it in chicken fat. In my teenage years, I went to an Italian restaurant for the first time. I asked for spaghetti and when they brought me a plate of spaghetti, I said, "No, no. I want spaghetti. *Spaghetti!*"

The Italians in our neighborhood lived to the east of us in small houses, but the Jews lived in apartments. Three-room apartments with maybe six kids. Try to figure that one out. You basically had a small kitchen, a bedroom, a living room, a foyer, and one bathroom. I slept for a period of my life under the stove. Well, I was young. But people were forever sleeping in the hallway or foyer. Or everyone slept in the one bedroom. At one point I slept on a folding cot. For years my sister slept on a small bed at one end of the bedroom while my parents slept together in a big bed in the same bedroom. But that was for a family of four in three rooms. When you had a family of six or seven it was like the Marx Brothers. The concept of having a room of your own didn't exist. There was no such thing. Sometimes you'd see it in the movies and you would wonder what it was. I mean somebody with their own room, their own bed, their own dresser? What is that? That was somebody else's fantasy about another kind of life. It could have been on Mars.

In our building of around fifty families, no one had their own phone, but there was one phone and it was in the hall on the ground floor. Because we lived on the ground floor, when the phone rang— and it could be for anyone in the building—I answered it. And that went on for a good part of my life there. I'd answer the phone, "Hello, who's this?" "I'm looking for Irving Schnabel." "Okay. Okay. Wait a minute. I'll ring his bell." And I would go outside to the hallway entry and I would ring that person's bell three times. That was the acknowledged signal. *Ding ding ding.* Then I'd go back into the hall. The person would open the door upstairs and I would yell, "Telephone!" "Who is it?" "Didn't say." "I'll be right down."

What a nutty idea! But fortunately phones were in such infrequent use we'd get only a few calls a night.

My mother was the person who said that I could do anything in life. My father was the one who said prove it. It wasn't as antagonistic as it sounds. He was a man with modest aspirations. A timid man to a large degree. A very decent, hardworking man. But he had no sense that great achievement of any kind was possible. He knew that he was meant to work. And so he worked twelve hours a day every day of his life. But my aspiration to be an artist was something he didn't fully understand because he couldn't figure out how anybody could make a living from that.

The most touching thing that occurred between my father and myself was when I went to visit him in an old-age home in Florida, six or seven months before he died. We were sitting, talking, when he said, "You know, you did the right thing." And I said, "What do you mean?" "You know, you decided to be an artist. I resisted then, but you were right. It turned out to be the right thing for you."

You don't get that confirmation often in life. It was like a benediction. Because all he wanted when I was young was for me to be able to make a living.

I have a standard story about the origins of my interest in the visual world. My parents were going out to some kind of event so they asked a cousin of mine to babysit. He came to the house—I was five—he came with a paper bag. I didn't know what the bag was. He said, "You want to see a bird?" and I said, "Yeah." I thought that maybe he had a bird in the bag. But when he reached into the bag he pulled out a pencil. He then drew a bird on the side of the bag.

I think it was the first time that I had ever seen anybody draw something that looked like something outside of a child's crude scrawl. It was as if he had created life in front of me. A bird had materialized out of nothing. Out of a bag and a pencil. I suddenly realized that I was going to spend my life creating life. That I could make something magical occur. I have to emphasize that this was a revelation. It wasn't logical. I almost fainted. It was like a blinding light. Suddenly! It was like the hand of God had come down. It was that important.

In some cases there isn't an event like that. There's just a slow accumulation of things. I think it happens differently to different people, and it also happens at different ages. Or the realization doesn't occur while you're that young. You don't know what to call it, right? You don't have a name for it. It's just an interest of yours.

I became a working artist by drawing pornographic pictures for the other kids. "Can you do a naked lady?" "Glad to be of service." In addition to my own satisfaction in life, I realized there was a job to be done for others and that you could satisfy.

And then, of course, I went to the High School of Music and Art. It was a very optimistic place. It was part of the optimism of that period, where the feeling was that anything is possible. That was a consequence of the emigration of people who were leaving a circumscribed life where they saw no possibilities to the sense that they could prosper and grow and that their children would have a better life. How strange it is now that that has flipped over—the idea that your children are not going to live as well as you. I think that's a great sadness.

Music and Art High School was one of the great institutions of the city. It's not fully appreciated for how much it shaped the aesthetic of the city. It created the audience for both music and art. It's hard to imagine what the city would've been like without that school. I think at one point probably two thirds of the New York Philharmonic were graduates of Music and Art High School. The statistics are astonishing. But more than that, it created so many generations of graduates committed to either the world of painting or the world of music.

Once Leonard Bernstein came to conduct the senior orchestra at the school. That orchestra was fantastic. They were doing Beethoven's "Leonore Overture No. 3," which has a big trumpet solo in it. It was played by a very proficient kid who could really play the trumpet. As the kid finished the solo, Bernstein yelled out, "You're hired!" And while he was still conducting, he hired him for the Philharmonic.

I grew up with the extraordinary idea that this was the promised land and that you could achieve anything. I was promised a scholarship to Pratt Institute, because the dean there had come to Music and Art to look at portfolios. He said, "Young man, I'm giving you a four-year scholarship to Pratt." I said, "Great." So I didn't apply anywhere else. Then I took the entrance exam to Pratt and I failed it. I called up the dean—I think his name was Boudreau—and I said, "I didn't apply anywhere else and I haven't got a school to go to because you promised me a scholarship." "Well I can't very well give you a scholarship if you can't pass the entrance exam, but I have an idea for you, young man. What I want you to do is to go to night school, and if you succeed in night school for one year, I'll give you a three-year scholarship for the remaining time in the day school." So I took the night-school exam and I failed the night-school exam too. I think I'm the only person in the world who failed that night-school exam. Then I took the Brooklyn College exam and got in. After three months of commuting from the Bronx to Brooklyn for two hours each way on the subway, I said I can't do this and left. I got a job and then got into Cooper Union.

Lewis Hyde wrote a wonderful book on how primitive cultures use gifts to diminish hostility but you can't keep the gifts. You have to pass them on. In most cases, these gifts are physical, but in our civilization you realize that the gifts are cultural and in the arts. That they're music and painting and they're architecture and so on. What is this persistent need for music and art and for beauty?

What the hell is beauty? Why do we have to keep making pictures and making music? Why?

Everything else is driven by money, greed, and power. The only remaining barrier to all of that is the arts. This recognition that there's something other than material issues in life. It's what bonds the species. It is the only thing that has no intention other than to make you feel you're part of something larger. It really serves as an alternative to religion. And it's experiential. It reaches a different part of the brain. You just see something and you are changed. And everybody who sees that same thing and is moved by it now shares that feeling too. And you share something that can't be sold. Something that can't be made into a commodity. Leonardo's *The Last Supper*, although it was created as propaganda, as most religious paintings are, makes us feel a spiritual longing. A longing to share an experience with others. That's the only reason that I can imagine that art exists.

This is my life. Art chooses you. You don't choose art. You become possessed. This is my commitment and I've never deviated from that.

MILDRED S. DRESSELHAUS

*Physicist, recognized for her original work in
nanotechnology and carbon molecules; Institute Professor
and Professor of Physics and Electrical Engineering,
Emerita, at the Massachusetts Institute of Technology*

(1930–)

WHEN I WAS YOUNG, WE MOVED FROM BROOKLYN TO THE BRONX, to one block from the Bronx House Music School, where my older brother had a violin scholarship. What happened ultimately was sad. My parents' resources all went into that move, but my brother's teacher, who was the reason we moved, died a few months after we got there. So people at the school recommended that we go to Greenwich House in Manhattan. That's what we did, even though it was a long ride on the subway from the Bronx to downtown.

My brother was the talented one. He was very devoted to the violin and worked hard at it. He was also a good performer. He started playing violin when he was three, getting scholarships from that age on. I got a scholarship only because he had one. I think my parents and the school both thought I was going to be something like him, but I wasn't. I loved music, but I always liked academics more, even though music became the gateway to opportunities I wouldn't have had otherwise.

The kids growing up in our neighborhood didn't normally leave the neighborhood. They just stayed there. Roosevelt High School was our district high school. It wasn't too bad but it was just satisfactory. It wasn't Hunter. I found out about Hunter High through the music school and the middle-class parents whose kids were there.

As part of my scholarship to Greenwich House, I ran errands for them and became a music critic, starting at about age eight. A couple of years later I saw the movie *Fantasia*, which made a terrific impression on me.

For everything that I did I had to write a report. That was good training for the future. Everything that I did there turned out to be pretty valuable, but who would have known that at the time? Even in public school, my teacher said to me early on in sixth grade that attending class would be a waste of time for me, so she gave me work to do for the school. I was like an administrative assistant, learning how to run things. And that's been kind of useful in life too.

I had no help for passing the exams to get into Hunter High. The teachers told me, "Forget about applying. What they ask on the exam is nothing that we teach you here." Which was true—but I learned it by myself, getting into Hunter High by having a perfect score.

The problem in junior high school was basically the behavior of the kids. The teachers had almost no time for teaching. They would just try to keep order, which wasn't an educational experience. For instance, we were told to go to the bathroom at home before we went to school, so we wouldn't have to go while we were there. It seemed that going to the bathroom was a bit dangerous because girls would get mugged there.

My mother was the breadwinner in the family. She started working at an orphanage, which was a twelve-hour-a-day job. She also had to travel to and from work, which made her days very long. So at age ten I took over the cooking for the family. My father had been emotionally destroyed by the events of the Holocaust and was a manic depressive. That was the diagnosis at the time, but I can't really say for sure. My mother was very loving and my father loved me too, but he was very disturbed for a long time and couldn't deal with reality. So it was tough on him but also tough on everybody else.

That particular kind of disease has ups and downs so when he was in the active mode he would be violent, which meant you had to stay away from him. Sometimes we just abandoned the house. My mother had a friend who lived on the east side in the Pelham Bay area, where the neighborhoods were much better. I used to seek refuge there. It was hard because Hunter High School was even farther away traveling from there, but despite that I recognized I was doing pretty well in school and that kept me happy. I'm still that way. I really like what I'm doing, in that I wake up in the morning excited about doing it. And I was that way when all this trouble was happening.

When you grow up like I did, you're at a big advantage because you're already taking care of yourself. You've been on your own. Nobody made it happen for you. You were making it happen yourself. So when you go to college or whatever you do, you have your own inner drive and confidence. I work in a man's world. But . . .

I've always worked in a meritocracy. And I'm still working productively—because I love doing it.

∾

Note: I saw Mildred Dresselhaus for the first time in Oslo, Norway, where she received the prestigious Kavli Prize for her original work in nanotechnology and carbon molecules. The king, Harald V, was present when Dr. Dresselhaus, in her acceptance speech, talked of her immense gratitude for the honor. She then announced that she was going to give her prize of $1 million to young scientists for basic research. She encouraged others to do so, as well. I was immediately taken with this brilliant person who had such a spirit of generosity.

A few months later, I took the train up to Boston to record a conversation with Millie, as she encouraged me to call her. We met at her offices at the Massachusetts Institute of Technology, where she sat at her desk behind a mountain of papers. She apologized for working on some recommendations for students, which were due later that afternoon. The Bronx accent and down-to-earth manner were familiar to me. In the course of our talking together, Millie told me that she was less interested in the perks of seniority, such as a larger office, than simply doing the work that she loves.

REGIS PHILBIN

TV personality, actor, singer

(1931–)

OUR NEIGHBORHOOD HAD MOSTLY APARTMENT BUILDINGS, BUT MY great-aunt Victoria owned this two-family house and that's where we lived. There was an empty lot next door to us. I think it's a parking lot now. My family planted corn and tomatoes there. I loved it. I had a great childhood. I even delivered the *Bronx Home News* right up Cruger Avenue to all those houses, and up and down Pelham Parkway to the apartments that faced Bronx Park East.

My great-aunt was a tough old Italian woman. I could hear her going down the stairs into the cellar to turn off the heat every night at nine o'clock. And I said to my father—my father was Irish and he didn't understand those Italians at all—I said to him, "How can Aunt Victoria go down into that dark cellar? Isn't she afraid somebody's down there?" And he said, "Well, if I was a guy down there, I'd be afraid of what's comin' down those stairs."

On cold winter nights when I was really young I used to listen to the radio. That's when I discovered Bing Crosby on WNEW, which was the premier radio station in town. They had a half hour of Bing every night from nine thirty to ten. And I just—gee—I was attracted to his voice, the sound of his voice. It was so clear, so beautiful. He had such a way with a song.

I was about six or seven years old. It was in the thirties. The Depression was going on. I kept hearing songs like:

When skies are cloudy and gray,
They're only gray for a day,
So wrap your troubles in dreams
And dream your troubles away.

The words meant something. "Wrap your troubles in dreams." It made me feel better, even though I was just a little guy. I knew all the lyrics to his songs. I was deeply attracted to Crosby. I wanted to be him. I wanted to be Bing Crosby. And then, of course, his movies came out, and I was so happy for him when he won the Academy Award for *Going My Way*.

Now the years are going by, and my mother is saying, "What do you want to be? You've gotta plan now. You're going into high school, then college. You gotta concentrate on what you want to do."

She was very nervous for me. How could I tell them I wanted to be Bing Crosby? I know in my heart it's ridiculous. I'm not a singer. I've never even taken a lesson. So I said, "In college. I'll tell you in college." Meanwhile, the pressure's on. When? When am I going to know what I'm gonna be?

In four years at Notre Dame I never tried out for anything

because I never thought I had any talent at all, but deep down I still wanted to be Bing Crosby. I had these friends, guys I used to hang out with at school, and this guy, Gus Falcone, played the piano. And I remembered I had told my parents that by the day I graduate I'm gonna tell them what it is that I'm gonna be. I said, "Gus, do you know a song, 'Pennies from Heaven'?" "Of course I do." So I sing it for him and then say, "You know my parents are coming for graduation, and I want to tell them that I want to be Bing Crosby." "Really?" and he looks at me a little weird. And I said, "Well, at least a singer like Bing Crosby."

So we rehearsed every day. Whatever time we had. My parents came a day early for graduation. They ran into this thunderstorm in Elkhart, Indiana, so when they arrived they were a little shook up. But I said, "Don't say a word, because I'm here to tell you what I'm going to do. Just follow me." So the three of us walked across the campus of Notre Dame to the Music Hall. And they don't even see that big engraved sign, "Music Hall." And Gus is waiting in there. He says, "Hi, everybody," and starts to play "Pennies from Heaven." And I sing the song to my mother, to tell her after the song that's what I want to do.

Well, midway through the song I notice my mother is crying. Crying violently. Very Italian. And my father, ex-marine, has fire in his eyes. He wants to hit me. I know he does. And I have trouble going through the rest of the song. I can see it's a disaster, and I say to them, "You know, remember those songs I used to love that Bing would sing? No, you're right. I can't. I'm not Bing Crosby. Get real with yourself. By the time I get out of the service"—the Korean War was winding down and I was going into the service—"I'm gonna know what it is, and it may be in television, but I'm not gonna sing."

I did go into television. After working my way up from a number of different jobs on TV, I even replaced Steve Allen on his late-night television show. Now I got on this little plane and I go to Cleveland, Baltimore, Pittsburgh, all the cities that had stations, and when I got off the plane, these guys would say to me, the television critics, "Steve Allen is a talented man, plays the piano, writes music, sings, he's funny. What's your talent?" I mean, I got hurt. I didn't know what to say. What was I gonna say? That I was Bing Crosby once when I was six years old? So I didn't say anything. And I felt terrible. Well, that show didn't make it.

At one point after that, Joey Bishop called. So I went with Joey. He had seen me do a TV interview with a really tough radio guy. Joey says, "Hey, this kid's got talent." I said, "Really, Joey? What's my talent?" Those comedians love to be challenged. They can end wars. They can do anything. What is the talent? He said, "You— you are a great listener."

So now we're doing the show but, you know, he was nervous about it. He's a comedian, not a talk show host. So every day we would take about a forty-five-minute walk up Vine Street—to Hollywood Boulevard and back down—to relax him. And when you walk and talk with somebody for three years every day, it gets down to what did you want to be when you were a kid. I said, "Joey, what'd you want to be?" "I wanted to be a comedian. Ten years old I'm on the corners of Philadelphia telling jokes, making people laugh. People would be falling down laughing." I said, "You did it! Hanging out with Frank and Dean and Sammy. Geez, that's great!" He said, "What did you want to do?" I said, "When I was six years old, I wanted to be Bing Crosby." "What?" I explained that I used to listen to Bing on the radio. There was no television, nothing, just the radio, and I listened to Bing Crosby sing. I knew all the songs, all the words, and for a while there, you know, I actually thought I would be Bing.

Four months later Bing Crosby is a guest on the show. Well, I couldn't believe it. He's gonna sit next to me. I was so nervous to meet him in person after all those years admiring him. It brought back memories of my cold kitchen on cold nights, or the hot kitchen on warm nights, singing with Bing and learning those songs. It was just a thrill.

So Bishop remembered what I told him. And he said, "Bing,

see this kid? Biggest fan you ever had. It would be a thrill for him, Bing, if you would sing a song to him." Crosby looks at me and I look at him. So Bing sings, "Over in Killarney, many years ago." He sings an old Irish song that he sang in *Going My Way*. We go to commercial break. Geez. What a thrill. Bing Crosby sang and dedicated a song to me. We come out of commercial break, Bishop hasn't had enough. He says, "Bing, that was very nice. I'm sure Regis enjoyed it. But let me tell you something. This kid knew all of your songs. All the lyrics. Regis, sing a song to Bing." I'm thinking, *Oh, my God!* And Bing Crosby turns. I smile, but you know those blue eyes. I'm thinking, *What was the last song I sang?* And I go back to Gus Falcone in the Music Hall with my mother crying and my father. So I started singing "Pennies from Heaven." I sang the whole song, including the verse. And Bing comes in a little bit—a buhbuhbuhboo. And the next day I get a telegram from Mercury Records about them wanting me for a recording contract. But Joey reads the telegram and says, "Somebody's playing a joke on you." He throws the telegram away. I say, "Geez, maybe that's true. I don't sing."

Next day the guy called up from Mercury Records in Chicago. "Well, what is it?" I said, "I'm in!" And I made the record.

∽

Note: I didn't know Regis when we both lived in the Bronx, but we ended up living in Manhattan on the Upper West Side in the same building and on the same floor.

The prize-winning documentaries The Bronx Boys *and* The Bronx Boys Still Playing at 80 *are both about the reunions of a group of fifteen men who grew up in the same neighborhood in the Bronx and who kept their close friendships with one another, mostly from kindergarten. Two of the Bronx Boys are George Shapiro and Howard West. They were interviewed separately but because they told one continuous narrative their two stories are combined as one.*

GEORGE SHAPIRO
(1931–)
AND HOWARD WEST
(1931–)

Agents, producers, personal managers

GEORGE SHAPIRO: I MET HOWARD WEST, WHO WAS A NEW KID TO our school, when we were both eight years old, in third grade. Maybe the reason why we bonded so much was because out of fifteen of us just Howie and I, at eight, nine, ten years old, became

Brooklyn Dodger fans. The Yankees were so dominant and the Dodgers were like colorful guys. The underdogs. We both rooted for the underdog. Our other friends were kind of cocky, walking around saying, *Go suffer with the Bums.* They weren't wrong. We suffered a lot with them. Then when Jackie Robinson came along it was so emotional. The Brooklyn Dodgers were the first all-white team to hire a black ballplayer. We were rooting for them when they broke the racial barrier. I may have gotten that from my mother, who talked about racial equality and instilled it in my brother and me. Pee Wee Reese, the shortstop, was my favorite player, and when Jackie Robinson came along in the late 1940s he was Howie's favorite. One of the most emotional times was when the Dodgers were playing in Cincinnati, where they were so racist at that time, and Pee Wee put his arm around Robinson. Howie and I, we followed our hearts. Recently there was this movie, 42, which was the Jackie Robinson story. I must've cried seven or eight times watching that movie.

Howard West: Here's the deal. I got to be a Dodger fan because of my dad. He always rooted for the underdog. Georgie and I were the two Dodger fans surrounded by friends who for the most part were Yankee fans and Giant fans. There were three great ball clubs in New York. Great players. We'd stand in front of a building called 75 West Mosholu Parkway and fight and argue about who was the better player, which was the better team. We'd argue, and we'd have baseball cards. It was a great time. Jackie Robinson, to this day, is my favorite all-time player, although not in skill. There were better all-around players, but in that era he was an exciting player. Mickey Mantle and Willie Mays could hit well and field well, but with Robinson it was emotional. We grew up on radio. So we were listening to the old-time announcers, Mel Allen and Red Barber. And then when baseball was televised we'd look at some of the stuff in black-and-white.

My grandmother lived in the Amalgamated houses and across the street was a golf course. One day when I'm about twelve years old, I'm looking around and I find a golf ball. A couple of guys come around beating the bushes on their side of the fence, looking for their lost golf ball. I say, "Is this yours?" And the guys say, "It looks like it." And I throw the ball over so they can see it. "Yup. Thanks, kid." That happened to me one more time, and then a lightbulb went off. I'm in business! I couldn't *wait* to go see my grandmother, because I'd hang out and collect the golf balls, hold them up, and make the golfers' fingers come through the fence. Then I'd turn the ball and let them look at it, and almost without failure, when it was theirs, *Yup, that's fine. Throw it over. Well, this is ten cents. Give me the money first.* Then I'd throw the ball over. I'd make a couple of dollars. I told nobody. I just kept the money hidden and then I'd buy ice cream or comic books, like *Batman* or Marvel comics.

GS: Our local movie theater was originally the Tuxedo Theater. *Those were the days, my friend.* We went to movies at ten a.m. and saw two complete double features, cartoons, short subjects, Pathé news, and the great serials the *Green Hornet* and the *Lone Ranger*, which were cliff-hangers. Then we'd get out of the theater at four.

My dad gave me an allowance, like twenty-five cents a week. It cost a dime to go to the movies. For six hours of movie pleasure it was ten cents. Eventually, it went up to twelve cents and then it went up to a quarter. Thinking back, we were noisy. In the kissing scenes, the love scenes, we would all boo. During the comedy, whether it was Abbott and Costello or the Marx Brothers, we would just laugh loudly and applaud, but if there was a romantic kissing scene we'd go "Booooo." When the bad guy got shot in a Western we'd yell "Yay, yahoo" and clap. "Serves you right, you bastard." That wasn't such a bad word. We used bad language but "bastard" is as bad as it's going to get for now. After six hours in the theater, when we went out, we were blinded by the daylight and brought back to reality. No complaints.

HW: We'd go into the Tuxedo Theater and we were talkative. Sitting there, waiting, we'd make spitballs to throw at the girls in front of us. And when we talked too much, the matron would come with a flashlight and then we'd shit in our pants, *Matron coming.* We'd duck down, and she'd leave, and we'd do the same thing all over again. The matron, fear, the spitballs, the girls—we were unruly, as they would say. *Unruly!* We had a great time.

So we're older now and we're dating. And we're on a double blind date. Someone fixed us up. Neither one of us ever met the dates before. And you're going to recognize the name of this theater—the Loew's Paradise, this magnificent theater with the stars in the ceiling where they gave away dishes and stuff. Now this was not a very good double blind date. Georgie and I said to the girls, "We gotta go to the men's room," whatever. And we went and never came back. That's not nice. We never came back. We left. All because we didn't like the looks of the girls.

GS: There was this metal railing on Mosholu Parkway, where all the kids used to sit. It was better than any singles bar today. People would just come and go. It was the park and you were meeting girls. It was a gathering place where we talked and flirted, even at night when we were out of P.S. 80. We also had parties. Pot wasn't in, but if it were available then, I'm sure we would've been smoking it. We had delicatessen and drinks. We all drank and then some of us would throw up, rest a little, and walk home. We always found places to have a party. No one had a car so we all walked. That was one of the beauties of growing up in the Bronx. You were so mobile. You walked to schools and to the parties or you took the subway or the bus.

HW: We drank a *lot* at the parties. *Whose parents aren't home? Who has an empty house? Whose parents are away? Whose parents don't come back until midnight?* We drank and ate and tried to have sex, mostly unsuccessfully. You'd find a bedroom. Someone would stand guard.

GS: When we were seventeen years old, Howie and I stole a car. You're asking embarrassing questions, but I say to that, "No tengo miedo." *I am not afraid*, in Spanish. I speak Spanish because in southern California es muy importante hablar español. Porque todos personas hablan español.

Before we could officially drive, Howie and I used to dream about having a car. People who had parked their cars on the street would often leave the doors open, so we'd go in and sit and talk about when we could drive and go out on dates with girls, or to be able to go up to Yonkers Raceway. Places that were hard to get to without a car. So one time we were in a parked car and we saw there was like this little switch. It wasn't a key. We turned the switch and it started. We knew a little bit about driving because one of my uncles had taught me to drive in his car. So we drove around up and down streets, you know, not far—but it was stolen. We stole it—and then we brought it back. We had our joy ride and then we parked it again a block or two from Howie's house on Kossuth Avenue.

HW: When we saw the car, it was parked close to one of our favorite candy stores, Mr. Baum's. I lived a block and a half away from there. *There's a car*—and I opened the door. We got in and challenged each other. We didn't know it could start. We turned a knob in the car and it started. *Let's go for a ride*. So we did, and then we started to crap in our pants. That we'd be in a stolen car, we'd get stopped, we'd get locked up, we'd be in jail—and we'd better go back. We went back and parked the car exactly the way we found it, including turning the tires the way they were.

We both lusted to drive so we both decided to buy a car together. I'm checkin' the *New York Times* and I find an ad. A Mr. Levitt. I still remember his name. A 1940 Oldsmobile and he said, "It's a cream puff." Five hundred dollars. It was 1949 so that was a chunk of change for us, but we bought the car. For two working kids in college earning their own money—we put over two thousand dollars into that car. By comparison, a new Ford was twenty-six hundred dollars. We were just pouring it in. So I have the car on my weekend and it's one of those snowy days where there's ice on the road. I'm going down a hill around the corner from my house near

Montefiore Hospital, and I hit the brakes to slow down, but there was the ice and I crash into another car that's parked. We get it repaired—we always split everything—and now I'm warning Georgie, "Don't do what I did. It's icy. Tap the brakes lightly." A whole repeat. He has to see if I'm right. He does the same thing I did and smashes up the car.

GS: We worked in the Catskills on the weekends and on holidays, at Grossinger's and a place called the Flagler Hotel. There was an agency where you could sign up to work and get tips, and that helped pay my tuition to NYU. So we borrowed our friend Elliott's car, which was a 1937 Plymouth. The car was fourteen years old. A creaky little car. We were heading down a hill when we hit a bump and all of a sudden we saw that the engine of the car got dislodged and bounced out of the car. So we're at the top of the hill, rolling down, and we're watching this engine rolling down the hill in front of us. I was driving. *I guess we'll coast down to the bottom of the hill*, and I steered over to the side of the road. There was no way that the engine was gonna work again since it was all battered and beat-up. I think that the car is still there to this day.

We didn't have suitcases, so we had our stuff in bags, like big laundry bags. We looked like refugees. We hitchhiked to the Flagler Hotel and called Elliott. "Elliott, your engine fell out and the car's on the side of the road and I don't think it's ever gonna work again." I must say he was pretty gracious about it. Another reason I love the boys from the Bronx. He understood that the car was old.

HW: Waiters, busboys—we worked all over the place and we didn't have a car for some reason, so we borrowed Elliott Liss's old beat-up car. That car was called *The Poop*, it was so bad. It's huffing and puffing when the engine falls out. We abandon the car and decide to take the license plate off so they can't trace us.

Did Georgie tell you what happened at the Flagler? Did he tell you where we slept?

The place was full, and they had nowhere for us to sleep except across the road in a barbershop. The only thing available to us were barber chairs. So we slept in the barber chairs. That's what happened to us when we went to the Catskills. We slept in the barbershop in the chairs.

GS: Howie and I, we went to school together, we bought our first car together, we became lifeguards together, we worked at William Morris Agency together, and when I came to LA I brought him out to work at William Morris in California, and then we formed this partnership together, Shapiro/West Productions.

HW: Georgie and I are like glue.

GS: I always felt lucky, happy, and so nourished in the Bronx. For the time I had my mother and my father, they just showered me with love. I carried that with me and I passed this essence on to my own kids. The other guys from the Bronx had similar experiences. And don't forget the freedom we had. Those reasons are why you see the joy in *The Bronx Boys Still Playing at 80*. A lot of the guys who live on the East Coast ended up in Florida, so I'm going there for New Year's. We'll go to a Thai restaurant for dinner, then we'll go to Lenny Kulick's house to celebrate with champagne.

MARK CASH

Lawyer, with a specialty in tax law

(1931–)

WE HAD BEEN LIVING IN WESTCHESTER AND I MET—I CAN'T remember his name right now—a very bright person who had gone to our elementary school. We were on the train together, and he told me about a celebration of the fiftieth anniversary of the construction of P.S. 76. There was going to be a gathering at the school, so I called up my sister and I called up my cousin who had lived across the street from us in the Bronx, and I told them I'd meet them there.

We left late, and I got down to our old neighborhood to go to

P.S. 76, and there were cars all over the place. When we grew up there were never any cars. This was really the first time that I had driven around those blocks. I drove around looking for a place to park when it dawned on me that in all the years I had lived there, I'd never even been to the east side of P.S. 76. The east side was Italian, and to the west of the school it was basically Jewish. That's the way the neighborhood was set up. We lived to the west of the school.

My grandparents and my aunt lived across the street from us on Arnow Avenue. They were Orthodox Jews. The rest of the family wasn't. Out of respect for my grandparents, my mother kept a kosher home, but I was very interested in *not* being Jewish. In integrating. My grandmother spoke Yiddish. Only Yiddish. I refused to speak it. I would listen and I would understand, but I wouldn't speak it. Now I live on the Upper East Side. There are all these young kids wearing yarmulkes all the time. This is something we never saw when we were growing up. We never saw any religious young Jews in our neighborhood, although there was a synagogue across the street and the rabbi lived at 788 Arnow Avenue. Most of us in our building shied away from the "old country."

Our parents, by the way, let us run all over the place by the time we were six, seven, eight years old. One Passover we were going to have a Seder at my grandmother's. I got dressed up in my holiday suit and then I went downstairs to where all the kids were playing. I don't know how we wound up there, but we found ourselves late in the afternoon in the park. We were actually playing in Bronx Park, and I'm wearing this suit. We went down to the Bronx River, and there's a mattress lying at the bank of the river. The mattress looks like it would make a great boat. We got on the mattress in the water, maybe two or three of us. It looked sturdy enough. We launched the mattress into the river and the next thing we knew we were sinking. We actually thought that we would just float away. We didn't think of where. Once the mattress started sinking, we figured we had to get off that thing. Fortunately, the river was shallow there so I got off. I walked home dripping wet in my Passover suit.

The Depression and the losing of jobs and money were a big influence on us as kids. I think that most of the families in our building were relatively small because of that. There were even a lot of single kids in our building although I had a sister and we lived in a one-bedroom apartment. Once while I was sleeping in our living room on a hot day, we left our front door open to the hallway so the air could circulate. I woke up in the middle of the night with a big dog licking my face. It was common to sleep with the doors open in the summer. Because of the stories I had heard about the Depression, I think I definitely knew that we were a lot luckier than many who lived before us, in tenements.

But at about that same time, something happened that was really terrifying. That's when the polio epidemic hit. Everybody was affected by the fear of getting polio. Our parents knew about the 1918 flu epidemic, where people in New York were dying like flies. In Philadelphia, they were lying out on the street. My parents never told us anything about it. Never mentioned it. When polio hit, they were terrified all over again. A few kids in our building even got polio, as I remember. It made my mother very protective. I couldn't go to the pool in the summer and summer camps were closed because of the epidemic. When we were kids at that time in the 1940s, I think that some people wore something around their necks to ward off polio. It was some superstitious thing. I don't remember what it was. Maybe it was a clove of garlic.

ARLENE ALDA

Author, photographer

(1933–)

WE LIVED IN A ONE-BEDROOM, ONE-BATHROOM APARTMENT. Mother, father, older sister, older brother, the mutt fox terrier Spotty, and me. We ate our meals, played cards and board games, did homework, and told jokes in a small area adjacent to the kitchen, called the dinette. I can easily picture my father sitting at the dinette table telling us one of his favorite jokes about these three American soldiers, lost and thirsty in the desert during the war. "Two of them called for 'Water, water,' and this Jewish boy called out—." My father's belly laugh drowned out the punch line

even though it tried to gurgle to the surface. *What's the punch line?*
What's the joke? Please! He'd manage to blurt it out, "Seltzer, seltzer."

My parents were immigrants from Eastern Europe—Lithuania
and Poland, or was it Russia? I never really understood when they
told me that the borders kept changing according to the wars, with
the winners taking this piece of land or the other. Tell me again
where you were born? What language did you speak? Where did
you go to school? Who were the Cossacks again? Why did they
hate the Jews? What was a pogrom? With its details of shootings
into houses and hiding in basements, our family history was both
exciting and confusing to me. I was a kid from a Bronx neighborhood, a place where I could freely roam in the streets of our own
mostly Jewish ghetto without fear of meeting up with some wild
men on horses who with their guns and their hatred of Jews could
kill me and my family.

My brother Harry was an avid builder of balsa wood model
airplanes when he was a young teenager. The smell of the glue
stank up the dinette as well as the rest of the apartment—and I
loved it. I also loved the finished airplanes that actually flew once
the rubber bands were wound tightly around their propellers. His
warnings of "Don't touch!" were words that I listened to, mostly
out of fear rather than understanding. I had no idea how that anger
might materialize, but Harry was ten years older than I was and
I wasn't going to test it either.

My mother, Jean, who was patient enough with the mess that
we kids always left in the dinette, also wanted it to be unique and
stylish. My father usually went along with her wishes. The dinette
was wallpapered and decorated many times. *Simon, I think the room*
needs something new on the walls. Something cheerful. Maybe a flower
pattern. He hand-stencilled the walls with a repeated pattern of
a drooping tulip with pink and white stripes.

On the windowsill of our well-decorated dinette was a small,
wooden rectangular box filled with dirt. Originally, this box held

a brick of orange American cheese sold by the pound and sliced to order in our local Allerton Avenue Appetizing store by the behind-the-counter man, Moish. If I'd politely ask Moish if he had an empty Breakstone's cheese box, he would give me one or tell me to come back in an hour or maybe tomorrow. The box was a treasure: an indoor garden where my sister Shirley and I planted petunia seeds from packets we got from P.S. 76, our local public school. I wanted to water the seeds often because I was impetuous and impatient, unlike my mother and Shirley, who seemed to be able to wait forever for things to happen, like chicken to roast or a cake to rise or clothes to dry on the indoor bathroom clothesline. The petunias miraculously grew into cascading trumpets of pink, white, and purple, despite my sneaking in some extra watering when no one was looking. To this day, old-fashioned petunias are among my favorite flowers.

My mother's sewing machine was also in the dinette. The word "Singer" stood out in bright golden letters across its black background. My mother was a skilled dressmaker who designed and sewed her own clothing and also earned money by sewing dresses for others. What was a skill and an asset for her was sometimes a curse for me. *Why is the machine so noisy? Why does she sew her own clothes into all hours of the night? Why does she have to make my clothes? Why can't I buy them ready-made like Diana down the hall?* My feelings would erupt. The targets were my mother and her machine.

"Stop sewing."

She'd try to placate me. "In a few minutes."

"Stop now. I can't think."

No answer, except the rebuke from the incessant drone of the motor with the needle moving up and down, up and down, up and down. My mother hates confrontation. She ignores me. I storm out of the dinette crying. I slam the door to the one bedroom in the apartment.

It wasn't just that I was most probably a spoiled brat, wanting what I wanted when I wanted it and often getting it. I was also hopelessly stuck, falling over and over again into the same muddy emotional rut as I watched my mother sitting, hunched over, sewing, while she sang or hummed under her breath. My knowing how she spent endless days and nights working as a housewife—cooking, cleaning, shopping, washing, clothing her kids, and being on call for whoever—became such a clear message to me not to end up like her.

Thankfully she had the immigrant's dream. "This is America. Your life can be better than mine." I can't say I didn't love her for that. I can't say for sure, though, because I had no understanding of what love was.

Wearing beautiful clothing was important to my mother, but when she dressed up to go out the compliments she craved from my father weren't there. Maybe it had something to do with the old country and the evil eye. Or maybe it didn't seem manly to compliment. I never knew. *Simon, how do you like my new dress? How do I look?* She lived a life of silent and not-so-silent criticism from her loved ones without the counterbalance of positive words or understanding. I know that my father loved my mother in his own way, because when she died at age seventy his sadness included the sobbed words "I've lost my best friend." It took me many years to realize that my parents had a marriage not unlike a lot of other parents', especially immigrant parents at that time. Putting food on the table was primary. Open affection, friendship, and love were kept under wraps, maybe to be uncovered when the kids weren't around.

My father was quiet, introverted, and insecure in most situations that were new to him. He was a commercial lithographer, but often he was the last one hired for a job and therefore the first one fired when work was scarce. A vicious cycle. He took solace from the pressures of his life with its unemployment and financial insecurity by playing cards with his friend Max from the third floor of our building and placing bets on horses with the local bookie. His dream was to make a small killing, not in the stock market or in the lottery like today's dreamers, but at the racetrack.

My parents argued about money, but it was often one-sided. She told him that the household allowance he gave her was too little, and complained bitterly about his spending some of it betting on horses at Belmont Park racetrack. He'd retreat to the living room to silently read the newspaper. There even came a time when I, taking my mother's part, wouldn't or couldn't talk to my father because of some disagreement or other. I wish I could remember the tipping point, but I can't. That's just what it was. A tipping point. An accumulation of the strain of parents simmering just below the boiling point, the lack of privacy and space, and the noise—amplified in my ears by my growing desires for independence.

In between my bouts of discontent were long periods of happiness. My friends were important to me, as were my babysitting jobs, which paid enough so that I could buy whatever a few carefully saved dollars could buy. I had also started taking clarinet lessons, an instrument I wanted desperately to play. Some of the more nosy neighbors would challenge me with their usual prying. "A girl playing the clarinet?" That always bothered me, but not enough to stop my working toward the goal of becoming a professional clarinetist. My teenage years were spent being in love with my instrument, my high school, my new friends there, and the freedom I had to travel to different parts of the city. That included going with my sister and her friends or just hanging out with mine. It was during those high school years that I started to go to concerts at Carnegie Hall. My horizon was expanding and I loved it.

Eventually my brother Harry married Norma, who lived in our building, and my sister Shirley married Carl, who lived in our neighborhood. The arguments between my parents petered out, coinciding with my father's early retirement. By then I was totally consumed with the clarinet. The sound of the sewing machine became a distant background hum to my incessant practicing on the instrument, which, by the way, neither parent, both infinitely patient with me, ever complained about.

By the time I was in college the sewing machine had been moved from the dinette into the one bedroom, which my parents had reclaimed from Shirley, Harry, and me. The dinette, with a narrow cot pushed against one of its walls, became my bedroom. There was an eerie quiet in the apartment when I became the only child left there. I especially missed my sister, because I forgot to mention that I was a tag-along kid. Where Shirley went, I wanted to go, and most times did. By the time I was in high school we were the best of friends. When she married I felt a deep loneliness, but by then I was already in college, fulfilling my mother's immigrant wishes without realizing it. "This is America. Your life can be better than mine."

MICHAEL BRESCIA

Physician, cofounder and executive medical director
of Calvary Hospital in the Bronx

(1933–)

WE HAD A FOUR-ROOM APARTMENT IN A WALK-UP BUILDING. My
three sisters, believe it or not, slept in one of the two bedrooms,
in one bed. My parents had the other bedroom. I slept in the living room on what's called in Italian a *branda*, a foldout bed, that
was kept in the closet when it wasn't used. It was great when one
of my sisters got married because then there were only two sisters at home, but I still didn't get a bedroom. At times there'd be
conversations going on around me or my sisters would be entertaining their boyfriends on the sofa in the living room, while I'd
be lying on my branda in the middle of the room.

The insulation in that room was bad. It was freezing in the winter, and we had no blankets to speak of. My father would put his heavy coat on top of me when he came home from work. That was my blanket. Other than that, there was only like leftover cloth and stuff that my grandmother brought over on the boat from Italy. The bedsheet was made from sacks that originally held rice that they stitched together. This was about as comfortable as sandpaper. I would've frozen to death if my father hadn't given me his coat.

But I had no negative feelings because I didn't even imagine how others might've slept. I felt very loved. My three sisters spoiled me as much as you could spoil any kid in the Bronx. I was this little prince when I was born, and to this day I'm very spoiled. When my dad was up in the morning, I could smell the coffee brewing even before I got out of bed. That was such a wonderful smell. Such a wonderful memory. There just was no room. We were stuffed into that apartment.

My dad was an extremely wonderful guy. He had no education, but he was determined to get himself a civil service job so that after the Depression he would be more secure. He was hit hard by the Depression because he was out of work a lot. He finally got a job with the Housing Authority and became a supervisor in one of the projects in 1938. His dream for me was to be a plumber.

He pointed out that it was complicated to change a pipe. At that time all the pipes were steam-fitted. He said, "Look, here's Nick the plumber. Look at the car he drives! Look at the house he has! He always makes a living no matter what's going on. And Mickey"—'cause he never had any great aspirations for what I was going to do with myself—"you gotta become a plumber, you gotta get a trade."

I'll confess that in P.S. 76 the teachers were anxious to get rid of me, to have me leave to go to Evander Childs High School. I was not a great student and spent lots of time with my friends in the streets. That changed when I went to high school.

I was challenged by this teacher, Mrs. Lubell. She looked at my

IQ test scores and said that they were definitely not my scores. She wanted to know where I sat. Well, I sat next to my friend Menasha, who was smart. Mrs. Lubell was sure that my test was not on the up-and-up because she knew me as a pain in the neck. She thought that I cheated, that those high scores weren't really mine. So I had to retake the IQ test and I suddenly found myself removed to another classroom, which was far more challenging, and Mrs. Lubell was my new homeroom teacher.

It was a bridge from my group of kids who I hung out with, who were totally unmotivated, to this other group who were motivated educationally. So I figured that I could sit in the class with the advanced kids but still have a leather coat, a ducktail haircut, and have lunch and hang out with the other guys.

I would do their book reports in the cafeteria during lunch. They'd get in line, and I'd say, "Tell me what the book was about." Like tell me what the basic story was. And they'd say, "Well, it's about this guy, he got shot and blah blah blah." So I would construct a page of stuff having never read the book. And the guys I did it for, they very much respected me 'cause I helped them out. That meant that I got respect in the street. I also got girlfriends.

When you grew up in that neighborhood, as far as a future was concerned, you were either going to take numbers, be a loan shark, or you were going to be an athlete or do some menial job.

One summer day we were outside. A big black car pulled up in front of my building on Bronxwood Avenue and somebody got out. He had a black bag and was a very good-looking elegant man who then went into the building and disappeared.

We all knew that one of our friends, Johnny, was sick and wasn't able to come out for a while. A crowd formed around the building. This Dr. McLeod came out of the building, tipped his hat, and went into the car. Everyone was impressed, because apparently the doctor had diagnosed what was wrong with Johnny. There was a lot of talk and excitement about this guy, this doctor. I was absolutely awed and said, "That looks like something I'd like to be."

So it was then that I got the idea to be a physician. I was thirteen or fourteen at the time.

I talked to Mrs. Wilson, who was a teacher at P.S. 76. I went to see her because I heard that her son was a doctor. And she said, "You don't need courage to take care of sick people. You need courage to do your studies. That's what you need." It was an impetus for me to change. That and Mrs. Lubell. I needed to get my act together.

I knew that I wanted to be someone. I didn't want to be a housepainter or a plumber. I wish I could say that at that point I wanted to help people, but my goal was to "make it" somehow. I was the first one in my large extended family who went to college.

I wanted to be revered by the family. And that did happen. Not only by my immediate one, but my extended family as well. First cousins, second cousins. They all were so excited when I finished medical school that they had this large party for me. I still have the pictures. Actually, it spawned many other doctors in the family whose fathers said to them, "Forget about being a wallpaper hanger. If Mickey could do it, then you could do it!"

∿

Note: During a commercial break on TV, I saw an ad for Calvary Hospital in the Bronx. Pictures of a Dr. Michael Brescia caught my attention. He had the same name as a boy I remembered from my classes at P.S. 76 and Evander Childs High School, so I wrote to him at the hospital and found out that he was indeed the Michael Brescia I knew from childhood.

We agreed to have lunch at an Italian restaurant near Arthur Avenue in the Belmont section of the Bronx, which is still an Italian neighborhood. I tried to put together the picture of the kid I remembered from school with the face of the mature person sitting opposite me in the restaurant. The pictures fit, but when I heard Dr. Brescia's stories I realized that, although I could remember him, I actually knew nothing about his childhood. After high school we had lost touch completely.

EMANUEL ("MANNY") AZENBERG

Theatrical producer, educator

(1934–)

I TOLD MY FATHER WHEN I WAS SIXTEEN THAT I DIDN'T WANT TO
be a doctor. It was traumatic. In the Bronx High School of Science, you had to put things on various applications. I put "premed" because I couldn't put down "pre-nothing" or "I have no
idea." But at sixteen I finally said, "I don't want to be a doctor."
There were a lot of kids who went to my school who were going
to become doctors whether they wanted to or not.

I joke and tell my students that there were two questions that
were asked by my parents when I was a junior and senior in

college: 1. What are you gonna do? and 2. When are you getting married? If you woke up at three in the morning there was your mother going, *What are you gonna do and when are you getting married?* If you didn't want to be a doctor or lawyer, they'd stick their heads in the oven. My parents struggled financially to send me to college, so it was a big deal.

If you went out on a date with a girl and it cost six or seven dollars, you knew that you had to earn it. You had to *earn* it. So you had a job. Everybody had a job in the summer. Many of us also had jobs in the winter. If you really wanted to make money during the summer, and if you were diligent, you'd get a construction job. Those guys made real money. And if you had to just make some money, you became a waiter in the Catskills or a busboy or a bellhop there. And if you kind of faked it, like I did, you were a counselor in a camp. So you didn't make five hundred dollars. You made two hundred dollars. And since everyone had a job the value system of working came with the job. You wound up respectful of work. You put in eight hours you got paid four dollars. If you put in eight hours you went out on a date.

I joined the ROTC in college and went into the army as an officer right after college. I met people there from Arkansas, Kentucky, or whatever. It was then I began to discover what I had taken for granted—my upbringing, my schooling, living where we lived. It was much more valuable than I had realized. I had a bigger adjustment to the discipline, though, in the military. But once I adjusted I knew my way around because I knew my way around the streets from being brought up in the Bronx. When I got back, I knew that I was going to work in the theater, but truth is I found out what work really was while in the army. And I said, I don't want to do *that*!

I was drunk two times in my life. One of them was when I was in the army, when we got orders *not* to go to Korea. We were the first company of young officers at Fort Benning who did not go to Korea. The other time was before that, when I was a teenager.

I was seventeen at a party. At age seventeen I had never been drunk in my entire life. I never knew what that was. And the Bronx Science mentality of seeing people drunk and out of control made no sense. How do you allow yourself? So I was going to disprove the theory. I hated the taste of hard liquor—so I had eight doubles of Four Roses in thirty minutes. The first twenty minutes nothing happened, and that's about all I remember except for lying on the floor. The guys took me home on the bus. I was not very happy. I was throwing up and I was moaning at home. My younger sister was frightened. My father understood and said, "Let him alone." It was a terrible experience. I didn't like the taste of it, and I was deathly ill, but I got that out of my system.

My father came from Poland. He had lived in London from 1910 to 1929. Then he immigrated to America. He spoke six or seven languages. He was a very bright man who did what he had to do to make a living.

I went back for the Bronx Walk of Fame thing. They install a street sign with your name on it. It was a Bronx moment. There I was with my son, and I said, "Do you want to see where I grew up?" So we sat at Franz Sigel Park just looking at the building. It was at 760 Grand Concourse, right near Cardinal Hayes High School. When I looked at my old apartment building it seemed so small. Our apartment itself had two bedrooms. My parents were in one and I shared the other with my sister. The whole apartment was tiny. I think the rent was seventy-six dollars a month. The honor itself, being on the Bronx Walk of Fame, has its own ambivalence. The recognition—what does it really mean? And yet the acknowledgment is wonderful.

We were in front of the courthouse when they unveiled my name. And that was two blocks from where I grew up. As part of the ceremony, my seventeen-year-old son was going to hold up the sign with "Manny Azenberg" on it. I couldn't help but think of my immigrant father, who had lived two blocks away. That thought transcended everything else. There was his grandson, who he never knew, who's unveiling a sign that has his name on it. *Azenberg*. All I thought of was if my father could only know that his family name was on the Walk of Fame on the Grand Concourse in the Bronx and that I was there with my son, Charlie Azenberg's grandson. In Hebrew there's a name for it. *Hemshekh*. Continuity. It's continuity.

AVERY CORMAN

Writer, novelist

(1935–)

THE OTHER DAY, I WAS WATCHING SOME CHILDREN PLAY ON THE Upper East Side. There were organized groups, some playing Wiffle ball and some softball. Then there was another group I observed on Randalls Island. Parents sign their children up to play, and they pay to have referees, depending on the sport. In one case it was soccer, and in another it was flag football. It's all organized play. That was so far from my experience growing up in the Bronx that it's as if we were in two different solar systems.

The world that I grew up in, in terms of sports, was between

183rd Street and 184th Street on Creston Avenue and Field Place, the actual street where I lived. Those streets were just west of the Grand Concourse. If you went just a few inches south of 183rd Street there was a different group of kids. You didn't play there. The two blocks I played in were my entire world until the time I moved from that neighborhood, which would've been in the midfifties. I don't know whether the demographics have changed in terms of the numbers of children in the neighborhood. I've been back there many, many times. I went back for a novel I wrote. I went back to do articles over the years. I went back with other people who were asking me about my memories. Each time I saw hardly any children in the streets. Now maybe it's what memory does, but I have a feeling that the actual culture of just releasing your children to play outside has changed as well.

Our streets backed up to the school yard of the then Bronx High School of Science where there was a basketball court or at least a backboard and a rim. The neighborhood kids co-opted it. The school yard also had a wall, which became a place to play handball. There was a small area that became a place where we played punchball. And there was a little section where we played pitching-in stickball. There was also a side wall where we could play boxball. Playing ball was what we did as often as we could.

There was a famous basketball player called Bob Cousy. He was legendary. He played for Holy Cross College and then he was a major player for the Boston Celtics. And among the older guys in our neighborhood was Bob Santini. He played for Iona College so he was pretty good. Creston Junior High School was a destination school yard for good ballplayers and Bob Santini, who took a liking to me, would play there. I was small and he was tall, and he called me "Cousy." Well that was the greatest thing I was ever called in my life. There was nothing more thrilling for me than to play in a game and to be called "Cousy." We'd be making up sides and he'd say, "I got Couse." There'd be three-man basketball games, and he'd say, "Nice pass, Couse." It was around then that I realized I could actually play well enough to play. And that was thrilling.

Stickball was the most popular and most majestic of the street games. On our street it cut across ages because it was such an enthralling game to play. The older guys could play, and some adults even played with us. Younger kids too. To be honest, it was a game of great elegance played on a very rudimentary skill level because it was hard to strike out. The bases were marked with chalk, if we had chalk. If not, the DeSoto car was first base, the Buick on the other side of the street was third base, and the sewer was second base.

We had a ritual that was repeated by all. You'd steal a broomstick or a mop stick from your home and then work it on a manhole cover until you could cut the end off. And if it was a good stick, maybe that was *your* stick. Just the way baseball players have their favorite bats. That was your stick. And it was played with a Spaldeen. It wasn't tolerated easily by the police and building superintendents because you could break windows with the ball. If the police came by and they caught you, they would confiscate your stick and therefore break up the game. You wouldn't be arrested, but there was always friction between the kids and the cops. The squad car would drive down Creston Avenue and if somebody spotted it they'd alert the hitter and hide the stick, usually under a parked car. "Chicky—chicky, the cops!" Then we'd pretend to be playing punchball, which was completely implausible, because stickball players could be a city block away and there's no way we could punch a ball that far.

And then the street games ended. They didn't end in the school yards, and they didn't end on the sidewalks, but we never played in the street again. The Second World War ended, and with that it was as though someone turned a light out on us. During the war there had been gas rationing and there wasn't a lot of money around. It wasn't what you'd call a car-owning neighborhood. There'd be no real reason to have one. But then when the war ended and gas rationing ended, we were literally driven out of the streets by the automobiles. Once in a while you might get a stick-ball game together, but it was impossible because there was so much traffic coming through. My friend Ben Miller had a father who drove down Creston Avenue in a Buick the size of a house, it seemed. And with that Buick it was over. It wasn't Ben Miller's father who ended it, but we just couldn't be in the streets anymore. My street-game universe ended. At the end of World War Two, my ball-playing-street-game life ended.

I. C. ("CHUCK") RAPOPORT

TV and film writer; Paris Match and Life
magazine photographer

(1937–)

People don't realize that the Bronx is so hilly, especially where we lived in the Macombs Road area. There was a huge flight of steps going up from the street below to Davidson Avenue, where the entrance to our building was. Our apartment was on the first floor facing the back so because of the hill we were at eye level with the Jerome Avenue el. I was watching the trains go by when I was about five years old. What I saw were subway cars filled with men in uniform. When I asked my mother who they were, she said, "They're soldiers going off to war." I couldn't fully under-stand this at the time, but she said it with a lot of sadness in her voice. When the war ended in August of 1945, we were away on my bubbe and zayde's farm in Winsted, Connecticut. My mother told me and my cousins to go up and down the country road so that we could bang on pots and pans with a spoon to announce that the war was over. I was eight years old at the time.

In the Bronx your neighborhood was also like a small town. You didn't leave it. If you went downtown, you were going into the city—Manhattan. Or summers you might be lucky enough to go to "the country," usually meaning someplace in the Catskill Mountains, or in our case my grandparents' rural cottages, where you were surrounded by the same people. Since my neighborhood was like this small town, I was provincial in my outlook. I was this naive kid. Maybe it was just in our family, but for instance we didn't listen to music in the house even though I took accordion lessons. We didn't even listen to music on the radio. We listened to comedy shows.

There was no library in our house. We had a set of classics but they were never opened. When I finally started writing, I went from illiteracy to writer overnight. And as for my being a photographer, I didn't want words. Words were the enemy. I was uncultured in an uncultured world as far as my eye could see. Even my friends didn't talk about books and reading. I had to read for school but I never liked it. Thankfully in high school there were lots of different kids from all over the city. I found out that the whole world wasn't brought up the way I was. I went to the High School of Industrial Arts. I could draw. I think I got in because my older brother went to that same school. He was a very good artist. They'd always ask me, "Are you related to Mel Rapoport?"

I had this love/hate thing for my brother. And I definitely wanted his approval so often I'd play dumb so as not to compete with him. I was the good kid and he was the boss over me. My parents would leave us alone without a babysitter. They said that if there was ever a problem to just call the super. My brother and I were jumping from bed to bed and one of the beds collapsed. So we called the super and he jerry-rigged it. When my parents came home, my father figured it all out—and my brother got blamed. My father hit him with a belt. My brother was about nine years old at the time. I was six. He was humiliated and scared and hurt and he hated me for it. My reaction was don't get into trouble. I steered away from pushing those buttons, but my brother wasn't so lucky. Maybe he had ADD, which wasn't diagnosed in those days.

When I went away to college in Ohio I was still kind of naive. If you grew up Jewish anywhere in New York, you were still a New Yorker. Jews from Cleveland were different. They had their own midwestern shtick. It was culture shock going away to college. The students drank. In my house while growing up there was no drinking. There was no such thing as social drinking. We had cream sodas or milkshakes. I thank my parents for that.

Although I was naive and didn't know about the world, I did have some street smarts. When I was still in the neighborhood, some of the kids got together to form a gang. We had taken an oath where we swore to protect each other. The threat was mostly from the Irish kids in the neighborhood, especially at Easter. That was the brown-shoe, black-shoe period. The Irish Catholics wore black shoes, and when you saw that you knew right away that you were in trouble. They weren't killers or anything like that. It was mainly humiliation. You ran when you saw them, but sometimes you were cornered. You were made to sing or dance. You couldn't escape it. *Sing the National Anthem*, or *Say the Pledge of Allegiance*. You were stuck there and they'd laugh. We figured out that we had to travel in groups, calling out so other kids in your gang would come running. Sometimes there were fistfights, and eventually adults would break them up. Both sides would split if cop cars came.

Those street smarts got me through a lot of different situations. I basically felt I could manage and survive in the real world.

When I was working for *Paris Match* I was sent to photograph Marilyn Monroe, who was going to leave Columbia Presbyterian Hospital. There were three of us from the same magazine. I was standing with them and thirty or forty other photographers so I decided to go to the apartment building across the street for a unique angle. I went to the third floor and rang the doorbell. A little old Jewish lady went to the inside of her door. "Who's there?" I explained who I was and that someone was coming out of the hospital any minute and that I had to photograph her.

"Who's coming out of the hospital?"

"Marilyn Monroe." *Ching, ching.* The door locks opened. I was let in. I went to the opened window and put my arms on the windowsill. I had the Bronx chutzpah to ask, "Do you have a pillow I can lean on?"

I took a series of pictures that really told the story of what Marilyn Monroe was like, with all of these people surrounding her. She had been followed out by at least a dozen and a half people. She stood on the street near the curb, talking to the radio and TV guys—she never stopped posing—and I got a series of pictures different than anyone else. The problem was, they didn't use any of my pictures. You have my permission to use this one.

COLIN POWELL

Retired four-star general in the United States Army,
chairman of the Joint Chiefs of Staff, and
U.S. secretary of state

(1937–)

I WASN'T MUCH OF AN ATHLETE AS A KID, BUT I LIKED PLAYING ALL
the street games, especially one that involved kites. Do you remember the trolleys? We'd take some empty soda bottles, put them
into tin cans, and then put them on the trolley tracks. Then when
the trolleys came by they'd smash the cans and pulverize the glass
so that it was like a powder. We'd glue the powdered glass onto
the kite string and attach razor blades to this long tail we had made
with torn-up sheets. Then we'd fly the kites on our rooftops and
try to cut the kites of the other kids, and some of those kids were

on rooftops a block away. It was our version of being in World War Two, shooting down planes.

We never thought of ourselves as living in the slums. We lived in tenements, not slums. We didn't think of ourselves as terribly poor. Our parents worked hard and their aspirations and all our relatives' aspirations had to do with getting an education and getting a job. Not necessarily getting a college education, but working and earning money to support oneself and one's family, with the highest goal that of getting a job with a pension.

I was fortunate to have a tight family. Outside of my immediate family of my mother, father, and sister, there were also aunts, uncles, cousins, and close family friends who lived on our street, Kelly Street, in the Hunts Point section of the South Bronx. The Bronx is like a small town, where everyone knows everyone else and everyone else's business. I found that comforting. The neighborhood was warm and embracing with everything I cared about being within a few blocks of where I lived: the schools, the church that we went to, the library, the stores. The stores especially defined the neighborhood for me.

There was Teitelbaum's drugstore. My sister was best friends with their daughters. Across the street was Kaiserman's bakery. Then on 163rd Street there was a tailor and dry cleaner. There was the Puerto Rican bodega, the Chinese laundry, a kosher chicken market, and then there were the candy stores, also usually owned by European Jews. Remember the egg cream? It never had an egg in it. The candy store also sold newspapers. No one in the neighborhood ever read the *New York Times*. The only newspapers we read were the *Mirror*, the *Post*, and the *Daily News*.

There was an Orthodox synagogue across from Teitelbaum's. I used to earn a quarter to turn the lights on and off on the Sabbath, which religious Jews are not allowed to do themselves. I was the

Shabbos goy, the non-Jew who was able to work on the Sabbath when Jews were forbidden to do so.

Starting at age fourteen, I worked in a store owned by Jay Sickser, a Jewish storekeeper in our neighborhood who sold baby furniture and toys and spoke with a thick Jewish accent. It was there that I eventually picked up some Yiddish words and phrases. The customers, of course, never knew that. I understood enough to be able to report what I heard to Mr. Sickser so that he knew what the customers were saying to one another about getting a good deal. With that information he would be able to talk to the customer and close the deal.

But the best place was Sammy Fiorino's, the Italian shoemaker's shop, which was where we used to hang out and play poker. Nickel-and-dime stuff. There were off-duty cops who were playing with us when some new cops came in to break up the game. They left us alone when they found out who was there. We set them straight.

I had a bike and I used to ride it to Pelham Bay Park, which was a good distance, but when our family went to Orchard Beach, which was part of that park, we all jammed into our car. Once a year, though, we had to go to Jones Beach, for a dip. We went there because our parents believed that the dip would protect us for the whole year against getting sick. Orchard Beach was on Long Island Sound. It wasn't the ocean. Jones Beach was on the ocean, and that made a big difference to them.

Do you remember those Dollar Savings accounts? I used to save my earned money in my account and my parents also put money aside for me. By the time I graduated from college, my father emptied that account and gave me six hundred dollars. That was a lot of money in those days.

Early on in school I was just trying to survive, but there were a lot of things I learned that were part of our education that I will always be thankful for. We had something called arts appreciation.

I'll never forget listening to Ravel's *Bolero* and feeling how beautiful that music was. And seeing a Rembrandt painting, probably shown with an old lantern-slide projector.

They also had something called religious instruction. That meant that on Tuesday afternoons you got out of school an hour early to go to the church or synagogue that you belonged to. The Catholics went to their church, the Jews went to their shul, and the Episcopalians, like me, went home. I loved that.

In our whole large family we have a lot of professionals, and there has never been a divorce. That doesn't mean that everyone was always happy, but it does mean that the family itself was valued and keeping it together was important.

LLOYD ULTAN

Historian, author, educator

(1938–)

I WAS BORN IN 1938, AND I LIKE TO SAY THAT I'M AS OLD AS SUPER-
man and Bugs Bunny and one year older than Batman. I guess it
was in my DNA or I got it from osmosis or something like that,
but from the time I was a toddler I'd ask my parents, my aunts
and uncles, what happened before I was born. The question was
usually about what happened with my family—with my grandfather, and even my great-grandfather, who was still alive when I
was young.

My parents were caught up in the Great Depression. My mother used to laugh when she'd say she went to Theodore Roosevelt High School—in one door and out the other. She actually quit to take care of her family. She therefore always felt the lack of education and so she educated herself. She did crossword puzzles to increase her vocabulary. She listened to classical music concerts with Arturo Toscanini and the NBC Symphony on the radio, and she read historical novels. She said that was the best way she could get to understand history. My father, on the other hand, wanted to be an architect. He was in his first year at City College when he had to leave to take care of his family. My younger brother got my father's interest in architecture. I got my mother's interest in history. So I'm a historian and he's an architect.

When I was two years and ten months old, we lived one block west of the Grand Concourse. There was a hill there. We were walking when my mother suddenly grabs me and we run up the hill with her holding my arm. We stand on the barrier that separates what would be called the service road from the main part of the Grand Concourse. I have no idea why we are there. I remember so distinctly that across the way, on the opposite barrier or mall, there was a woman with a pageboy haircut wearing a print dress. Suddenly this woman leans forward, turns to her left, and starts applauding like a seal. I look in the direction she's looking, and coming up the Grand Concourse is a car. And in the back of the car, talking to a person next to him in the backseat, is our president, Franklin Roosevelt. I turn to my mother, who is still holding my hand, and I say, "President Roosevelt? Here?" Of course, as far as I was concerned as a kid, Roosevelt's first name was "President." But I knew that he was an important man because everyone knew his name. Everybody talked about him. And every time there was an election, my mother took me into the voting booth and I watched her cast her ballot.

The Grand Concourse was also a big parade route, especially on Memorial Day and July Fourth. There would be flags, bands, veterans' groups, and after them the civic groups. Because these parades were huge, the massing of units would occur along the side streets. They would come into the Grand Concourse as the last contingent in front of them passed by. I think because of that, every Thanksgiving morning I turn on the television to watch the Macy's Thanksgiving Day Parade. To this day, I love a parade.

Between the ages of seven and fourteen I had asthma so I really couldn't do much in the way of athletics. Whenever I ran, even just a short distance, I'd find it difficult to breathe. So I never developed any skills of hitting or running with a ball. One result of this was that I turned to books. I read a lot. The first book I ever took out of the New York Public Library was a history book. The book was a historical novel, called *Og, Son of Fire*. Toward the end of third grade, the teacher said, "Next year when you go to class, you'll have two new subjects, history and geography." I said, "Ooo!" and the kid next to me said, "What's that?" I was sort of in my own world, and I was perfectly happy with it.

Even though my parents didn't have much money, they were determined that their kid was going to get everything that New York City had to offer. So every weekend we went someplace else. One place we went was the Bronx Zoo. First of all, it was free. I found out later that you had to pay on Tuesdays, Wednesdays, and Thursdays, but nobody went there on Tuesdays, Wednesdays, and Thursdays. I got to know what all the animals were and where they were. The African Plains had already been built so I saw the animals roaming around in what was close to their natural habitat. I can still walk around the Bronx Zoo and know exactly where I am, even with all the new installations.

My parents made it very clear when I was in elementary school that if I wanted to go to college either I had to get a scholarship or I had to do very well and get into one of the city colleges. So I got into Hunter College in the Bronx, which was only eleven minutes away by subway.

After World War Two, they wanted to integrate Hunter to get their hands on the GI Bill money. They couldn't do it as an all-girls' school, but they could preserve the all-girls' atmosphere by keeping the Park Avenue branch that way and integrating the Bronx campus. When I got there, in the freshman class of 1955, Hunter's president, George N. Shuster, said that this was the first Hunter College class that had an equal number of men and women.

For my graduate work, I bless Nelson Rockefeller because I was able to get a New York State Regents College Teaching Fellowship to Columbia University, which is not very far away from the Bronx. That paid my entire tuition plus room and board. They gave the money in one lump sum for me to decide how to spend. Whatever was for tuition was tuition. But as for room and board? I stayed at home in the Bronx instead. And of course Columbia University, at that time, had some of the top historians teaching there. Richard B. Morris for colonial and American revolutionary history, Harold C. Syrett, who at that time was editing the papers of Alexander Hamilton, and William Leuchtenburg, who taught nineteenth- and twentieth-century histories. These were the top historians of the day and it was wonderful.

In 1977 two things happened in the Bronx, both in the same month, and within days of each other. In October 1977 Jimmy Carter was at the United Nations to attend meetings and speak before the General Assembly. At lunchtime, he gets into his limousine and of course he's followed by all the press. He goes up to the Bronx to Charlotte Street, and suddenly he's walking on rubble. Block after block of rubble. The print photographers take out their cameras when they see Jimmy Carter walking along Charlotte Street and the television cameras do the same thing and suddenly—*poof*—this is seen all around the world. The image of the Bronx until then, at least in many eyes, was that of a largely middle-class area, upwardly mobile, healthy. And then all of a sudden these pictures come on and people's jaws drop. Then the New York Yankees are in the World Series that year and it's a night game. The Goodyear Blimp is circling overhead for occasional shots from that angle. You see this shot of Yankee Stadium from above, gleaming in the darkness, and suddenly the blimp moves, Yankee Stadium hovers out of view, but the narration is still going on. And this is on ABC television. It's broadcast nationwide and also picked up internationally. You see the outline of the streets and the little pinpoint streetlamp lights and the rest is all blackness. And then somewhere, about ten blocks to the east of the Concourse, what hovers into view is a huge tongue of flame leaping to the sky. Howard Cosell is the broadcaster and he says, "Ladies and gentlemen, this is what Jimmy Carter saw. Ladies and gentlemen, the Bronx is burning." And I'm at home going "Aghhhhhhhh," grabbing my head. The combination of the two really shook the image of the Bronx.

A few years later, the nail in the coffin happened with the filming of the 1981 movie *Fort Apache, the Bronx*. People in the neighborhood are complaining to Paul Newman and Ed Asner about all the negative things in the movie. So Newman and Asner meet with these people at a local diner and explain that they can't stop production because all this money has already been spent. They have to go ahead. But they did promise that at the beginning of the film they would put in a disclaimer saying that not everything is like this in the Bronx, and that there are good people living in the area, etc. etc. etc. And true to their word there is a disclaimer at the beginning of the film. But I defy anybody by the end of the film to remember the disclaimer at the beginning! Danny Aiello is also in the film. He plays a bad cop. In one of the most shocking parts of that film, he's standing on the top of a triangular burned-out building, and he takes the perpetrator, puts him over his head, and throws him over the parapet to the streets below. Shocking! Before that scene is shot, Aiello is approached by the director. "Danny, come up with me in my car. I'll take you to the set." When they get there, the director says, "Now you go to the top of that building and shoot the scene." Danny Aiello takes a look at the building and says, "That's my house. That's where I grew up!"

DION DIMUCCI

Singer, songwriter, guitarist,
multiplatinum recording artist

(1939–)

I LIVED A BLOCK AWAY FROM THE BRONX ZOO. BY THE TIME I WAS sixteen I think I saw every animal alive on the planet Earth. I was five feet away from lions and tigers and gorillas and monkeys and seals and snakes and giraffes and rhinoceroses and hippopotamuses and llamas and just every animal imaginable. And in those days you could get really close to them. So what a fortunate person I was. I'd jump over the fence on Southern Boulevard and meet giraffes and hippopotamuses. I mean, it was wild. You could get a few feet away from an elephant. Where else can you do this?

I was also just a hop, skip, and a jump from the Botanical Garden, where we'd swim. We'd dive off bridges into the streams and climb trees and what seemed like mountains. You could be Tarzan for a day. I feel very fortunate that these things too were like a stone's throw away from me.

But there's a lot of angst and fear and anger when you don't know how to do life. I wasn't getting that kind of guidance from my parents. Maybe they didn't get it from theirs. We're all part of something bigger than ourselves. Whatever the reasons, none of us in my house knew how to deal with emotions, so I grew up with this fear of people. I don't mean just economic insecurity. I don't mean fear of people punching you in the face. I mean in an emotional sense, where you don't know how to handle things. It's kinda like—you become this kinda macho guy. You cover up all your feelings. You hide some deep psychological weaknesses. I had this feeling that I was supposed to be born knowing everything. Of course, that wasn't the case, but you'd pretend that it was by acting that way.

I lived one block away from Tally's Pool Room on Crotona Avenue and 183rd Street. Once, Willie Mosconi came and played with the neighborhood champion Joe Rock, and what a wonderful day that was. It was like a saint or royalty was coming through, all dressed up in a suit. It was unbelievable. We looked at him—*we're not worthy*. He was like the Pope of Pool.

My father had a lot of wonderful qualities, but he never had a real job. He would paint and sculpt and he would take me to the museums in New York, but he didn't work. I had uncles, though, who were wonderful electricians and policemen and they were hard workers, all of them. They were also tall. They looked like John Wayne and Jimmy Stewart and Cary Grant to me, but they weren't in my neighborhood.

What was in my neighborhood, up on the corner at Joe's bar, were these mafioso-type wannabes. I had a number one record and they told me, "Give us the record and we'll put it in the jukebox and when the kids come out of school, they'll pass the bar, they'll hear the record and they'll buy it." *It was number one!* They said, "I want you to be with me." I said, "I am with you." "No, I want you to be *with* me." I said, "I am with you." And then we go a little more into it. I said, "I can't kiss your ass. I'm not a 'yes' man, I'm a rock 'n roller. I can't do that. I can't be like these people who walk around kissing your ass."

I had a passion for music early on. When I went to Junior High School 45—I think the new name is Thomas Giordano Middle School—there were two black women music teachers who encouraged me to sing these Hank Williams and Jimmy Reed songs. There was also a superintendent of a building that was on Crotona Ave around the corner. His name was Willie Green. He encouraged me too. He lived in tenement buildings and he played blues. And I loved this guy, Willie Green, and he would teach me these songs, and when I'd go back to J.H.S. 45 I'd get encouraged there as well. The Reverend Gary Davis, the great blind blues man, also lived in the Bronx. I used to go to his house. *Teach me a chord. Teach me this.* At that time, he would play in Harlem on the streets.

Mount Carmel Catholic Church was the heart of Little Italy where I lived. Monsignor Pernicone used to talk to me about virtue. "Dion, what muscles are for the physical body, virtues are spiritual muscles for the soul. So you have to build yourself internally." The guys in the neighborhood, I thought I knew where they were at, but they didn't know where I was at. Monsignor Pernicone would also teach me in these conversations we had. I was walking around with questions like, *What is truth? And who has the authority to define it?*

There was also this guy, Dan Murrow, who became one of the closest friends in my life. He was a Jewish guy from Boston. He was a social worker and my father didn't like him. He said to him, "You're getting paid for what you do?" So Dan Murrow gave up his job and he'd come into the neighborhood without getting paid and we'd sit and talk for hours. He was an extraordinary guy who loved people. There are not many on the face of the Earth like him. Because of his coming into the neighborhood, and infiltrating the gang and talking to me personally, asking questions about my purpose and direction, what he said and what he did meant a lot to me. I loved talking to this guy and we remained friends all of his life.

When I look back, I say, *Why did I gravitate to these good people when others used to smack 'em in the head?* They were threatened by them. I was too. Then I saw the reason why. Because if they're right, then I'm a failure. That's frightening. These were extraordinary people.

When I went to Italy and started connecting the dots, that's when I started grabbing on to higher ground. I was very lucky because I had a hit record at an early age. I was twenty when Columbia Records sent me to Italy. I had a five-year contract with them for half a million dollars. Guaranteed. One hundred thousand dollars a year. They wanted to expand their distribution so they sent me to Italy. I went to Milan and that's where I fell in love with Italians. And, you know, I'm Italian and I wasn't crazy about Italians until I traveled. It was there I saw the beauty and the history and the architecture and the poetry and the music and the spirituality. You can't look at Jews, for instance, hangin' around Long Island, or Italians hangin' around Jersey, and know those groups. You have to look farther than that. In Italy, I got to understand what the culture's truly about. When I went to Milan, I saw my neighborhood. Milan looked like the Bronx, and the people walking down the street looked like they were from the Bronx. My God! I grew up with these guys in my front yard carving marble steps and stoops—and my grandmother would even come out and wash them with soap and water!

If you're raised in a borough, you're very much on the surface of things. Then you grow up and you can see that all of these traditions have a lot of depth. They're not old-fashioned. There's more to it than that, you know.

That first time I went to Italy, I was into all the artists. I looked at Michelangelo, at Raphael, their sculptures and their paintings, and the architecture there. From my perspective, each time I went, I went deeper and deeper. The second time I went, I was saying, *These artists are glorifying God. Look at these artists. The Sistine Chapel, Saint Peter's, and the architecture.* The third time I went I realized why Rome was so important. It was the place where these two guys died. Peter and Paul, these two little Jewish guys, were martyred there. Paul's head was taken off and Peter was hung on a cross. Upside down. That's why Rome is so important. Not because the Vatican's there. Not because of the architecture or the art or anything else. It's because these two guys gave their lives for their beliefs.

I'm gonna tell you something I'm very proud of. I'm going to brag about myself. I got an honorary degree from Fordham University this past year. And you don't know how that made me feel. I don't even know how to explain it. I was sitting there up on this platform on graduation day listening to the commencement speeches and looking out on the lawn with these mothers and fathers and faculty surrounded by these beautiful buildings on this beautiful day.

I'm sitting there being honored and, you know, it felt like it came around full circle. I was born in Fordham Hospital. It connected so much for me. The past, the present, and the future. I was so honored. I grew up a block away from there, not able to even think about going to Fordham. I used to climb over the fence and get chased out of there. My wife said, "They're giving it to you because of your life experience. The way you affect people now." Getting that honorary degree was one of the greatest experiences of my life.

BARBARA NESSIM

Artist, graphic designer

(1939–)

Our apartment faced south. It was the last house on the Grand Concourse so we could almost see downtown. I just somehow knew in my heart that where I lived was really special because I said, "Dear God, thank you so much for making me be born in the Bronx in New York and not in Kansas." I had no idea why I chose Kansas. I hadn't even seen *The Wizard of Oz* at that point, and I knew nothing about tornadoes.

We're Sephardic Jews so we come from a close-knit family of uncles, cousins, whatever. My father came from Turkey and my mother was born in Egypt but her family came from Greece. The cooking, Passover, everything was different from the Ashkenazi Jews from Eastern Europe. My parents spoke the antique Spanish from 1492. Ladino. That wasn't for us to learn, but for them to tell secrets.

We lived in a two-bedroom apartment. My younger sister and brother and I shared one bedroom and my parents had the other. I would stay up late doing my art homework in my parents' bedroom. I had a little corner there with my table and my chair. I'd put my pads and my T-square underneath the table and I would work all night. I don't know how they managed. My father was a postman and got up early in the morning while I would be up all night with my light on, when they were going to bed. By the time I was about ten I knew that I was going to be an artist.

My parents were traditional, but they trusted me. I mean, I knew how to get pregnant, and I knew that I wasn't getting pregnant. I didn't want to have kids. I wanted to have a career. I remember when I was fifteen, I was figuring out my future and I was sitting there thinking, Okay, I'm fifteen and I have to finish high school and that brings me up to sixteen, and then I want to go to college, which my father was against. He said if I was too smart, nobody would want to marry me and then, at twenty-five, my face would crack and I would be a toy in every man's arms. "Dad, maybe one day I will get married, but not now." I don't think my mother had dreams for me. I was always pretty self-directed, so if she had a dream for me, it would be for me to be happy. And I was happy, so she got her dream.

When I was fourteen, I had an epiphany. I was ice skating at the Wollman Rink in Central Park with my friend Vivian, whose mother had breast cancer and had one breast removed. She kept the falsies in a shoe box in the apartment. Vivian and I put on her mother's falsies to look older. We were fourteen and we looked sixteen. I guess it was the end of the day, when the ice was very uneven, because my skate got caught in a rut and I fell. I heard my leg go *boop,* and it broke. I used to call it "my lucky break."

I was in the ninth grade and I had to get home instruction. I had Mr. Stonehill for three hours a week for academics, and then I had Julie Mahl as my art teacher. She was the one who encouraged me to go to a specialized art school, like the School of Industrial Art. She loved the work that I did. She used to tell my mother I was a sponge. I just soaked up everything. She told me something, and then I did it, so I felt very empowered. I finally learned how to learn, academically.

Before I broke my leg, I wasn't really a great academic student at all. Somehow learning escaped me. I was always a dreamer. If I got a seventy-five in class I'd be happy, but it eroded my confidence. The one-on-one was very good for me. With Mr. Stonehill, I learned how to pay attention. I learned how to learn, and I liked it. Heaven forbid. I liked school! Because of the tutors, I knew I could be a better student.

I also never felt very popular in middle school. Because of my upbringing, I wasn't allowed out that much so I wasn't integrated into a social group. Everyone was out after school, making friends, but my family was more strict. I said to myself, when I go to high school, I'm gonna completely change myself and I'm gonna go with the crowd I want to be with. That's what I did. That was my epiphany. I was going to like myself better.

You know, I was an artist even then. I was really the same person as I am now. When you're young, you think you're gonna change when you grow up. Somehow you think you're gonna be different. When I was ten, I thought, What am I gonna be fifteen years from now? And at twenty-five, I used to think, I wonder what I'm gonna be like when I'm forty? I was exactly the same. Now [in 2012] I'm seventy-three. I'm exactly the same. I'm not any different than when I was younger.

PART TWO

I SAY IT'S THE TEACHERS ... DESTINY

It was a separation toward self-creation.... It's the process of coming from a place—your family, your neighborhood—and then creating something new. I knew that change was not about money, but an interior process about understanding who you are. What you see the world as being. There's a kind of self-confidence that comes with that.

—ROBERT F. LEVINE

AL PACINO

Award-winning actor, director, producer

(1940–)

REMEMBER THE DOVER MOVIE HOUSE? MY MOTHER WOULD TAKE me to the movies there when I was about three or four. Movies were our entertainment. It was sort of like having a big television, only no one had TVs in those days. We had radios but no TVs. I remember going past a storefront and there was this little box on display, and in it was Milton Berle in black-and-white and it was fun to look at. You couldn't hear anything, because the set was in the store. I have a very vivid memory of that—the first time I ever saw TV—in a store window.

The Dover theater is where I learned how to understand some of the more sophisticated movies. I'd have some vague memory of the movie, which I'd sort of repeat at home the next day. You know how kids have this memory? It gets imprinted when you see those pictures. So I'd act out all the characters that I saw and remembered. I was addicted to those stories. It was a lot of fun for me because most of the time I was home alone with my grandmother. My mother and grandfather were out working during the week.

I adored my grandfather. He originally came from Sicily but came to New York and lived in Harlem before he moved to the Bronx. He was a great storyteller. We'd both go up to the roof with chairs and newspapers. We'd put the newspapers under the chairs because otherwise they would sink into the soft tar that was the floor of the roof. Then he'd tell me stories about what life was like then, growing up. I relished those stories. He was a simple guy but very intelligent. You know how it is—intelligent but uneducated. Smart. I listened.

And you know—it was beautiful. I mean the world up on the roof. It was like our terrace. I wish I could describe it to you artfully. It was as close to poetry as I could get. It was spectacular. The sun would be going down. You could actually stand there and see the Empire State Building and the skyline from the South Bronx. And imagine—all these people who had come from different parts of the world would be up there. And at night—at night, there was this cacophony of voices, especially in the late spring to late summer. You would hear the different accents. We had them all. There were Italians, Jews, Irish, Polish, German. It was like a Eugene O'Neill play.

Summers were hot. We used to sleep on the fire escape of our apartment. Get the breeze out on the fire escape! My mother and I put blankets and pillows out there in the summer. That was a big thing. We had one bedroom, a living room, a bathroom, and a kitchen. It was hot inside.

Sometimes there were seven or eight of us in that three-room place. My uncle came back from World War Two, and then sometimes there were cousins too. There were a lot of beds that would come out at night. At one point, I even slept between my grandmother and my grandfather.

In first grade at school, I was extremely obedient. In about the second grade, the teacher started putting me in school plays. And then she had me read for the assembly. The Bible! I was the guy who got up and read the Bible to start assembly.

There was this teacher, Blanche Rothstein, the drama teacher, who went to my apartment to talk to my grandmother and to tell her things about me. To this day I don't know what they were, but I think they had to do with encouraging me to be an actor. She actually climbed those five flights of stairs to say that to my grandmother.

This is why to this day I say "It's the teachers." That's why when anybody says "teacher" I light up. There it was, in this South Bronx public school, recognizing something I was doing that made her say that there was real hope there. I don't know, because otherwise I think I was pretty hopeless.

The conduct thing started when I hung out with kids that sort of pulled you with them. You were influenced by them. They were influenced by you. It worked both ways.

After third grade, my mother had to come to school pretty much once a year to talk to the teachers. Their conclusion? That I needed a dad. My mother was adamant. She said it was because we were poor and, because of that, she had to work. And besides which, she said, I had a great relationship with my grandfather.

As I got older, I noticed that I would become close friends with males who became my father figures, like my grandfather had been to me—like Lee Strasberg of the Actors Studio, for instance.

When I was a young teenager, three or four of us hung out together. We were extremely close. We played tag on the roofs, believe it or not. We'd hop from one roof to the next. One time I was running full out to leap over to the next roof when I saw this alley between the roofs. I pulled myself back just in time. I swiveled around and went back because I knew I was going to go down. We also scaled the roofs when we were about ten or eleven. Remember those TV aerials? We'd kind of hold on to them as a balancer—and we'd walk on the edge of the rooftops. Now I couldn't even look down if I had to. Nobody ever fell, thank God.

Some of my closest friends, like my friend Cliffie, became drug addicts. They started taking drugs at ages fourteen, fifteen, but they had IQs that went through the roof. At the same time they were into drugs they had little pocket books of Dostoyevsky in the back of their pants. I was very fortunate. I wasn't into drugs.

My mother kept me off the streets on school nights. My friends weren't controlled that way. They had the kind of freedom and abandon that led to drugs and difficulty. I was so angry with my mother for keeping me home when I wanted to go out. It wasn't until later in life that I fully realized what she had done for me. What can I say? I hope my kids don't take that long.

ROBERT F. LEVINE

Entertainment lawyer, literary agent

(1940–)

A s a kid I was fat and I was smart, and my mother supported me unconditionally. When she took me to the family doctor who told her, "You know your son is too fat and you should do something about that," her response was, "My son is too fat? Look at your wife."

I was always at the top of my class in public school. I was smart enough to manipulate my world to avoid activities in which I couldn't be the best. Even now, I find myself gravitating toward things that I'm good at rather than changing myself. For instance, I don't want to ski. I'm not interested. It comes from a combination of built-in fear and wanting to excel. I figured out how to manipulate my world so it worked for me. I avoided sports because I wasn't good at them. I hated phys ed because I wasn't good at it. I found climbing ropes really hard. I wasn't good at it. Instead of building my body and learning how to climb the damn ropes, I figured out how to avoid the class.

In retrospect, it limited my life. And not being good at sports was a source of some humiliation for me. I was good enough at other things so it wasn't held against me, but it bothered me. When you're used to being the smartest in the class and then you're the last one picked for the team, it feels like shit.

When I went to Bronx High School of Science, my views expanded because it was a window onto the world. When you grow up as a working-class, lower-middle-class Jewish person in a Jewish neighborhood, the world is very small. The world is your neighborhood. The world is your building. You know everybody in the building. The kids in the building play together. You know all the people in the neighborhood because they all play together. When I went to Bronx High School of Science, all of a sudden the world got bigger. Really much bigger. One weekend you'd go to a party in a Bronx tenement. The next weekend you'd be at a party on Park Avenue. The high school had kids from all over, which is why it worked. There was this mix. Upper-middle-class kids from Manhattan professional families went to school with kids like me who were from these very limited Jewish neighborhood places. Seeing how other people lived made me want to get away. To get out of my small world, my parents' world.

My mother grew up during the Depression and that defined everything. The people who grew up that way had a level of fear about the world that was scary. My mother was one of the most frightened of people. She was terrified. Terrified of risk. Everything needed to be secure. The intention of life was to be safe, so I grew up with a fear of taking risks, of being out on a limb. You have to have a safe job. You have to be a professional. I bought into it, I guess.

I was very young in high school. This was a period when kids were skipped in school, meaning you skipped grades if the teachers thought you were very smart. They would keep pushing you forward without any sense of where you were socially. So I graduated high school just before I was sixteen and I managed to get myself out of the Bronx. *I have to get out. Go to school out of town.* My parents said, "Why can't you go to City College or Queens College?" I knew that if I stayed my world would stay small. *I gotta get out!*

I was able to get into Cornell. I went to the Industrial and Labor Relations School, which was what I was actually interested in. I did this all by myself, even though I was only sixteen. The school gave me scholarships, and my parents helped out a bit with some money. My first dorm room at Cornell was shared with this six-foot-four farmer from the Midwest who had gone to one of the fancy prep schools. There I was, this sort of fat Jewish kid. I didn't even know what clothes to wear. I was two years younger than everybody, which made it hard for me socially. So I graduated in three and a half years, not four. At that time, I was nineteen and a half and still on a fast track.

After college I went into the Air Force Reserve so I could get that over with. That was the era where there were lotteries and a draft, and all eligible guys had to serve. Can you imagine what basic training was for someone like me? I don't know how I survived. After that I went straight to Harvard Law School. I moved forward without taking a breath. Without looking back for a moment.

When I was at Harvard, I had the good fortune to work with Derek Bok, who at that point was a professor of labor law at Harvard Law School. He went on to become dean of the law school and president of Harvard University. He and I used to have lunch on a regular basis. When he heard about my life and the way I had steamrolled myself through all of these activities, he said, "You have to stop for a minute."

"I don't know what you're talking about."

"I think you should spend a year in Europe to start living a little bit."

I still didn't know what he was talking about. But he prepared me for applying for a Knox Fellowship, which was given to promising students to study at universities in the United Kingdom. I got the fellowship and went to England, to the London School of Economics. Cornell was another planet, but this was another universe. I took a course in industrial labor relations and for the first time in my life I didn't do the work. I carried this one textbook around for months. I remember it so clearly. It was called *Industrial Democracy in Great Britain*. It couldn't have been more than two hundred pages and it took me months to read. I really didn't need another degree, so during that one year I traveled all over the world. A condition of the Knox Fellowship was that twice a year you had to write to the dean of the law school and tell him what you were doing. I did that, but for the first time in my life I shirked my other responsibilities. It felt great and it changed my life. Somehow I realized that I didn't have to be on a constantly moving fast train through my life. I could take some deep breaths and make some decisions that were not simply based on a forward trajectory.

It's very interesting. When I look to formative processes, like in therapy, look at leaving my family, it wasn't an unpleasant separation. It wasn't that I had a family I had to get rid of because I was being abused. It was a separation toward self-creation. That's what I think about when I think about the process. It's the process of coming from a place—your family, your neighborhood—and then creating something new. I knew that change was not about money, but an interior process about understanding who you are. What you see the world as being. There's a kind of self-confidence that comes with that.

SUZANNE BRAUN LEVINE

Feminist writer, author, editor

(1941–)

I LOVED NATURE AND BEING OUTSIDE, SO WHEN WE MOVED TO Fieldston from Washington Heights, the idea of living in a place with a lot of trees and private houses was very appealing. Fieldston, which is a section of Riverdale, looks a lot like Larchmont or Scarsdale, but unlike Larchmont or Scarsdale it has hills and rocks so the houses aren't in straight rows. Some are up on big outcroppings of rocks, and others, like ours, are below on the street level. I don't think I knew that Riverdale was part of the Bronx. I don't think I was aware of the boroughs at all.

I was a tomboy. My favorite outfit was my flannel-lined jeans with matching flannel shirt. You got dressed up in a skirt or dress when you went "into the city," and I didn't want to get dressed up, so I avoided going into the city. The Fieldston School, which was a few blocks from my house, was my home base.

I loved being on the basketball team. I loved the practices. I loved getting on the bus to go to away games. I loved having a number. Seventeen. Years later, Title IX (legislation that banned sex discrimination at government-funded educational institutions) changed the nature of sports for girls.

In my day, teams like the one I was on were second-class citizens. We played in an old gym, while boys monopolized the new one. No one came to watch us. Even our parents didn't come. I guess it didn't seem as important a school event as, say, a class play. When I got to college there was no girls' basketball team at all. It's hard to imagine today; my daughter played volleyball all through high school and college and now plays on a coed city team. She loves volleyball the way I loved basketball and she's been able to make it part of her life. Title IX was too late for me, but it has affected me in watching my daughter. I think it was one of the major achievements of the women's movement.

Being popular was as important at Fieldston as anywhere else in the fifties, even though the Ethical Culture philosophy that guided the school made a big point of community building and respect for each other. Socially, the goal was to be "a fabulous kid." It meant you were a team player. That you were well rounded. But most of all, it meant that people liked you.

There were a hundred and three kids in my class. One day, one of them, who was a friend of mine, said, "You're so great and you're so popular and you're head of the student council—and I only know one person who doesn't like you." I went bananas and I got out all the yearbooks and I made lists of who it could possibly be. It obsessed me for weeks. And later—years later—it dawned on me. *I know who that one person was. It was the person who told it to me.*

Like most women of my generation, I expended a lot of energy trying to be liked. I never asked, *Do I like this person? Do I want to be with this person? Why am I working so hard to make somebody like me who I have no interest in?* Now I do.

Also like most women of my generation, I was ambivalent about being smart. This came out most clearly in our advanced math class. The three or four of us girls in the class all suffered from what came to be called "math anxiety." Because everyone "knew" that girls weren't good in math, we always felt that if we got the answer to a hard problem it was a fluke. No matter how many flukes we achieved, we were sure that we would get the next one wrong. Our teacher, Hans Holstein, loved giving the class challenging problems, and he never understood why we were so stressed while the boys were so exuberant. "Math anxiety" was something else the women's movement helped us understand— and overcome.

Something I never really outgrew was my lack of interest in clothes. My mother would take me to Loehmann's, the big department store near Fordham Road. They had this big open women's changing room, and everybody tried on clothes in front of everybody else. That was my first experience seeing older women's bodies. And girdles. Those orangey skin-colored girdles. It was fascinating and a bit shocking. The women there were not only big, they were loud and demanding. They would yell at salespeople. They fought over garments. It was a real Bronx experience. I don't think anybody who used that changing room would ever forget it.

STEVE JANOWITZ

Comedy writer, retired math teacher

(1941–)

I NEVER HAD A FOCUS OR A CLEAR DIRECTION AS A KID. THAT WAS one of my issues, I think. I was always getting into trouble, fooling around, trying to be a little bit of a wiseguy. I used to hear about the gangs, like the Fordham Baldies, but I never saw them or saw the action. Basically, I hung out with a bunch of young Jewish kids, but we would hear these stories and try to be cool and tough ourselves. So we had pompadours, and we smoked cigarettes when we were twelve or thirteen years old, and we wandered around like we were a bunch of tough kids—which we weren't.

Once in a while, though, we'd get into fights. This is the thing—I was always a very careful person. They were like . . . Jewish fights. One guy would get hit and the other would say, "I give." And that would basically be the end of it. And I'd always make sure that the guy I was fighting was someone like Arnold Katz, who is now a physicist, or Jerry Zelinsky, who had thick eyeglasses and looked nerdy. Guys like that. So we'd fight once in a while among ourselves, but no one would get hurt.

Our neighborhood was middle class, but there was one really tough guy there. I'll never forget this guy. His name was Billy Flanagan. People were terrified of Billy Flanagan, with his perfect pompadour. There were all these stories about him and how he would break people's heads. One time he was in the barbershop on Eastchester Road at the same time I was there. The barber was literally trembling because he was afraid he was gonna mess up this guy's hair when he cut that perfect pompadour.

In junior high school, a group of my friends and I decided that we should start our own gang. *Yeah, that's a great idea. Let's have our own gang!* There was some sort of carnival taking place out of our neighborhood. It might have been on Gun Hill Road or somewhere like that. So how're we gonna know we're in a gang? By dressing alike and wearing that uniform to the carnival that night. Our uniform was black pants and a white shirt. We must've looked like we were going to a school assembly or like we were accountants. Now that I think back on it, me with my black pants, white shirt, glasses, I think I looked like a cross between Arnold Stang and Alfred E. Neuman.

So we're at the carnival doing the games and walking around in our black pants and white shirts, maybe about five or six of us, when two other kids come up to us. And they looked tough! "We heard you're a gang now. Wanna fight our gang?" Our guys looked at one another, and within three seconds it was like, "Gang? What's that? We're—no, no—we're a club. A club!" Next thing you know, we're on the phone with one of our mothers. *Get us out of here!* At that point, we realized that even though we were trying to be tough, smoking cigarettes, our hairdos—all of that—it really wasn't for us. When I think back on our Jewish gang, I think we should've called ourselves Price Waterhouse or maybe the Accountants.

Fortunately, about a year later, the Beatles hit. As soon as I saw them, even though I thought they were weird-looking with those haircuts, I knew those guys were really good. That's when my focus changed. I listened to the music and started the shift toward peace and love.

MARGARET M. O'BRIEN

Sisters of Charity nun, educator

(1942–)

Education was very important to my immigrant Irish parents. They told us that we were all going to go to college but that we needed to get scholarships. My brother, who was probably five at the time, said, "Mommy, I'm going to get a scholarship. Mommy—what's a scholarship?"

I was in seventh grade when a nun came to talk to us about what we called vocations. She was an older lady, and I can remember her saying, "If you have this little voice, this little idea in your mind that doesn't go away, maybe you need to pay attention to it." At the time, I was thinking, *That's me*. My sister Ann and I were sitting in front of the mirror of the vanity in our shared room, and I said, "You know what that nun said the other day? About that little voice and paying attention to it?" And my sister said, "Oh, you're hearing things." But I thought about it a lot through the high school years and then I did it. I entered the Sisters of Charity a week before my eighteenth birthday.

In those days it wasn't unusual to enter young, right out of high school, although some entered out of college or nursing school or older. When I entered, I was very homesick, but I thought of my mother coming to America at age sixteen. She had relatives here, but still, within a few weeks she was out working, "living out" as a maid. I thought, *If my mother could do what she did at sixteen, then I can do this.*

I became a nun and taught in Scarsdale at the Immaculate Heart of Mary. Then I went to teach on the Lower East Side of Manhattan. What an awakening! From Scarsdale to the Lower East Side. In the Lower East Side Parish, St. Brigid's, there was no convent so we traveled in each day. It was the late 1960s and we wanted to be in the neighborhood, so we found an old tenement to live in. It was an unusual place, where the stairs were crooked and small and went up at an angle. If you looked at the front wall, there was a gap between it and the side wall, which was eventually pulled together with cables. Six of us moved in. We loved it. We were young. Those were incredible and wonderful times for us. Wonderful community. Wonderful experiences in the parish. The school looked right out on Tompkins Square Park. That was in 1967, when the park was the center of drug activity, but we weren't fearful. The school was broken into one night, so several of us stayed there the next night to make sure that nobody would break in again. When the police found out they nearly killed us.

I knew deep in my heart that I was very happy in my work, but when I was in my late thirties and early forties I went to Berkeley, California, on a sabbatical. I looked around and noticed, *Gee, everyone's in couples.* It was during that time of upheaval when I wasn't sure who I was and what I wanted. I started therapy out there and wasn't ready to come home. That was when I had to kind of rechoose. I think of that as having been a very healthy searching. I was so young and inexperienced when I entered, and so I had to rethink my decision on an adult level. My ties to the community were close so I didn't leave, but I did live in California for those twelve years. I had a friendship and that was one of those things that really made me stop and think about whether to recommit. I was at a funeral of a sister who used to pray for me all the time. I was kneeling, talking to her and kind of thanking her and also realizing at the same time that we were in the chapel of a retirement home for this funeral. I remember thinking, *I hope I can die here too.* And then I realized what I had said. I had basically already made up my mind.

I grew up in Kingsbridge Heights, one of the highest points in the Bronx. On our block there were apartment houses, private houses, lots of trees, and empty lots across the street with tree roots that looked like little rooms so you could play house in them. That neighborhood was wonderful, full of places to explore and plenty of kids to explore with. I even have a picture that someone's father, a photographer, took. There were maybe fifteen of us all sitting on the trunk of an old tree that had fallen down. I can still name most of the kids in that picture.

When I was a first grader, my parents would give us a nickel each to put in the collection basket. Some Sundays my nickel never got to the basket. It was spent on candy on the way home. It got to the point, when I was eleven or twelve, where, *Oh, there's a little change on the table* and it got into my pocket. I wasn't getting an allowance then. My parents caught me and then I was in big trouble, but my punishment was mostly interior. I felt embarrassed because I was supposed to be a good kid. My parents learned from it, though, because we started getting an allowance after that. It was small, but it was an allowance. Thirty cents

When it was report card time and we were young, they used the report card as an incentive. I got a nickel for every A or mark over ninety. A good report card was worth a dollar ten. The only time I got a B was because I talked in church. That mark came under "reverent and religious duties." With it all, I was a studious girl who loved to read. I loved to sing. I loved plays. I loved history and learned it just by reading.

We were very secure until my mother got ill with several brain tumors when I was just coming into adolescence. Those were uncertain times, let's put it that way. We thought she wasn't going to make it. She survived, partially paralyzed, blind in one eye and deaf in one ear. She was forty when this happened, and lived until she was ninety-five.

My mother was very dominant and so we toed the line. There were five of us, with me the oldest. I struggled with that control when I was a teenager. I would be fresh. Talking back. Disagreeing with her, but really mild stuff, like: "Get in there and do those dishes." "We'll do them at the commercial."

I also wanted a pair of heels. How long it took to get stockings and heels. My mother gave me a gift one Thanksgiving of stockings.

I went to dances and there were a couple of boys that I kind of had my eyes on, but I never really dated. We didn't step out of line too much, but my siblings tell me that they learned by watching me fight to just be quiet—and then to do what they wanted.

There was a girl, Annette, who I used to argue with. I didn't like her. My mother refused to get involved. *You got into it. You'll get out of it.* That's how you learned life, you know? You got a sense of yourself by being away from your parents but knowing that they were still there. I feel sorry for children today who don't have the freedom to just be with other kids, especially to work out their difficulties and relationships. Our kids have a harder time today.

JOYCE HANSEN

*Writer/children's book author specializing in
African American themes*

(1942–)

ALL OF THE ACTION IN OUR WORLD TOOK PLACE ON THE STOOP.
It was our town square. We played dolls and jacks there and jumped
double Dutch in front of the stoop. The stoop was also the place
for news and gossip, which was mostly done by the adults and
older girls. Those of us who were younger had no news or gossip.
Only lies or stories we told, just to have something to say too.
There was one neighbor who, when I think about it now, must've
known everything about us. I can see her sitting in her third-floor
window, with her arms folded, leaning on the pillow she kept on

the windowsill. She sat at that window morning, noon, and night, in all seasons. She was the neighborhood watch before that term was ever used.

I don't know anything about the West Bronx, Jerome Avenue, over there. We rarely traveled to that section of the Bronx. That was like another country. We lived farther east and north in the Morrisania area. I think in the early fifties, when I realized what was going on in the world, when I was about ten, that's when drugs started coming in. We never felt threatened, though. It's very interesting. Back in those days, you didn't hear about women being attacked on the street or old people being held up. You didn't have that. We lived in a tenement, 919 Eagle Avenue. There were also some private houses down the street, little private houses. One family—I remember them so clearly because they were doing so well—they had a house and they had a store.

Our neighborhood was primarily African American. There were a few, but very few, whites. Most of the whites had moved but there were two little girlfriends that I had, Patsy and Barbara. I guess they were the last two white children left in the neighborhood, and they just blended. They played with us all the time.

But though you had African American families of different economic levels, we were all in the same place. There was a musician who I'd see with his horn in a bag, going to work. There were a couple of nurses. There were some older kids who were going on to college. Then we had some very poor families. In our building there was a great mix. I guess to outsiders, all of us were poor, but although my family didn't have a lot of material things, my mother and my father created a safe environment for us right in that apartment.

My mother read to me before my two younger brothers were born, which was before I could read on my own. Reading on my own was a big wish of mine. I'd beg her for *Alice's Adventures in Wonderland*, which she read to me over and over. She'd do that no matter how many times I asked, but in later years she confessed that she didn't like that story at all and couldn't understand my fascination with it.

My father had his own business. A photo studio in Harlem. When we were young, we had no idea of the years he'd spent, even before we were born, documenting cultural and historical events there. He had taken pictures of Duke Ellington, Count Basie, and many other big bands, along with other famous people such as Mary McLeod Bethune, Eleanor Roosevelt, Mayor La Guardia, Martin Luther King Jr., Malcolm X, and so many others. He also took pictures of confirmations, baptisms, weddings, and many street scenes with ordinary folks, and always took pictures of us so that he didn't waste any unused film. He documented our lives too.

My mother worked off and on, but she mostly worked in factories. And like I said, she tried to create a good environment for us. So we didn't know how poor we were, materially.

As far as I knew, all the men in our neighborhood had jobs then, and there was a man, a father, in every household. You hear so much about these African American families, especially now, with the stigma that there's no man in the household. There are only single women. It wasn't like that when we were growing up. The men could get jobs and the families were together. They may not have been the best jobs or the highest-paying jobs, but they all worked. And if you were on home relief, as they called it then, that was a shame. You didn't even talk about it.

Our next-door neighbor, who was also the super of the building, was the first person in our tenement to own a television. My brother Victor and I, along with the super's grandsons, spent as much time as we could watching, but we were only allowed to stay for one program, the *Howdy Doody* show. My mother kept a check on us and warned us about wearing out our welcome. It was a happy day for us kids when my father finally bought a TV set. I watched the *Mickey Mouse Club*, my favorite, every day. Though back in those days there were no black kids in the club I related to Annette Funicello, who stood out from the others.

Like everything else, the TV set wore out, but you didn't get a new television just because the old one was broken. Things got fixed or patched up or you improvised. My brothers and I improvised. We took turns standing behind the TV, holding the antenna to keep the picture going. We'd tell the person holding the antenna what was happening, but when it was time to switch, whoever's turn it was, that person invariably whined about the length of time spent behind the TV instead of in front of it.

Our parents weren't involved in this craziness. Neither had time to watch television. This is just what we had to do if we wanted to watch. One of my grandmothers lived with us. We came home for lunch when we were in elementary school, and if my mother wasn't home my grandmother would be there, looking at the television. She loved Liberace. Oh how she loved Liberace! But she would be there for us.

I had a happy childhood, yet when the drugs started seeping in, I remember someone was hurt in the hallway. She was a junkie and she was shot. That's when my father made the decision. "Okay. It's time. We gotta get out of here." I was fourteen. That's when we moved to a house he bought on Belmont Avenue.

We left the old neighborhood, and then the world changed for me. When I entered Theodore Roosevelt High School, it was at the beginning of an influx of African American and Latino children from various parts of the Bronx. The lunchroom was segregated with all of the black students sitting together at two or three tables. Some of the teachers didn't seem to like us much either. I can remember a few teachers who were superb and who didn't seem to care who we were, as long as we learned. Not all of them were like the teacher who counseled college-bound kids. When I went to his office, I was told that college was for smart kids. I can't even remember how I responded. I think that I probably believed him for a moment, but I still had my books, and by that time a dream. I wanted to be a writer. High school, where I discovered Langston Hughes and even wrote horrible poems imitating him, was the beginning of my journey. I ignored the school counselor and took college courses at night while working as a secretary during the day.

My mother's love of books and writing and my father's love of history and telling stories through his photographs influenced me, but dreams have to be supported. I continued taking night courses and worked during the day until I received a bachelor's degree in English literature. What does a person who wants to be a writer do with a degree in English literature? You become an English teacher. But as the saying goes, "Man proposes and God disposes." I discovered that teaching reading and language arts to middle-school and special education high school youngsters was what, in the end, I was supposed to be doing. I wrote and published seven books while I was still teaching, but I thought of myself as a teacher first and foremost. My last teaching assignment before retirement was in a middle school in Morrisania in the same neighborhood I grew up in. I had come full circle.

ROBERT KLEIN

Actor, comedian, author

(1942–)

My parents were ultracautious. "Yoyishtanem." It's a Hungarian expression, and it's usually not good. *What are you doing? Watch out for that lamp cord! Wear white when you go out at night so the cars can see you! Don't cut that bagel! You'll slice your neck!* I've not read of too many beheadings while cutting a bagel.

When someone rang our doorbell at 6F—*Who is it?* Even the sound of it. *Who is it?* "Da *da* da." It was automatic that no one came into the apartment. And if you didn't recognize the voice, you looked through the peephole in the door. I remember even later, while on my own, when I already had a track record in show business, I'd get a phone call from my parents in Florida.

"What are you doing tonight?"

"I'm staying home."

"Good!" *How about some bubble wrap around me?*

I never leave my thirty-year-old son, and I see him twice a week, without saying, "Drive carefully! Watch out. There's rain." My son boulders and does some rock climbing. The bouldering is not a Klein tradition in any way, shape, or form. He only goes maybe seven or eight feet up on a rock with special shoes. You don't have far to fall. But it's not as safe as Ping-Pong, for which I insist he wear a helmet.

Early on, the ability to make others laugh enhanced my image. I showed off in the first grade by making Joy Wyman, my classmate, laugh at my silliness. Things like imitating the teacher when she left the room. I always made the class laugh. I was always the class clown.

We are three generations, my father, myself, and my son, three consecutive generations whose parents had to go to the principal because the boy was fooling around. My father told me, "Don't be a clown. It doesn't pay!"

Our block, on Decatur Avenue, had three vacant lots that were used for playing. Our enemies were broken glass and dog shit. There were no *curb your dog* rules. People never even thought of doing it. These were active lots anyway. We played softball on this one lot facing up—home plate was downhill. And in the warmer weather, these women would sit outside in their folding chairs where it was cooler and they'd sit behind home plate. *What are you doing with this ball?* They had absolutely no concern for the fact that this was where we played.

We played softball on the lots, but we played stickball in the street. There were two kinds. The one where we played across the street on the Woodlawn Cemetery wall, where we aimed for the box on the wall with a broomstick with no real fielding. If you hit my building, it was a home run. If you hit above the fourth floor it was a triple. The other kind of stickball was fungo. You yourself throw the ball up. No one's pitching to you. We played association football only in the colder weather, and if there was traffic you'd yell, "Car! Car!" and you never said that without its being true.

There was a sensible aspect to life there. It was a walking life. It was a public transportation life. There was a sensibleness to walking to grade school, walking to junior high school. Walking to high school. There were routines. Sunday mornings were special. My father would go to the bakery, and we would get six small rolls, which are known as kaiser rolls, but these were a more sensible size, and I would have a roll with cream cheese on one side and butter on the other. There was Freddie the barber who cut my hair from the time I cried when I was too small and had to sit on a little seat until I went away to college. In his shop there was this beautiful calendar of Babe Ruth in heaven. There was also a picture of a very handsome Jesus looking over the barbershop on the calendar at the other end.

Despite those good memories, I really didn't like where I lived. I wanted something else. I wanted a backyard when I lived on Decatur Avenue. There were veterans coming back from the war and getting good loans. Moving to Westchester. Moving to Levittown. Going to the suburbs. My father used to take the subway downtown to work, but he took the New York Central back. The trains said, "Northward, to Chatham" and "Southward, Grand Central Station." I wanted to go northward to Chatham. There was a kind of claustrophobic feeling I had where we lived. I wanted what I saw on television.

When we were very young, someone in the building on the second floor had a TV set before we did, and we'd come home from school, go to our neighbor's, and watch *Six Gun Playhouse*. Or Republic and RKO Westerns with a young John Wayne, which often featured children galloping on a pony, usually white, across expansive plains. It appealed to me so much that eventually I learned to ride quite well in camp. That was one of the ecstasies in my life, galloping. Now, of course, I'd be afraid to gallop. So anyway, west and north were my favorite directions. The West Side. I didn't like the East Side. And going west. I didn't get to California until I was twenty-five, but then the smell in October of jasmine, when it was getting nasty back east, and every traffic light there turning green. I wanted more space.

I went to camp as a kid, and even though those were my father's worst years because he was a terrible businessman, he still provided. Even in the worst year he'd take a place in Monticello or in Peekskill, which isn't even twenty minutes away from where I live now. I loved the trees and the smell of the grass and I loved camp. All those experiences made me think that I wanted less concrete.

I have a couple of acres in Briarcliff, fifty minutes away from where we're sitting in Manhattan. The view of the Hudson is unbelievable. There's no building across the way. It's north of the Tappan Zee Bridge. It's one of the great places. It's the views. It's the Hudson River School of painting. I never get tired of it. So when I come to the city it's more of a novelty for me.

There were things in the Bronx everyone seems to think of nostalgically and positively, but part of that is because we were young and we had fun. Sunday nights I do *not* have fond memories of. It took me many, many years to get out of the slight gloom, because Ed Sullivan was on and the next day was school and as much as I'm thankful for the most wonderful free education it was dull, except for a few courses in high school and a few in college.

At my age, I realize another important thing about that life. It had to do with women. When you live compactly, you know everyone else's business, and it's amazing how they pretended they didn't, but the women were incredibly strong for each other. Much more so than the men. Men in the building—there'd be some talk, and this and that, but the women, they bonded, they knew each other's business. Even women who didn't see each other socially would confide in each other. I remember the word "divorcée," the women talking about this other hardworking woman with two kids, a divorcée—the very sound of it scared me—and that with my parents arguing every day. I didn't know if there'd be a divorcée in our family. I didn't know anybody who was divorced.

I have a collection of books, mostly from the Bronx Historical Society and the Museum of the City of New York, with pictures of when the Bronx was farmland. I love those pictures. Farmland! These beautiful photos are of something that will of course never exist again.

JULIAN SCHLOSSBERG

Theater, film, and TV producer, movie distributor

(1942–)

LONG BEFORE THE JAVITS CENTER, LONG BEFORE THE NEW YORK
Coliseum, there was the Kingsbridge Armory. The Kingsbridge
Armory was the largest armory in the world, and I lived across
the street from it. In that armory there were motorboat shows
and car shows. All the things they now show downtown, in Manhattan, they did in the Bronx. And what's so extraordinary is that
in the middle of the Bronx, in that same Kingsbridge Armory,
there were rodeos. Bucking broncos, catching steers, roping heif-
ers. Unbelievable! And there I was, eight, nine years old, going

to these shows. It was extraordinary. It was so extraordinary that I was able to meet, in person, my Western heroes, Buster Crabbe and Johnny Mack Brown. Buster Crabbe was a big Western movie star who also did *Flash Gordon* serials. For a kid, he was a giant in that field. And Johnny Mack Brown was one of the many cowboys. That was an amazing thing. A rodeo with those Western heroes right across the street from me in the middle of the Bronx.

I knew all the local stores in our neighborhood. The barbershop, the cleaners, the candy store, and the bowling alley, for instance. Every time there was a new show, any show, at the armory, these shopkeepers would be given two free tickets for opening night. I'd go around and say to each of them, "If you're not going to the show, would you save your tickets for me?" So I would get their free tickets and then sell them. So instead of, let's say, three dollars a ticket, I would sell them for two dollars. My concept at eight or nine years old was to give them a discount. One third off. Well I wasn't paying for them, so I thought I would at least give them a break on the price.

I was never caught, except for this one time. There was a comic book called *Scrooge McDuck*. This character, Scrooge McDuck, was Donald Duck's uncle and probably the granduncle of Huey, Dewey, and Louie. He had a pool full of cash. In the comic book, he would go up on the diving board and dive into this money. So I spread these dollar bills from my ticket sales all over my bed—my mother was out working—and I'm diving into them, about seventy or eighty dollar bills, throwing them into the air, when my mother unexpectedly walks in. She comes in and goes crazy. "Where'd you get this money?" I tell her and she says, "You must promise me that you won't do that again." And I promised, "I won't do that again." Of course, I was referring to diving into the dollars and she was referring to my not continuing to work the armory.

Even at that age I knew what money was, and I wanted it. It wasn't as if my parents were misers, or that they really loved money. All they wanted to do was to pay the rent, which sometimes they couldn't quite do and so they hid from the landlord. They always paid, but sometimes a little late.

At about ten years old, I actually worked in a drugstore, delivering prescriptions and milk of magnesia. I was hired to do these deliveries, which I did for two weeks. Two weeks later I'm dusting the shelves and sweeping up because the regular delivery boy came back from vacation, but no one had told me. They weren't kind enough to let me know that I was now the cabin boy of the ship and so I quit.

But I didn't quit until I had another job. I was now eleven years old and got a job working for a dry-cleaning store, Dorsey Cleaners. I was the delivery boy. I got a little more than sixty-five cents an hour. About two dollars for three hours. That part was okay except the hangers dug into my hands when I delivered the clothes and the people at the other end weren't always home when I arrived. There weren't any doormen in these buildings, so I'd schlep the clothes there, and I'd schlep them back.

Then I got a bit more industrious and went to the bowling alley underneath the cleaners and became a pin boy. That was the hardest job I ever had in my life. This was before automated pins. Even before semiautomated pins. There go the balls, and there come the pins! Those pins go flying, and I'm sitting in between the two lanes. I'm working two alleys and I'm eleven or twelve years old. And those pins are coming up and I'm hitting them down, at nineteen cents a game. That was really tough stuff. It was backbreaking. The bowling alley guy knew I worked upstairs at the cleaners, but the guy upstairs didn't know I worked downstairs. I decided that I had to wear sneakers and run with the clothes, run back, go down, do a couple of games, and run up again. It was an interesting way of being industrious.

Later on, but still at a very young age, twenty-seven, I was made head of a theater chain called the Walter Reade Theaters. At that time, I was supposedly the youngest head of a theater chain in that business. Whether it's true or not, I don't know, but that's what *Variety* said. When I went to meetings with all the studio heads who were in charge of sales, to a man they would ask, "Where's your father?" You know, *Who are you?* They really intimidated and wanted to intimidate. So the first thing I did was to grow a beard, because I had read somewhere that a beard made you look older. That helped a little bit.

What was fascinating was that these men had risen through the studio ranks, but they had started in Texas, in Oklahoma, in Iowa. They didn't start in New York City. I was a city kid. I knew how to handle myself. They had the advantage of age, but they didn't have the street smarts that I grew up with. Those streets made you grow up quickly and you learned from your experiences.

ANONYMOUS

Writer

(1942–)

I WAS A VERY SHY GIRL AND PRETTY MUCH OF A LONER. MY SISTER was six years older than I, so my pal was my cousin, who was a year and a half younger. She was more social than I was, so naturally she wanted to have other friends too. Whenever that happened, I would tell her that the other person was no good. I just didn't want her to have other friends. I knew other kids, but I never really hung around with them or played with them. I was also very frightened of people. I think a lot of it had to do with my father, although it's unclear how early things started with him. I think it may have started when I was about five years old and lasted until I was seventeen. I don't know if I've told you. There was incest in my family between my father and me.

He would say that it was all about what he did for me, so that I could have a house and, you know, how hard he worked. Basically, he said, I owed him. If I got a gift or an ice cream cone or a bicycle, there was a payment to be made. That colored my whole life. My sense of reality was never really developed because he also told me that whatever was happening to me was not happening to me. I was told there's nothing wrong with what he was doing, but yet don't tell anyone because then they'll think that I was crazy and then he would have to institutionalize me. You know, he was really demented. As you can imagine, I haven't even talked about this in years, but it sure did color my trust of people and of being around people. I was afraid that someone would find out. I had this terrible secret that if I told I would be put away in an insane asylum. And that it would also kill my mother. I think that my mother knew, but she couldn't deal with it.

So that was why I couldn't be around other kids. And on some level, I didn't know. Didn't this happen in everybody's house? I just didn't know.

I didn't even confide in my sister because my sister was, until the day she died, one of the meanest people on Earth. I actually didn't tell anyone until I was nineteen. Now don't laugh. I told my charm school teacher, after I had moved from the Bronx.

I was most happy in my imagination. I was happy on Saturdays when I went to the movies or when I was playing. You know, when I was in a whole other world. I can still picture the playground where there were these big concrete tunnels that you could climb into. God, I'm really remembering things I haven't thought about. I used to run away a lot. I used to run into the playground and hide in the trees, or I'd hide in the tunnels, or I'd hide wherever I could. I would come home from school, change into my play clothes, and then not come home. They'd be calling for me all over the neighborhood, but I would be hiding. Sometimes I'd go to a neighbor's apartment and nobody would know I was there. And the neighbor wouldn't know that anyone was looking for me. I would kind of disappear. I think that I was just hiding from life.

My father died in 1974 of a rare disease at the age of fifty-eight. It seemed fitting that this was his fate. There was this big funeral for him in Paramus, New Jersey. He was well liked by mostly everyone, never having revealed his dark side. To them, he was a kind, friendly, benevolent person when, in truth—well, we know the truth.

At the graveside, the rabbi gave me something to read and I gave it back to him. I couldn't do it. I couldn't grieve or cry or feel anything but relief.

RICK MEYEROWITZ

Artist/illustrator, writer

(1943–)

THERE WAS THIS FULL-CITY-BLOCK EMPTY LOT ACROSS THE STREET from our building. It was filled with gravel, broken bits of glass, sharp pebbles, crabgrass, stunted trees, and mounds of garbage. And we played there day and night. We played in that lot because we were told it was safer than playing in the street. "Because of the cars," my father said. And you'd look up and down the block and there'd be maybe six cars parked on the entire block because this was the forties and nobody had cars. And I said to him, "What was it like when you were a kid? You told me you played in the street all the time." And he said, "Well, yeah, we didn't have to watch out for cars because there were no cars when I was a boy growing up on the Lower East Side, but you had to watch out for horse shit because the streets were filled with it." And I said, "Well, that must've been awful." He said, "I don't know. It made sliding into second base pretty easy."

On the corner in our old neighborhood there was a bank. Manufacturers Trust bank. And right next to it was a New York public library. We played stickball for hours against the wall of that library. You could hit a rubber ball easily three times the distance you could hit a softball. And the speed of it! I once hit a line drive and it went into a city bus. Through a window of a moving city bus! I held my head in my hands. It wasn't that I worried I might have fractured somebody's skull with a hard-hit ball. I was worried that I lost the ball because it went into the bus. It all happened in a split second, but the bus kept moving, and then I saw there was the ball on the other side, bouncing in the street. It had gone through the opposite open window of that bus. What are the odds of that happening? The driver didn't even slow down. It may have happened so fast that nobody in the bus even noticed that this ball flew through the windows.

These are the things that make childhood so remarkable. Something like that stays with you all these years. Let's see, Jefferson had on his gravestone that he was the author of the Declaration of Independence, that he was the writer of the Virginia Statute for Religious Freedom and the father of the University of Virginia. Will mine say that I hit a ball through a Number 3 bus and it came out the other side?

There was a particular look to the Bronx. The look of the architecture and the streets. The feel of being under the el and the light coming through. I didn't know Berenice Abbott had already made the photograph that was in my own memory. The light coming through under the el used to mesmerize me. I would walk with my mother and she'd go into a store and I'd stand in the street and I'd look at the light filtering through. Beautiful sunlight. Through the tracks.

If your childhood was a happy one, that becomes a place that has magic to it. And that was our Bronx in those days. We felt no threat. The war was over. And we were alive and there was a sense of real possibility. Possibility. There was a world opening before me. I didn't know what I was going to do with myself, but I didn't dwell on that too much. I knew I was going to draw and read and go to college.

There was another thing. There was a smell. It's hard to describe. The smell of a thunderstorm. The change in the barometer as the sky would turn a kind of a deep gray-green and the summer thunderstorm would come over and the dust would lift from the street. It was like the rain or the falling barometer actually drew this stuff out of the ground into the air. You'd breathe it in. You could smell the storm. The aftermath of it was clean. The Bronx was an extraordinary and fertile land to grow up in.

My father once explained to me the difference between a Bronx accent and a Brooklyn accent, 'cause I had said, "I don't get it, what's the difference?" And he said, "In Brooklyn, they would say 'I'm gonna moider da bum.' In the Bronx, they would say, 'I'm gonna muhdah da bum.' There's a lot of 'duh' in it." My father would then say, "Either way, the guy's dead."

Before television, men and women went outside at night from spring to fall to sit on beach chairs, or whatever chair they brought out, in front of the building. The women talked, the kids played, and the men smoked cigars and belched. It was after dinner and everybody came out, and that was the sound track of my early days. If a fight or a baseball game was on the radio inside someone's apartment, that person would open the windows so everybody outside could stand around and listen. Things changed when television came around and families went inside to watch TV. They didn't go outside anymore. And you had air-conditioning, so you didn't have to go outside to cool off. Suddenly you didn't know your neighbors. The world began to evaporate for us. The reason it seems so magical in my memory is that it's a world that's gone.

In his acceptance speech at the 1968 Republican Convention, Richard Nixon recalled that when he was a child, he would lay in bed in Yorba Linda, California, hearing the frequent rumble of freight trains as they passed through town during the night. He wondered where those trains were going, and if he got on one, where it would take him in his life.

Nixon and I had similar experiences. Drowsing in my bed half a block from the Westchester Avenue el, I would fall asleep while listening to the passing trains every night. But unlike Nixon, I didn't wonder about the final destination of those trains. Where they were going was no mystery. On a Saturday afternoon that train would take me two stops east to Parkchester, where the admission to the Circle Theater was 25 cents. And I could buy an insane amount of candy, and watch two movies and ten cartoons.

JOEL ARTHUR ROSENTHAL
(JAR)

Artist, jewelry designer

(1943-)

I GET SO ANNOYED WHEN PEOPLE, EVEN PEOPLE I KNOW, INTRO-
duce me and say that I'm from Brooklyn. *He's from Brooklyn!* I've
been to Brooklyn three times in my life. Actually, I'm going there
tonight for pizza, so that will be the fourth time in my life. At
openings I've had or openings I've been to, people will sometimes
come up to me and whisper, *I'm from the Bronx.* Whisper? *Why are
you whispering?*

Bette Midler has a foundation that creates gardens in neglected
parks and open spaces all over the city. I went back to the Bronx
with her because I wanted to have a garden there to honor my

mother. When we got there I saw that the space for the garden was on Fox Street, which was amazing. My mother grew up on Fox Street.

I went to Music and Art High School, where I felt I belonged and fit in because I was surrounded by an entire school full of kids with whom I had many things in common. There were kids who drew, who were really good. There were musicians who were outstanding. I guess by then I was already an arrogant little bastard. There was a wonderful teacher, Julia Winston, who taught our watercolor class. She'd walk around correcting this paper and that. Once she corrected something on my paper, and I said to her, "You're the teacher. We're here to learn, but don't you ever draw on my paper again." Total silence in the class. But she never did it again, and we became really good friends.

I don't think I was spoiled except by love, but it was in high school that I started spoiling myself by realizing that I had the capacity to make beautiful things. I did pretty good watercolors and I was a pretty good draftsman so I knew how to get attention. That was not the goal, but when you do a beautiful drawing and someone looks at it, it makes you feel pretty good. I think that artists and musicians do whatever they do to get attention, consciously or not. I don't think there's anything wrong with that. It's inseparable from what we do.

I once said to my parents, "How did you know how to bring up a kid?" "Just instinct, that's all." I was an only child and I didn't play baseball in the lots. I didn't play stickball. I had no apologies to make, and my parents made me understand that I had no apologies to give. They encouraged me to express my opinions and not the opinions of others. They raised me to respect what I thought and not to waver from that. Taste and opinions. I got into many fights about those, and I still do.

I think I was the head of the yearbook in high school and somebody wanted to do a cover that I thought was too modern. Too ugly. *If I've been given the power to decide what this yearbook looks like,*

I'm gonna fight for the cover. I prevailed. They were all annoyed with me, including Julia Winston, the watercolor teacher. And yet, and I know this sounds odd, I'm very shy. I was head of Arista, the honor society. There was a general meeting of the heads of Aristas from all the different schools. We were each supposed to make a speech and I said no. And I didn't do it.

Recently, the head of Christie's in Paris came to our office in Paris bringing all these guys I've known for years. Five of them along with François, who's been a friend for five hundred years. He wanted me to explain something. I couldn't. I couldn't talk to them. I can talk to you alone. Maybe two of you. But I can't expound in front of people. I wish I were Barbra Streisand, and then maybe? I just cannot do these things.

Eleven years ago we did an exhibition of my jewelry in London. Then friends gave us a ball for about four hundred people. At the last minute they told me I had to make a speech. The logistics were that two other people would make their speeches first and then I would be tapped on the shoulder and they would give me the microphone. I was sick. Absolutely sick at the idea. After agonizing over it, I decided that I would say, *Thank you, Eugenie. Thank you, Nicola. Thank you all for coming.* Period. I was numb even thinking about it.

When the time came, they gave me the microphone. I said the first thank you and then burst into tears. Lily Safra was at the table, and she said, "You're always such a pain in the ass. Come outside with me." She knew what she was doing. She saved me. I went outside with her and I sobbed for five minutes. It was then that I decided that I would never, *never* under any circumstances try to do that again. I never will.

Maybe this is my way of dealing with the public and my shyness, but when they asked us to do this current show at the Metropolitan Museum, and when I conceived of the exhibition, I didn't think of myself as the person having the show. Instead, I thought of this little kid walking up the steps of the Met, being taken there by his parents. He was the one having the exhibition. That little kid, who was always very happy to go to the museum every time his parents took him. Who did drawings there when he was ten. Seeing the little kid there instead of me, the grown-up, keeps the experience away from me, even now.

MILLARD ("MICKEY")
S. DREXLER

Businessman, CEO of J.Crew

(1944–)

IN THIRD GRADE, I WAS GIVEN A PUNISHMENT THAT INVOLVED
math calculations. Five digits multiplied by four digits. And the
punishment was to do thirty or forty of these different multiplica-
tions. It's hard, right? But I did them. The next time I figured out
that the teacher didn't check out the answers, so I just made up the
numbers and handed them in. She never checked, but after that I
didn't misbehave. I didn't like being punished. In the fifth or sixth
grade, after the regular public-school day, I also went to Yiddish
school. I went for a few years, but then was kicked out for misbe-

having. I misbehaved because I always had trouble with authority to a degree. Especially with people who weren't nice to me. Even to this day, I'm very sensitive to people being rude.

When I was punished in Yiddish school, my teacher, Mr. Schneid, said, "Mordecai"—my Yiddish or maybe my Hebrew name—"you will go home and write, 'I will be good in shul. Ikh vel zayn gut in shul.'" Maybe it started with my writing this twenty-five times. I misbehaved the next time. "Ikh vel zayn gut in shul." Fifty times. I got more angry. I couldn't stand these stupid punishments. I was sitting in the apartment of my aunt Frances, who was a bit of a renegade. With her encouragement I wrote, "Ikh vel zayn gut in shul x 1000." I handed it in, and that was it. I was out. I was bored out of my mind when I was there. And I think also, somewhere in my eleven- or twelve-year-old head, was the fact that I couldn't stand the guy.

You know what's interesting? I didn't grow up in a home environment that said, Do your work. Be successful. Work hard. That was the usual Jewish DNA message in those days, but not in my family. I was the only one of eight cousins who made it to college. Somehow or other I was lucky. I realized that I needed others as role models. My seventh-grade math teacher was someone I loved. I was always good in math. I excelled in it. Mr. Barrett gave me the confidence to feel good about myself. At home, my mother was either ill or depressed, and my father didn't pay any attention to me. Ambition and education were not values in my family. I never heard, for instance, Be a doctor. Be a lawyer. Be a dentist or a businessman, for that matter.

There were two things that introduced another world to me, other than the one I knew at home and in the neighborhood. The first one was going to sleepaway camp. For the first time in my life, I met kids who lived on Long Island, Westchester, and even Manhattan. And I'm thinking on visiting day fancy cars are here. I'm looking, and even a kid knows that if you had a Cadillac you were automatically rich. Wow! And then I met this girl who went to a private school in Manhattan. Dalton. I couldn't imagine going to Dalton, a private school on the Upper East Side. I had never met anyone like that before. I got a tour of the school. I'm looking around and saying, This is another world. Private school. You pay. And it's in Manhattan. Mecca to a kid from the Bronx.

The second introduction to the world at large was when I went to Bronx High School of Science. One of my best friends there was Jack Friedman, who lived in Riverdale. A three-bedroom apartment, a housekeeper, and a father who was a stockbroker. I couldn't get over the wealth. I had never seen this before. A maid, a remote control on the TV—his father had the remote—and three bedrooms.

It was lucky that I went to Science, because everyone there was expected to go on to college. I didn't get that from my home, as I've said. If you were affluent, then you could afford to go to a private school. At home, there wasn't even a discussion about which college to go to. When it came up, it was automatic. City College or State University.

There was a hunger that I had growing up in the Bronx. It wasn't financial. It was an emotional hunger. I was lucky that I had aunts in the neighborhood who balanced out what I didn't get at home. But I had this added hunger to go out into the world. It was an achievement hunger. It was a pass to get out and the training was the Bronx.

When I worked in San Francisco, I was out of my natural habitat for eighteen years. There's something about this town, New York. You feel it. You see it. It has the highest level of intensity, of humor, of creativity. And none of that gets separated from where we grew up.

As you grow older, you can grow in any environment because you have exposure and the possibilities of learning every day. And I'm still learning. The way I grew up turned out to be the best thing that ever happened to me.

ANDY ROSENZWEIG

Retired policeman, detective, chief investigator for the
Manhattan district attorney

(1944–)

I GUESS SOMEWHAT TO MY DETRIMENT AND CERTAINLY NOT TO MY
benefit I was mesmerized by basketball. Playing it. Watching it. I
wasn't a very good player. A mediocre player in retrospect, but at
the time I thought I was terrific. Basketball was everything to me.
I even got to play with some very accomplished, very good players
from time to time.

I played in my backyard, Bronx Park. Sam Borod and my friend
Stan Golden, who passed on a few years ago, we'd be on the courts
shoveling the snow off with a few others. It didn't matter how much

it snowed. It didn't matter how cold it was. We'd even get brooms to clean off the courts, along with the shovels, and play there all weekend. Be there early morning until dark. We also played with Stanley and Leon Myers, a couple of young black men, African Americans, or we would have called them "Negro boys" back then. Stanley and Leon played ball in the park with us all the time. We never thought anything much of it, that they were black, I mean. I guess we had our social boundaries, but I wasn't too aware of those things at the time.

Even though I went to Bronx High School of Science, I didn't go to college right after graduation. I had thoughts about my future, but they weren't very clear. When I was seventeen, before I graduated, I told my mother that I'd like to join the Marine Corps. Her response was very clear. Over my dead body! I did eventually join the marines, but not until I was twenty. The Jewish family tradition was definitely not to go into the marines. It was a struggle to figure out who I was and what I wanted to do when I was fifteen, sixteen, seventeen. It took a while. Eventually, after the marines, I became a policeman and then a detective.

All the things that happened in the ensuing years, like the turmoil of the civil rights movement, were foreign to me. I mean, it didn't make sense to me because I had direct contact with African Americans and it never occurred to me that there was discrimination against them. I was in my late teens or early twenties when I started to get it, but it took a while. I was inured—not inured—I was blind to how badly other people could behave.

The Myers brothers, from my basketball days, we didn't stay close friends, but probably in 1967 or '68, which was, of course, in the throes of the civil rights movement and the Vietnam protests, I was on the police force. I was walking the foot post on a street called Wilkins Avenue near Boston Road. I had one or two years in the department, and who do I see walking down the road? It's Leon Myers. And I hadn't seen him in several years, not since we were younger fellas. I was really happy to see him. Leon was a distinctive guy. He was very tall and had thick eyeglasses. He probably would've been more accomplished in basketball if he didn't have such bad vision. I think he went on to work in the post office.

So I'm in uniform. I'm alone at the time because in those days you had a beat by yourself. I saw him and said, "Leon, it's Andy." And he says, "Oh God, they're taking anyone in the police department now, huh?" He had a good sense of humor. We laughed and chatted for a few minutes, and then he said, "Well, I gotta be going because this doesn't look so good for me to be talking to you in this neighborhood."

I kinda felt bad about that. I felt that way then, and I even feel that way now, so many years later. I've thought about it a lot through the years, and actually it was that racial divide that got to me. At the time, there was no thought of my being on any side, other than the one that I was on, which was being a policeman. But I look back on that sometimes with regret and I say to myself that maybe I was on the wrong side. I missed an opportunity in history. If I had it to do over again, I don't know. Maybe I would've been a freedom marcher.

KENNETH S. DAVIDSON

Hedge fund manager, investment adviser

(1945–)

THERE WAS AN EMPTY LOT NEXT DOOR TO OUR BUILDING ON Bronx Park East. The park right across the street had a playground and a lot of grass space where kids could run and play, but the lot was our place of choice. The land there was hilly and rocky with thick weeds and snakelike paths. There, we were away from supervision, away from the people in the park. That's what I liked about it. It was our own place where we were able to light fires.

There were eight of us in our gang, all from our same building. There were, maybe, three years separating the oldest from the youngest. Matty and Jimmy were the oldest, Mitch, Peter, and Steve were next, followed by Andy, Henry, and me. Age, overall toughness, and courage established ranking in the gang. When it came to courage, none of us could beat Mitch. He was slightly built and unafraid of any confrontation with anyone of any age. From the age of eight he lived with his grandparents because he'd been orphaned. His grandfather was a distinguished-looking German immigrant who always wore a cardigan sweater while he listened to the Metropolitan Opera radio broadcast on Saturday afternoons. I don't think he was the kind of role model that Mitch responded to. Mitch was described by the building tenants as a troublemaker, although some just called him "troubled."

Mitch was fascinated by fire and was never without matches in his pocket. He had book matches or those white-tipped Diamond brand matches that came in their own boxes. At age nine he could light a white-tip with one hand and a flick of his thumbnail, which he probably learned from the George Raft or Hopalong Cassidy movies we used to see.

We helped ourselves to the discarded newspapers in the basement of our building to help start the fires in the lot. As soon as the super, Mr. Hartmann, caught us gathering papers and junk, he knew what we were going to do, and he'd put a stop to it. Sometimes we'd be lucky enough to get a fire started before the super could stop us and put it out. To us, fire meant defiance and excitement, especially since I was expressly told not to fool with it. "You could burn your eyes out," was my mother's warning.

Our kitchen faced the lot and I can still see my mother leaning out of the window when she'd smell the smoke and see the flames rising. She'd whistle a two-tone birdcall that stopped me dead in my tracks. Then with her loud, shrill voice she'd blast my name until it echoed through the lot. Ken-*neth*! It was Pavlovian. I would stop whatever I was doing and head home to my apartment. At other times when she smelled the smoke on my clothes she'd say, "There was a fire. Who had the matches?" It was usually Mitch so I never had to lie.

Years later I got in touch with Andy, who had been my best friend in the days of the lots and the fires. When I asked if he knew what had become of Mitch he said, "I think he became a social worker somewhere in New Jersey." A social worker? If you had told me that he was running a numbers racket somewhere I would've believed it, but a social worker?

DANIEL LIBESKIND

Architect, founder of Studio Daniel Libeskind

(1946–)

W E CAME TO AMERICA FROM ISRAEL ON THE SS *CONSTITUTION* ON a voyage that was very long and very rough. After maybe fourteen days on the ship, my sister and I were awakened at five in the morning by my mother. "Get up. You're going to see the Statue of Liberty!" It was very powerful and moving. And then we were looking at the skyline of Manhattan. To see the cluster of skyscrapers—I was thirteen years old and had never seen these buildings before— was like a fata morgana. It was not just the massiveness of the buildings, but that people made them. It was like something out of a dream. That stuck with me. It was unbelievable in every sense.

As we got off the boat, what struck us was how friendly people were to us. *Why were people so nice to us?* When we went to Israel from Poland, Israel was only eight years old. It wasn't like it is now. It wasn't so easy to live there. Even jobs were hard to get.

We were probably some of the last immigrants to arrive in New York by the Statue of Liberty like that iconic picture of the immigrants on a ship. And then we went straight to the Bronx. We went to the Bronx and that was it! We went straight from the boat, literally. We didn't speak English. None of us. Not a word.

Before the war my mother was an anarchist. She didn't believe in government. She knew the founders of the cooperative apartment buildings in the Bronx, the Amalgamated. Some of them were old anarchists from Emma Goldman's time, but there were also Socialists, and Social Democrats, and so just through the grapevine our name, through my mother, was why we were able to get an apartment there. In the beginning, we lived in the Sholem Aleichem houses. In Israel, at that time, Yiddish was neglected and not very well tolerated. Hebrew was and still is the official language. They didn't even want to talk about Yiddish. Can you imagine what it meant to us that there were buildings named after Sholem Aleichem, the beloved Yiddish writer? Then we moved to Building Number 1, the first residential cooperative building in the Amalgamated Houses, the oldest middle-income co-op in America.

Mr. and Mrs. Straus, very elderly Jews who were our friends, lived in a small apartment there, but in it they had the complete works of Goethe, Schiller, the music of Bach. They were highly intellectual people even though they were working class. The people in the Amalgamated all worked in factories, but when I look back they had more books and literature than any Harvard professor would have today. The love of learning of music and art— how lucky we were. There was a cultural program every week, a small performance, or a poetry reading. There were gatherings.

There were places where painters could paint. We adapted easily because we could speak Yiddish and Polish with all the people around us. We thought that we had come to Utopia.

My mother would say to me, *Never worry about what other people tell you. Don't ever buckle to authority. Don't think that if you're getting good grades that means you're doing well. Don't be under the illusion that everything that is being fed to you is the truth.* My father was also very strong. He was very mild, very quiet, but he was very principled. We were not practicing Jews, even though my mother came from a very prestigious Hasidic dynasty, the Gerrer Rabbis. They were like the popes of Poland. People used to fall on the ground to kiss the ground, literally. My cousins are all in Mea Shearim, the ultra-Orthodox neighborhood in Israel, with their fur hats and their payes. My cousins—first cousins—have sixteen kids each. My parents rejected this. My father was completely unreligious. Even to his dying day, when religious people came to his hospital room to speak to him or to say prayers, he'd say, *Don't come in.* And yet when he died he saw Hebrew letters. He saw aleph, gimel. He was a Yiddishist.

In Poland, where I was born, I started playing music on the accordion, very early on. My parents were afraid to bring in a piano because of the neighbors and their anti-Semitism. Even though it was after the war, my parents were afraid of bringing attention to themselves. The accordion is like a piano, but it's portable. I wound up playing that strange instrument and I wound up playing in classical venues because I played only classical music, which I transcribed myself. Mostly baroque music, Bach and so on. Even though I was very short I had this very large accordion with four octaves.

When we were in Israel, I won a competition sponsored by the American Israeli Foundation, which brought me to America with my family. Itzhak Perlman won that same year. I remember that Isaac Stern was the head of the jury. Stern said to me, "Why are you playing this small piano?" But, you know, it's strange, when you play vertically, like on the accordion, it's hard to play horizontally, like on the piano. Then my interests drifted, because I loved art. I loved painting.

One of the first people I met in America was an Italian American, Tony Roccanova. I met him in junior high school. I didn't speak a word of English. He was sitting next to me, so I'd pick up something. *What is this? It's a pencil. What is this? It's a bottle. What is this? A cup.* So I had a list of all these words, and that's how I learned English. *What do you call this?* I had this list, which I memorized. We became friends and he became an architect as well. I'm still friends with him.

I found that people were not fake in the Bronx. I never met anybody with pretentions there. I never met anyone who was phony. People were very down to earth whether they were Jewish or Irish or Italian or African American.

If you're born here, you take what you have here for granted. My father was a Holocaust survivor. Until the day he died, and he was ninety when he died, he said, "If Americans knew what they had here, they would kiss the ground."

My father was very talented in art, but he never had a chance to explore it. He never had any education. When I was in the Bronx High School of Science, there were a lot of bright kids, doing experiments in genetics and physics. You had to bring in a project that you were working on. This was the height of the Cold War, so I decided to build a perfect model of an ideal nuclear shelter. I don't know why I thought that would be a great project. My father was a brilliant miniaturist and he built these exact replicas of cans of soups, which he painted and which I then used to stack the shelves. I also had a miniature mother, a father, and their two kids in the shelter.

Our apartment in the Bronx was small, and when I went to Cooper Union we had to make models and drawings often using a T-square. In our kitchen, there was one Formica table, with large rounded corners. I never knew if my T-square was on the right angle or if it was on the curve of that table. Those rounded edges began to play a big role in my thinking about architecture. Everyone always talks about the straight edge. Why are other angles so neglected?

I loved the Bronx. Maybe once I went on a trip to Brooklyn. That was like going to a place as far away as Africa. Even Manhattan seemed to be a distant country, but of course the subways were very cheap and the city offered so many ways to educate yourself. Museums were free. You could go to lectures. You could go to concerts. My education was in this cultural arena. Before that explosion of culture in the city, I remember being in the Museum of Modern Art virtually alone. I was also in the Metropolitan Museum of Art in these huge rooms, where I would sketch. I loved the building itself. I thought I was in Rome.

My upbringing was totally influenced by the fact that my parents were Holocaust survivors. Totally. I grew up in the void. I was born in Poland after the war. There had been millions of Jews before the war and there was no one left. I was walking with my father when I was a little boy in Poland. We would meet somebody who he didn't know and he would say in Polish, "Are you Amhu?" using the Hebrew word for Jewish. If they were, they'd immediately break into Yiddish. It was like a password. A secret code to find out if the person was a Jew.

We're now finishing a building in Warsaw. The tallest residential tower on the site of a former Stalin-era Palace of Culture building. It's right next to where my mother was born. It was an old Hasidic neighborhood and of course it was all bombed out. My new building is right across the street.

When we used to go to Warsaw, that Palace of Culture was the dominating symbol of the city and it was such an oppressive symbol, because it was built by Stalin to oppress the Polish people. And now my building is a totally different form. It has nothing to do with what was there. It's something *free*. And right near there is a memorial to my mother's family, a memorial to Rabbi Alter of that Gerrer Hasidic dynasty. It's a significant memorial. It means a lot to me to be able to come full circle.

Architecture isn't about stones and concrete. It's more about storytelling. Everybody has a story. Architecture beyond its being a science, an art, is a storytelling profession. Every building that's meaningful tells you a story. Only late in my life I discovered from my father that *his* father was an itinerant storyteller. He went from village to village telling stories. That was his job. He walked from shtetl to shtetl sitting in the market, telling stories.

I've had four lifetimes. There was a lifetime when I was a musician.

And there was a lifetime when I was a student and theoretician.

The third lifetime was when I was in Berlin for the Jewish Museum.

And the fourth lifetime was when I won the competition to oversee Ground Zero. Four lifetimes.

It's not a fake idea, America, New York, the Bronx. It's not some myth. It's a reality.

VALERIE SIMPSON

Pianist, singer, composer

(1946–)

Both my grandmothers lived in the Bronx and had pianos, but nobody in the family could play them. That was the setup for me to learn, because everyone could sing. I can only think that the pianos were there, just waitin' for me to come along—destined to play them because of the musical gift that was given to me. My grandmother put me in front of the upright and I just kind of knew it. I was four or five when I started playing piano by ear.

When I was about eleven years old I took piano lessons and learned to read music, but for a long time I fooled the teacher because she'd play the song and I would just remember and repeat it. Then she got hip to me and stopped playing, so I had to learn to read the notes. I played Bach and Chopin—classical music—and then I got a scholarship to a place called Chatham Square. It was at that time I realized I was never going to be a classical pianist and that I didn't want to be one. I quit and started playing more on my own.

I was raised on Jackson Avenue in a three-story building that my grandmother owned. When it came time for junior high school, our neighborhood school wasn't that great, so I was bused to Junior High School 22, which was a better school about fifteen or twenty minutes away. We were the first black students to go to that school so I felt a big responsibility because I was going to get this good education and I was going to represent the whole black race. *Don't mess up now!* I wanted to do well. Nobody told me that, but I felt it on my own.

In that junior high school a lot of good things happened. They had musical programs, and when the teachers found out that I played the piano I got out of class a lot. That worked out really well for me. I was recognized for what I could do musically, and they made a way for me to do it. Some of the kids saw me get that special treatment, like getting pulled out of class, so I wasn't exactly a favorite among my peers. I can remember almost getting into a fight with a girl because she thought I was stuck on myself, you know. Teacher's favorite. The girl was bigger than me, so my younger brother, who was bigger than both of us, intervened and got me home.

Because I was such a standout in junior high school, when I got to high school I became almost like wallpaper. I disappeared. I didn't want to be the one that got called out in that same way anymore, so I played very little piano in school in those days.

But I loved playing handball in the Morris High School yard, which was right across the street from us. I was really good at it.

I'd hit those low balls, you know. I still have a great affection for handball even though I don't play anymore. I play table tennis. I have a Ping-Pong table in my home that looks like a piece of art deco furniture and I'm real good at that game too.

One of my grandmothers was a minister and she gave me the job of being her church pianist. As a church pianist you come across many people who get up and sing but often start in one key and end up in another, so I learned how to follow. From that early training where the ladies get up with those big hats, full of the spirit and end up not where they started, I could play even if I didn't know the song. My grandmother paid me to be the pianist. Even when she didn't have enough money because the congregation was too small, she'd pay me from her own pocket. And she'd make sure she paid me what she agreed upon, because she said that a deal was a deal. She instilled certain values in me. A deal is a deal. Keep your word.

My grandmother was married and owned this house that we all lived in. I always liked the fact that although she was this minister when she came home she was the wife who cooked for her husband. She changed her roles and put on the hat that she needed to wear and didn't have a problem with that. She didn't have to be the head honcho at home. She was an interesting study for me to see—a woman who did many things and handled each thing in its place. Later on I could see how hard that was because some men might get jealous and not want a woman to be in control. She handled all of that really well.

It was through a church in Harlem, not my grandmother's church, that I met Nick Ashford. He was homeless and had come to New York to make his fortune as a dancer, but that didn't work out too well for him. He came to the church where he was told he could get a free meal. In addition to his dancing Nick wrote gospel songs, and since I played piano we were like a natural pair.

We all get honored in so many different ways as we go along, but the one that really got to me was when I was honored by the Bronx borough president Ruben Diaz Jr. to be part of the Bronx Walk of Fame. It touched my heart in a special way because it's where we come from. It's where we started. When I think that I represent the Bronx to such an extent that my name is on the Grand Concourse—that gives me a sense of real pride.

ARTHUR KLEIN

Pediatric cardiologist, president of the Mount Sinai
Health Network

(1947–)

I SPENT A GOOD PART OF MY GROWING UP LISTENING TO FAMILY immigrant stories—who brought whom to the United States, how they got there, how they ended up in the Bronx, which in those days they thought was nirvana. The immigrant stories always had adversity. There was suffering. There were bad times in Russia, and there were the Depression and the recessions when they finally got to the United States. But most of these stories were colored with humor. I think that was a very important cultural influence on me.

In our extended family, there were a lot of Sarahs, there were a lot of Roses, there were a lot of Helens, and there were a lot of Sylvias. My mother had two first cousins. One Sarah was Fat Sarah and the other Sarah was Dumb Sarah. I just thought those were their names: Fat Sarah and Dumb Sarah. Dumb Sarah was the most likable person in the world. She would do anything that you asked her to do, but reasoning was not part of it. She was always amenable. The other Sarah, on the other hand, she was the one you had to be careful about how much cheesecake you laid out when she came over for coffee and cake.

In 1948 my grandfather's first cousins, who managed to survive the Holocaust, were sponsored by him and came over. And to us, these people were forever known as "the Greeners," because the slang Yiddish term for newcomers was "greenhorns." I thought that was their name because they were never called anything else. The Greeners are coming for dinner tonight was what they said.

There was predictability to life that gave me, as a child, a tremendous sense of security. As the family grew, my grandmother couldn't prepare the Friday night dinner for everyone, so wherever you lived—our whole family lived in the Bronx, and for years we all lived in the same building and neighborhood—you went to my grandmother's for dessert and coffee. That was predictable. Our Friday night ritual.

The men played pinochle in the dinette, and the women were generally in the living room chatting. The kids were in the back bedroom doing whatever we did—mostly watching TV. My grandmother had a TV early on because she liked to watch *The Loretta Young Show.*

My grandmother would make an announcement that it was time for coffee and dessert, which meant that she moved the cut-glass fruit bowl from the kitchen into the dinette and put it down on the table, no matter at what stage the card game was. My grandfather was always pissed off because it was invariably in the middle of a game. And she would say to him, "Sha. Be quiet. Enough."

My grandmother also had this habit, which, by the way, to the day my mother died, she also had. She used to keep playing cards in the pocket of her housecoat or apron. Then she picked up crumbs or dust from the floor with the two playing cards, using them like a dustpan and a small dust broom. If my grandmother was sweeping the floor of the kitchen on Friday night, and if the men were playing cards and she didn't have cards handy, she'd go right over to the table and take two cards off the table—without asking, of course. My grandfather would say, "What are you doing? The woman's an idiot," and she would look at him with complete disdain and say, "What are you complaining about? You got a tableful!" Then—"The man's a meshuggener." A crazy one. Those last words were not said to him but to the broad air.

My grandfather had a view of America that was also part of the Friday night gatherings. We were to hear the world according to Grandpa. He was very clearly seen as the patriarch. That stability in the family was very important to me. There was a real sense that this was the family hearth. Even though it wasn't a big sprawling home or the farmhouse, it was the Bronx version of that.

When the Russians launched Sputnik my grandfather went crazy. "What's the matter with the Americans? Couldn't they see that the Russians were going to concentrate on this?" His notion was that Americans could be self-congratulatory and lazy. "This country has to wake up." The reason he had such a profound influence on my life is that he would always say, "The future is science." We have to beat the Russians. We have to be the technological leaders. We can't sit on our laurels of having won World War Two.

Quite frankly, if I were to be true to my real passion, I would've been a history teacher. But for my generation, and I've heard this from a lot of my friends, there was this pressure to go into a scientific career. That was the future of America, and we couldn't risk falling behind. It was patriotism linked with the sense that European Jews had made a huge impact on science in Europe and it was now our responsibility here. My grandfather was the one who taught me how many German and Russian Jewish scientists were involved with the Manhattan Project and theoretical physics. It all made a big impression on me.

I went to a Bronx school, yet I got the best secondary education I could possibly have gotten in the whole country. When I graduated from Bronx High School of Science, there were twenty-one of us in my graduating class who got into MIT. We were the largest single contingent from any high school in the United States going to one of the foremost universities in the country.

DAVA SOBEL

Science writer, author, educator

(1947–)

Usually when people hear my name, they think that my parents wanted a boy, but that wasn't so. My parents already had two boys and they wanted a girl. My father, who was a doctor, mostly an obstetrician, enjoyed making up baby names. That's how I got mine. He delivered a baby the day Alaska became a state and he tried to convince the poor woman to name her baby Ala.

Although I wasn't aware of it at the time, I was slightly more privileged than others in the neighborhood. My parents were better educated than most, and compared to the people next door, for instance, we had the larger house. We also owned a boat. My mother was a chemist, in addition to my father being a doctor. My parents had met in chemistry lab at NYU. But I know that I certainly didn't feel privileged, because at one time I wanted to buy something or other for myself and didn't want to ask my parents to buy it for me. I saw an offer for a kit of greeting cards in a magazine, which you could sell door to door to make money, so I sent away for it. When it came, my mother was horrified. She had to explain that I could not go door to door to our neighbors, who would be offended by my asking them to buy something from me. That was a revelation. I had no idea that it wasn't the right thing to do, probably because my parents were not at all pretentious.

My father worked at Harlem Hospital and we had a variety of people who came to our house. Everyone was welcome. He also had many patients who couldn't afford to pay and he treated them for free. They cooked for him. They knitted sweaters. They did what they could to pay him something for his services.

My parents had this forty-foot sailboat, which also had an internal motor. We kept it on City Island, and in the summertime when it was hot my mother and I would just stay out there and sleep on the boat. The sky was always there. My mother became very interested in astronomy and the constellations when my father became interested in sailing. She then went to night school to become a celestial navigator. My mother had a sextant and had even bought herself a little toy planetarium projector—a box that projects constellations on the ceiling of the room. It was probably a study aid for her to learn the stars of the Southern Hemisphere. So that's what I grew up with. If I have a love of learning, it was because my parents were always interested in learning. I was a studious girl. An obedient girl. I wanted to live up to my parents' and teachers' expectations. Early on in school, we were tracked for special interests. By third grade I was in science class. I found a report card in my mother's old filing cabinet.

There were long boxes in which to make comments. My third-grade teacher wrote that I was interested in knowing about life on other planets. How prophetic!

The Botanical Garden was a short walk from our house. My mother loved it. That made it more meaningful to me, as a kid, than they perhaps might otherwise have been. She was an enthusiastic gardener and visited often. She even had a vegetable garden on our roof, planted in five-pound buckets from the Burger King on White Plains Road. At the southern end of the Botanical Garden there's a waterfall and a building called the Snuff Mill. What a great place that was to go on dates, which usually involved kissing—not truly X-rated but what passed for it in those innocent days.

Although the Botanical Garden was right near us, I loved the area directly across the street from us. There was a huge lawn that was public property. It may have been part of Bronx Park, but it was separated from the park itself. On summer evenings, people would take their chairs out to sit and talk there or play cards. There were beautiful trees and it felt like ours. Once, coming home from high school, I saw a group of men cutting down a giant elm tree during the time of the Dutch elm blight. This particular tree was a monument. It was gigantic. I was so shocked that the tree would have to come down, and I stood there, bereft, when one of the guys said to me, "Poems are made by fools like me, but only God can make a tree." That was the Bronx. An unexpected mix.

My mother's younger sister, my aunt Ruth, had worked in the Roosevelt administration. She was a special assistant to the secretary of the interior, Harold Ickes. She's still alive, living in Manhattan. She's 101. Coincidentally, my brothers had gone to Christopher Columbus High School, where my oldest brother was a classmate of Anna Italiano, who later became Anne Bancroft.

In 2001, Bancroft was in a made-for-TV movie called *Haven*, which was based on my aunt Ruth's true story, which took place during World War Two. In the movie, Anne Bancroft portrays my grandmother. There's a wonderful scene where Bancroft is horrified that the secretary of the interior is sending her daughter, played by Natasha Richardson, into danger in the middle of the war. That danger referred to my aunt Ruth's assignment from Ickes that changed her life. During World War Two she was sent to bring back a thousand refugees. Most of them were Jews and many of them had been in concentration camps. They were gathered in Naples, some of them still in their striped prison clothes, and put on a ship with a thousand wounded American soldiers and Ruth. They were even attacked during the crossing.

My aunt Ruth spoke German and Yiddish and took down the stories of the refugees. At the time, it was very difficult for refugees to get visas to enter the United States. Her story came out because the newspapers wrote about how the State Department was pretending that the denial of visas was not going on. It was a scandal. Aunt Ruth has written and talked about her amazing life a lot. She's been a real role model for me because she was both a writer and a woman with children.

The Bronx was such a good place to grow up in because the boundaries were so fluid. The neighborhoods were mixed and so were the schools. People from many different countries lived there, people of different socioeconomic levels. However, at that time, I personally knew few Hispanics and African Americans. In fact, at Bronx High School of Science, out of a class of 860-something there were only eight black students. That made me very aware of social injustice. One summer I picketed the White Castle on Boston Road. I was thirteen or fourteen and had come under the influence of a boy, Peter, who was slightly older than I was and who came from a politically aware family. I think he was reading Marx by the time he was in junior high school. He told me about this protest at the White Castle. I thought protesting was a really fine thing to do, and so I joined in.

When I mentioned this to my father, he said, "What?" and said I was not to go there again because picketers had actually been shot at. However, when my aunt Ruth went to Washington for the March on Washington in 1963, she took me with her. On the plane we sat behind Ruby Dee and Ossie Davis. I was sixteen years old so the whole experience was exciting. When we got to D.C. my aunt had to write a story or something, so I wound up on the Mall walking by myself and listening to the Martin Luther King "I Have a Dream" speech. It was one of the most extraordinary experiences of my life. I think I must have known how historic it was. I had never seen so many people in one place before. And the spirit of it! I was there from another state walking alone, but everybody there was united in purpose. I remember that feeling, and I'm so grateful that I could be there to be part of it.

ROBERT F. X. SILLERMAN

Businessman, media entrepreneur

(1948–)

My father's fortunes went up and down, so my childhood was full of highs and lows, mostly measured by where we lived. My earliest memory is of a lower-class apartment building on Jerome Avenue in the Bronx. My father had lost whatever money he had at the time, so we had moved there from Manhattan. We were grandparents, parents, my brother and I—six of us, in that small space. I'm sure there were distinctive sounds and noises, but I don't remember them. However, I clearly remember the sulfur smell from the match you had to light for the stove.

After four or five years we moved to what I thought was the Taj Mahal—a two-family house in Riverdale on Vinmont Road. It wasn't large, but at the foot of Vinmont was the school with its baseball field, and that was like Disneyland. It was wonderful. And coming from a virtual tenement to a house, albeit a two-family one, I couldn't imagine that it could get better. Especially with the ball field so nearby.

But it did get better. We then moved to a postwar modern fancy apartment building with a doorman not a half mile from where the other house was, on the other side of the school to which the baseball field belonged. So I wasn't right down the hill from the baseball field but I was essentially right next to it, and in a beautiful apartment. And *that* was just wonderful.

We could also go everywhere on our bikes at any time of day or night to play ball. It didn't matter. Midnight on a Saturday or eight a.m. One day, in this very beautiful fancy apartment, my parents came to my brother and me and said, "Great news. We're moving again, to an even better place." And my first question was, "How far is it from the baseball field?" Each time we moved up it was because my father got more successful in his business. He had a radio network and made a lot of money. Then, in the late 1940s, it was said that radio with pictures was better. So he went into the television business. His company produced some of the truly great shows of the 1950s. *Private Secretary. Ramar of the Jungle. Lassie.*

His fortunes were definitely up when we moved into a house that was gigantic. Twenty or thirty rooms, four stories, a swimming pool, and acres of land. It was on Independence Avenue between 250th and 252nd Streets. Magnificent. Toscanini's house was right down the street. It happened to be not quite as nice as our house.

When we had moved to our first house there was a cook-maid. When we got to this mansion, there were a few maids and a separate cook. And from this new house, most importantly, I could still get to the baseball field. It was magical. Baseball in the fifties was a religion. It was *the* religion. It's what we did. The Bronx Bombers, the New York Yankees. At that time I also transferred from P.S. 81 to Fieldston, a private school that was also in Riverdale.

And as we got older my mother in essence said, "Riverdale is paradise." It was such an amazing time because my mother, who was a highly educated and cultured woman, insisted that we have the advantages of what was available in Manhattan as well as having the freedom and relaxation of Riverdale. So every Saturday from my eighth to my thirteenth year, except in the summer, we went to Manhattan and, if the time was right, went to the Young People's Concerts or a museum, had dinner, and then went to a show. Every Saturday. Every one. When we got to spring baseball season, there was a little tension, so it wasn't every Saturday.

I was recently telling somebody a story about what a Saturday was like during the baseball season. There was a baseball field with no organized games. We got on our bikes and went there and went home at six or seven, having gotten there at eight or eight-thirty in the morning. We were there all day. The entire day. I can picture exactly where my mother was standing one Saturday when she said, "What'd you have for lunch today?" "*Lunch?*" So the mothers got together and said that they were going to make sandwiches for us. They did, but we never ate them. They sent us with a big picnic basket and the reason we never got into any trouble was that each of these ten or twenty mothers made the sandwiches for a different Saturday. So only about once a year did that mother's sandwiches not get eaten.

But we did buy ice cream from Sam, the Good Humor man. Big thing was when Sam decided to stock soda instead of just ice cream. He was an entrepreneur. We also used our bikes to go to other places. One of the first Carvels was on the Riverdale–Yonkers border. Two for one on the opening Saturday. What we did—and only kids can do this—we went up, bought our two ice creams, finished them, got back in line, and ordered two more. Two for one.

Then the wheels fell off. When I was thirteen, my father went totally bankrupt. So we were evicted from our mansion. We then moved to Broadway, just north of the subway, where we were right across the street from Van Cortlandt Park. But the appeal of the park wasn't as strong. We were also getting older and baseball wasn't as important to us.

When my father went bankrupt that last time it was horrible. He was sixty or sixty-one and quite a bit older than my mother. He never really did anything more. Thinking about my father, probably during his lifetime before us he had seen fortunes come and go. Some people would've said, *I'm going to store it away for another day.* He said, *I guess I'm going to enjoy it while I have it.* When he lost money he was usually able to make it again, so maybe he wasn't afraid of losing it. That might've been part of his thinking. When you're a kid it is what it is and it's not until much later that you try to reconstruct those things.

My mother, however, went from being a philanthropist, head of the women voters, a real activist, to having to work. She then became a program director or fund-raiser or something like that for the National Council of Jewish Women. It was really rough for us all. I reacted a lot to all these changes. These were formative years. Age thirteen from the richest kid on the block to the poorest. Kids are merciless. I wasn't invited to parties. Kids made fun of me. Stuff like that. I felt ostracized. Father loses his money, friends are difficult, I say "piss off" to them. I had my own view of the rules. That's a nice way to say it.

I had the stability of the family but had to deal with the vagaries of fortune, good and bad. I remember taking a test in biology. There were one hundred questions. I got them all right. *They're going to think I'm a nerd.* There were the kids who were the brains and the nerds. And then there were the cool kids. It was a coed school. Puberty. I changed twenty of the answers to the wrong ones so that I wouldn't be considered a nerd. I went home and I said to my mother, who by this time was well on her way to becoming a serious alcoholic because of my father and our circumstances, I said to her, "I have to get out of this school. I'm at a school where I'm afraid to learn and afraid of being picked on as the nerdy kid." I went to the school and told them the same thing. Their response? *Whoopee! Are we excited. Get the hell out of here!* They were not unhappy to see me go.

To my mother's credit she found an educational consultant. He said, "You should probably go to boarding school." *Sign me up!* However, this consultant happened to be the dean of boys at Collegiate, and he also said, "You're a great kid and I'm gonna see if we can make room for you." And he made room for me.

In 2007 or 2008, I don't remember who it was, but someone started this program to show how many successful people had gone through the New York City public school system. I guess there were four or five people who were honored. Matthew Broderick and Liam Neeson introduced me. (*They* were the ones the event organizers really wanted.) I was talking to them. "My last year in a New York City public school was in third grade," I said. "Do you think I should tell them that?" "Don't tell them," was the answer. As part of that same program, I also went back to visit the school, P.S. 81. The last year I was in that school was probably 1956, which was about fifty years before. I had a car and driver with me and I said, "Do you have a couple of minutes?" Then we went behind the school to the baseball field—and I ran around the bases. I was little Bobby Sillerman from the Bronx again.

MAIRA KALMAN

Artist/illustrator, author

(1949–)

WHEN I WAS FOURTEEN OR FIFTEEN AND SOMEONE ASKED WHERE
I was from, I would say I was a Bronx Bagel. I liked the alliteration,
I guess, but I was a complete Riverdale snob. I think that's because
we were so close to Manhattan and to Lord & Taylor and the Bird
Cage, the store's restaurant. We also had a certain pride in being in
this little enclave. For me, it was really like an enchanted land.
Riverdale was Oz in a funny way. Well, we did also go to other
places in the Bronx. Loehmann's was Mecca. Literally Mecca. We
also went to Stella D'Oro. That was my first experience with

nonkosher food. I had a shrimp cocktail and I heard the angels singing.

My father's whole family was killed in the Holocaust. There I was living in Riverdale and the lullaby is, "Never again," coming from him in a most poignant and powerful way. He constantly told us stories about his family perishing. And that he went to Israel in 1939, joined the underground, and fought the British. My mother went there in 1932.

The people who built Israel had a tremendous sense of "We did something quite extraordinary, both by leaving our old lands and by coming to this new country." So part of the pride that I had was clearly instilled in me by my father and my mother too. Another story that's in my soul—one where my sister really thinks I'm insane—but to this day, to help me meet a deadline, I say, "What if the Nazis came, in, say, two hours, could I finish the work? If they were coming in, like, eighteen minutes, could I finish the work?" So somehow I use the danger of them coming into my safe place on Twelfth Street to help me with an illustration assignment. I do that all the time.

My parents were not the happiest couple. There was a lot of silence and distance. My father was a diamond dealer and would be gone half the year. He'd go to Belgium for diamonds. He'd go to Israel. He'd do whatever he was doing on his own, having a good time and wanting to be a player in a larger field. He was not interested in being at home. My mother never complained about him. There was just a tacit silence. He was gone, and we were doing our thing. And we had a lovely time. When I think about it, I think that his being gone was a relief from the tension. I don't mean to imply that it was some kind of horrific household. Everything from the outside seemed quite reasonable.

Because of my father's business as a diamond dealer, all these interesting characters from around the world would visit us. It was a small club in a way. They seemed very eccentric, but they were people who traveled the world, who dealt in these luxuries, in diamonds and jewels. They traveled well, they dressed well, they lived well. They also divorced frequently. It's so odd. My parents didn't have a good relationship, but they were very social and entertained a lot. They had a big circle of friends. There was a big crowd of other Israelis who were either stationed in New York for something or here on business. And there were relatives.

My mother opened up the world of culture to me. I had piano lessons with Mrs. Danziger and ballet lessons from Miss Nubert. My mother took me to the public library, and we read the books from A to Z. And every Sunday night we had Chinese food at Bo Sun. We became part of this cultural community in Riverdale. That's one of the reasons I went to the High School of Music and Art, because I was a pianist. My mother never was forceful in saying, "You have to be something or you had to be ambitious." It was just, "Here it is and do whatever you want with it."

It was wonderful that my mother allowed me to daydream—and the daydreaming allowed me to become partially the person that I am. There was no sense of needing to analyze anything or understand anything. I just kind of lived.

I spent a lot of time reading in the park that has a huge statue of Henry Hudson in it. I had the time to develop, on my own, a sense of language and love of language and love of the word. Coming to America from Israel and learning a new language at the age of four was wonderful. And the fifties were an optimistic time. When I got older and I started writing more seriously, I thought, *Ugh, this writing is terrible. All that imagery!* I thought that there's a way to express what I'm thinking in another way and I have to express myself. That was a given. There was no question like, "Well, what else would I do?" Saul Steinberg had a huge show at the time. And since I read a lot, I had looked at a lot of children's books. I looked at images and I looked at writing and said, "Wait a minute. There's something going on here." Combining images and writing looked like it could be fun. The word "fun" was really important to me. I had felt like this tortured writer with angst—this adolescent with angst. I just wanted to have fun.

I've had occasion to go back to my old lobby in Riverdale to photograph the plants that are there now and to see the views, both interior and exterior. And to go back to Mother's Bakery, where we used to buy our mocha cream cakes. When I did those things, I connected to moments of joy, pleasure, and self-confidence. A sense of well-being.

PART THREE

ALL THE NEWS THAT FITS, WE PRINT . . . THE GIFT IN THE RIVER

You had drugs going on. You had the gangs during that time. Everyone was doing their thing. So you became a graffiti artist. People were going to clubs, like hanging out on a Friday, dressing up, going to jams, but we dressed all dirty on Fridays, going into the subway. That was our mission. Our thing was subways.

—BG 183, MEMBER OF TATS CRU

What also amazed me about the Bronx River was that it was crystal clear. . . . So beautiful. It was like a secret I had discovered. The whole experience there was like opening presents when you're not sure what the present will be, whether it's going to be something you really want or nothing. Seeing and finding these giant turtles in the river is a present I'll never forget.

ERIK ZEIDLER

SAM GOODMAN

Urban planner

(1952–)

WHEN I WAS IN FOURTH GRADE MY MOTHER SAID TO ME, "DAD wants to meet you for dinner. Do you know how to count and do you know how to read?" And I looked at her. "Of course I know how to count. Of course I know how to read." She said, "You're going to take the D train to Forty-Second Street. You're going to be in the last car and when the door opens your dad will be waiting for you." I was in fourth grade—nine years old. I went on the subway by myself and I bought the subway token and I learned how to ride the subway to Manhattan. By the time I was a teenager

I knew every subway line and I could get anywhere. My parents were never reluctant to teach us how to make the city our home and they had the brains to show us how. Consequently, I've always felt at ease in our urban environment. It was, and still is, my home.

In the early sixties, as part of what was seen as the need to integrate grade schools in New York City, a pairing plan was established whereby underutilized elementary schools could be matched up with overpopulated elementary schools in other parts of the city. Buses would transport the students from one to the other. P.S. 70, which was my school, in the West Bronx was paired with an elementary school in the East Bronx and we all knew that the East Bronx had bad neighborhoods.

There were many senior citizens where I lived, and because of that we had relatively big schools with empty seats. The poorer neighborhoods, with primarily people of color, were overloaded with kids. There were these meetings where they were trying to figure out how to achieve this balance of integration without busing the kids out of their neighborhoods. It's important to remember that no one wanted the busing plan. The schools in the East Bronx wound up being as opposed to it as the schools in the West Bronx. So, ultimately, that whole thing didn't happen. I was in grade school at that time, and I remember that there were demonstrations with these loud angry people marching and screaming. The neighborhoods were changing and it was one more signal that it was time to move. Whenever people had the means, there was every incentive on every level, from the school system to the police department to the elected officials. They were all saying to people who lived in our neighborhood at the time, "Move. It's not going to get any better. Just move."

There was also a dramatic jump in crime in the sixties. People were being mugged, and I would hear stories. There was a little luncheonette that we went to in our neighborhood. We'd hear an older person talking about being pushed down a flight of stairs, about being held up in an elevator. There were robberies and windows broken and old people screaming to scare off strangers in the buildings. There was an article that came out in the *New York Times*, July 21, 1966, about how the Grand Concourse was going to change for the worse. My mother thought that Robert Kennedy's model cities program could offer the necessary guidance for places like ours, of mixed race, to become a national model. My parents took that article, with me in tow, to meet our congressman, James Scheuer. He told my mom, "Mrs. Goodman, if I were you, I would move. In twenty years we're going to bulldoze that whole place down." He further said that the City of New York could no longer afford to keep up the level of municipal services needed, and that a good option would be to move to Co-op City. That just smacked us right across our faces. That was in July, and in October we moved up to Connecticut.

The idea that my neighborhood, the Grand Concourse, could change from what it was in the twenties to—forty or fifty years later—become a slum was something inconceivable to me. I got angry about it. It prompted me to write a newspaper that I would distribute to the community called *Community Times*. "All the news that fits, we print." That was the slogan. I would type up interviews that I had with officials. I, a thirteen-year-old kid, would write a letter to some city official inviting them to our apartment for a community meeting. Then I'd write about the meeting and hand it out to everybody in the neighborhood. The captain of the Forty-Fifth Precinct or maybe it was the Forty-Sixth up there, came to one of the meetings, with his gold badge and all that, and told everybody how they could no longer rely on the police for their safety. Can you imagine a policeman telling people that the police department could no longer guarantee their safety? And he passed out a piece of paper that was basically a set of behaviors that everyone needed to adopt in order to protect themselves from being the victim of crime.

I was fifteen when we moved to Connecticut. I had watched this Bronx community that I knew—with both relatives of mine and friends of mine living there—I watched that community slowly fade away. When we moved I decided I wanted to be someone who would make the Bronx better rather than worse. At that time, I read a lot of news articles about the Bronx, and the articles were all negative. I would stuff them under my bed. I had hundreds of articles stuffed under my bed in my Connecticut bedroom. My parents actually encouraged all of this because they recognized that perhaps I would get involved in government in one way or another. People who still lived in the neighborhood called me "the kid congressman." Whenever I had a chance to write an essay about something I would write it about that community.

There were a lot of things happening in the 1960s. The living wage jobs for low-skill people were dwindling, because so many people were coming here looking for those jobs. The ability of a man with very little education, like my father's father had in his day, to earn a living wage was quickly vanishing. At that same time, there was this dramatic rise of primarily people of color from the South, who were coming here to escape what we know today was a hard situation down in the Jim Crow South. And the fact is these people came here hoping to achieve what they knew could be found here—only to be disappointed when it wasn't really there. To make up for that disparity, the city helped out with welfare assistance. Here's the weird thing about welfare assistance. You couldn't be married and qualify for welfare because the assumption was that, as a couple, one person could always find a job. You couldn't work and collect welfare at the same time. You also got a benefit if you had children, so the City of New York was discouraging people from getting married, encouraging them to have children without getting married, and making it very difficult for a person to earn a living if they in fact required welfare help. At the same time, if you were on welfare, where you lived was entirely up to the City of New York. My parents had a domestic who helped take care of our apartment but certain days the woman couldn't come because a social worker was coming to meet with her at her own place and she had better be there, because if she wasn't, and if they found out she was working, that would be the end of her welfare. This whole system was not designed to help people to come together, but rather to exacerbate a racial prejudice and economic stress, which is a foundation for conflict.

If young people, in particular, don't sense that they are welcome, or don't sense any opportunity, sometimes just out of desperation a person would do something that they would rather not do. And once it becomes socially acceptable for people to be that way, for whatever reason, the reluctance on the part of a kid to harm a senior citizen walking down the street is no longer an issue for that kid. My grandfather, on my mom's side, stayed in the Bronx well into the 1980s and ultimately didn't ever go out. He used to pay someone to do his shopping for him because he was afraid to go into the street. It irritated me because I knew that what was happening was not accidental. The officials chose to make decisions that they recognized were not necessarily in the best interest of their constituency. They hid these problems rather than addressed them. An elected official would not likely address a long-term problem because by the time that problem might be resolved the official would no longer be in office. So sometimes people in government would push the can down the road, because they knew they couldn't solve the problem quickly or easily. There was also rent control in effect in most of the apartment buildings in the Bronx. If you were on welfare, in some cases you weren't paying the full rent, or in other cases the welfare system offset the rent costs. Most of the people who were living in the buildings moved in when the buildings were first constructed, so these original rents were ridiculously low. My grandfather was paying a hundred fifty-three dollars a month for a seven-room apartment. From the 1940s to the 1960s the city was showing all these danger signs and no one addressed them until the 1970s, when the city went belly-up financially. At that point the whole house of cards came crashing down.

My grandfather on my mother's side, Abraham Mayer, always said that it wasn't how much you owned, but how much you could share. He used to say, "A rich man is not rich if he doesn't know how to use his money to help someone else." He would talk about the Depression and how he would buy dinners for people because he had the money and he knew someone else didn't. One of the most devastating aspects of the Bronx turning from a prosperous community to a poor community was that although our community, which was mostly Jewish, although it was of one color, one race, one ethnicity, and one religion, it wasn't homogeneous on income levels. There were different income levels within the community. I can remember people coming to my grandfather's apartment and they would go into a bedroom and after they would come out and leave my grandfather would say to me, "That man lost his job. You never want to work for someone else. You always want to work for yourself. I was able to help him because I work for myself." The point is that when the city started manipulating the way people lived in this community, it put everyone poor in one place. Well, if everyone in the building is just as poor as everyone else, where's the help going to come from? And when you create an entire community of people who are desperately poor, who don't want to be where they are, what is the inevitable outcome of that kind of lifestyle? If not one of violence, it's certainly one of resentment. I know people who worked in this office [office of the borough president] who would say, "I need to rent a post office box somewhere else, because if I give my real address as the Bronx, who would want to hire me?" So they would rent a P.O. box at Grand Central Station so they wouldn't have a Bronx address. This is what we'd done.

My father was trying to inspire me to be a lawyer and, in retrospect, I regret that I didn't follow his advice because he had a very successful law practice. During the summers, when I was a high school and college student, he would take me to work with him in order to expose me to his profession. And the more I was exposed to what he did, the more intimidated I got. I can remember one meeting with a client where my father was instructing this client as to how to answer the questions that the other side might pose. I was just bowled over, especially since I was a kid. I saw it as a chess game. And the whole point was that this was an adversarial thing where you have two sides trying to demonstrate opposite sides of an argument. This was my first case of law through my father's eyes and it turned me off. It scared me. This is not me. I'll never succeed in this. As a consequence, I followed a different career path.

When I finished college I started looking for that career. I had a BA in political science from Kenyon College, which in New York City meant I knew how to think. I didn't know how to make myself or someone else any money. I wound up driving a school bus in Westport because I couldn't find a job. This was in 1975 and things weren't so good, economically, so I decided to get myself a master's degree. If you majored in journalism as an undergrad, you could become a news reporter. If you majored in accounting, you could become an accountant. I was a political science major. What does that mean? What I understood was how government worked and how it didn't work, because of what I learned from watching and living in the Bronx. So I got my master's in urban management.

Things are different now. I moved back to the Bronx. I purchased the apartment across the street from where I work at the courthouse. The apartment is number 800 Grand Concourse. The reason I chose that building was because I remembered the building as a kid. To this day, it's a very well maintained Bronx apartment house, and believe it or not it was affordable. It's taken all these years practically until now for people to start to see the Bronx as a place to go to rather than a place to escape from. That's because it's affordable, it's a super location, and there's been a dramatic drop in crime and a diminishing fear of neighbors that appear to be different than oneself. I'm glad to say that things are looking up. The Bronx is New York's borough of opportunity.

CHAZZ PALMINTERI

Actor, writer, director

(1952–)

In my neighborhood, the Little Italy of the Bronx, I saw things. I saw a murder when I was a young boy. It's what I wrote about in *A Bronx Tale*. People always say to me, "Oh, my God, you must've been traumatized and horrified," but I really don't have an answer for them because I wasn't at all. I was young, almost eleven, and I just kind of stared at it. I had seen some violence before, like punches and fights. Kid stuff. But I never saw anything like that. I was sitting on my stoop holding my head in my hands, and all of a sudden I saw one car trying to back in and another car going forward. I thought they were fighting over a parking space, but they weren't. This guy who was backing in was after the other guy for something—something which my father never told me and my mother still to this day won't tell me after over fifty years. So this guy just pulled up, jumped out, and *bam!* Blood! *Bam-bam!* And then he kind of turned and looked at me. And I looked at him. But I wasn't scared. It's hard to describe because I was just kind of staring and looking at him. The next minute I knew, I was being dragged upstairs by my father. He had run downstairs. My mother had said, "Oh my God. Go down and get him." So he ran down and dragged me up.

That's when I got scared—when my mother started crying. *Mom! Mom! Are you all right? Why are you crying?* She was like, *Was the kid hit?* In the movie and in the play, the cops come up and knock on the door, and I go down with them because I was a witness. What really happened was that the cops did come up, but I didn't go down. My father wouldn't let me go down. He said, "He's not going. He's a kid. He didn't see anything. You're not talking to my son. He doesn't know anything. He's a kid." And that was it.

But the interesting thing is that the only time the murder would be vivid in my head was when I would sit somewhere, like at a table, and put my head in my hands. If I re-created the position I was in, it would come to mind. I never even had nightmares. But you know what? I told a shrink about it once and he said, "It did affect you." And I said, "How?" He said, "It was in your mind for a long time and you had to write about it. You wrote about it and you made it into art." But at the time the killing actually happened I wasn't aware of its effect on me.

I became a writer because I was desperate for work. I had been working as a doorman in LA and when I got fired from that job I remembered the words that my father always said—I even had cards printed up with that saying—"The saddest thing in life is wasted talent." *If they won't give me a great part, I'll write something myself. I'll do a one-man show. I'll play all the parts. They gotta notice me.* And I started to write.

I wrote a five-minute piece and then I performed it for my theater workshop. They loved it and each week I would write another ten or fifteen minutes, and after I performed it I would take six minutes from that and add it on. I literally workshopped it in front of a live audience for a year. By the time the year was over, I had ninety minutes of a very tight one-man show. *A Bronx Tale.* Then I did it and it was like a rocketship.

Now here's a guy—me—who came out to LA who had decent theater credits, but all of a sudden I went from not even having an agent—I couldn't get to William Morris, I couldn't get to ICM—to everybody wanting me. Everybody! *Wait a minute! I'm the same actor. How can this be?* And then a week later I'm offered $250,000 because they wanted to make *A Bronx Tale* into a movie. I had two hundred dollars in the bank. But they didn't want me to write the screenplay and they didn't want me to play Sonny, the mobster, so I said no. Then they call again and offer $500,000. I still said no. They go to one million dollars. Everybody wanted to do the movie. I remember Pacino wanted to do it. Nicholson came to see the play. They all came to see it. And I was just like—no.

There was such a bidding war after the play was a success. Big-time directors got my phone number and called my house. I had producers—huge producers—calling me. Following me into the bathroom in restaurants. *Listen, you got to take this meeting with me. You got to!*

The interesting thing is, the hardest offer to refuse was the first one, the $250,000. That was the hardest one because that came out of nowhere: *$250,000? What?* That's the one that put me through trauma. When I called my parents they said, "Don't worry, son. It's okay." My parents were behind me. They said, "You do what you want." After I turned down the initial $250,000, the rest just became numbers to me. I couldn't connect with them. I also do believe that

I'm just a very lucky guy. I've always felt that way. I felt that there was some divine intervention. That God was there and put his hand on my shoulder. *It's okay. You're gonna be okay.* And I thought, *Yes. It's gonna be okay.* De Niro saw me in the play and said to me that if I wanted to write the screenplay and also play Sonny, he would direct it, play my father, and on a handshake it was a deal.

When I went to Italy in 1998, I went to film a movie, about Giovanni Falcone, a famous anti-Mafia judge. Pretty amazing to be in Sicily in the towns where my family grew up. My great-grandfather was a poet and he would go to the town square and read his poetry to the people. So I was like, *Wow!* Because you know I was asking myself, *How did this writing come about to me? How did this happen?* Well, I found out that it's in the family.

They used to say that Sicily is a land kissed by God and cursed by man because of the Mafia. I have very strong opinions about depicting the Mafia in films. About showing Italians as bad guys. A lot of people put down *The Godfather* and they put down *Goodfellas* and they put down *The Sopranos*. Well, this is America. This is art. This is *art*. You don't have to like modern art, for instance. If you like traditional art, the Renaissance, that's fine. This is art. That's what gives us our freedom. I know that Marty Scorsese said that he made *Goodfellas* to depict how awful and bad these people are. *A Bronx Tale* is not about the Mafia. It's about working people. It's about my father—De Niro in the film. My father is a *working* man. He's the one who wins at the end. The Mafia dies. But to show the light you have to show the darkness. Every good story is about good versus evil. Otherwise you don't have a story. Are there some very bad Mafia movies where Italians are made to look like total idiots? And they and the movie don't have any redeeming value? Yes! That's the price you pay for having free speech. Tell that person you can't make that? Absolutely not. You can make whatever you like and that's why I live in this country. You don't like it, shut it off. Don't watch it. It's okay.

This is not a knock on my mother's brothers and sisters, but they all left the neighborhood where we grew up. They said to her, "If you don't get out of this neighborhood, your children will all turn out to be bums." They all left but my mother stayed. My mother said, "You worry about your kids. I'll worry about mine."

We stayed there until I was eighteen, nineteen years old. My two sisters and I, we're all very successful. One sister married a vice president of a bank. Then she started a travel agency, had twenty-five of them and sold them, and they both retired. They live in Boca. My other sister is a teacher in Tampa. I think she became an associate professor. Does very well. All three of us did very well. In fact, better than all of my cousins who moved out of the neighborhood.

People say, *Chazz, I feel so bad for you—your neighborhood.* I go, *No, no, no, you don't understand. It was great. I loved it.* It was a family neighborhood. We all loved it. My father said we might not have a lot of money but we have a lot of love. We have each other. What does a parent do? A parent can set examples for their children. They can say till they're blue in the face, *Do this, do that,* but what they do is what you pick up. My father was always kind. My mother was always kind and generous and nice. I had a great upbringing. I believe that the problem in this country is that we try to say, especially in affluent areas, they say, *My kid's gonna go to Harvard. You're gonna do this. You're gonna do that.* We're not teaching them to be morally good people. If a child is morally a good person, he'll be okay. He might not be affluent, but he'll be successful as opposed to just being a winner at anybody's expense. And that's important.

It doesn't matter where you're from if you have good parents. I think that parents are very undervalued. I always tell people when you create a child, that's not just a child. That's a universe because that child will grow up and affect a lot of people, like ripples in water. And they'll get married and his kids will affect even more people and they'll affect even more people. So if you treat your children as this incredible special love the world will be better.

I go to juvenile prisons to talk to the kids there. It's not a coincidence that the juveniles in these prisons all come from broken homes. Not one home with a mother and a father. What shot do these kids have? In Baltimore there was this young kid, in solitary. The kid was sixteen, in for a double homicide, a gang-related thing. I went in to see him. I said, "You can tell me right now to get the F out, and I'm good with that. But I'm here because I care. If you want me to stay, I'll stay. If you want me to go, I'll go." *You could stay.* I said, "Fine." We started talking and I said, "Did you ever have any aspirations to do something?" "Yeah, I wanted to be an artist." "An artist?" I thought he was going to say a bricklayer, a mechanic—but an artist? "What do you mean artist? What kind of artist?" "Well, I like to draw." Two weeks later I get this mail that this kid drew a horse's head. A beautiful picture of a horse. He had put my card, "The saddest thing in life is wasted talent," on his wall.

Here's the problem with him in terms of follow-up. They can't release him to anybody. There's no one! His father's dead, his mother's a crack addict. Who wants him? That's what they say to you. *Who wants him?* Some of these kids who want to get out, where are they gonna go? Are you going to throw them out on the street? They don't know what to do with most of them. There's nobody to take them. It's a vicious cycle so I really do believe the parents are key.

I go back to the neighborhood once a month to go shopping. I buy my pasta there, my olive oil, my cheeses, my muzzarell. In each store I get something different. In one store, even if they have the muzzarell, I won't buy it there. I'll buy the cold cuts there, but I'll buy muzzarell on 187th Street. The best muzzarell in the world. My cold cuts I'll get in Mike's deli, and my olive oil I get at Teitel Brothers. For my pizza I'll go to Zero Otto Nove. Every time I go back, I go to a different restaurant and they're all good. There's

Roberto's, there's Rigoletto's, there's Zero Otto Nove, there's Mario's, so I go to each one of them. I want them to know that, *Hey, it's not just one I like. I'm here to support all of you.* The neighborhood is a wonderful place. It makes me feel at home. It brings back great memories, 'cause I used to roam these streets when I was a young boy. It's such a strong feeling in me that I almost can't explain. Those are my roots. I grew up there.

DANIEL ("DANNY") HAUBEN

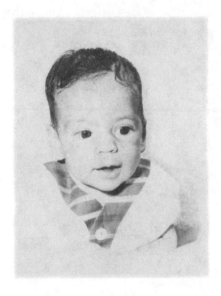

Artist, educator

(1956–)

I MOVED INTO THIS BUILDING WHEN I WAS NINE. I WAS VERY QUIET and shy, so my mother accosted every kid that looked like he was my age, saying, "I have a son your age. You have to come visit him." So there was this kid who lived down the hall, David Schwartz, and the two of us connected. The apartment building we lived in was newly built, and since we were the first tenants we had all of these empty packing boxes and cartons. David and I built forts out of the boxes. Then we drew a street map on a big piece of cardboard and colored it in with Magic Markers. My father brought home gears from the company he worked for and we'd stick them together with clay and make little vehicles that drove on the roads we created. We decided that the cars needed drivers, so we purchased small plastic Wishniks and Rat Finks from vending machines. My mother would even make outfits for them. Eventually these became the inhabitants of a town that evolved over the course of the next six years. We called the town Edge City, and it became more and more elaborate. We wrote laws and wrote about the adventures we had with the town. We had lights and we eventually even had water running to it. We created these elaborate organic dwellings, with Plexiglas windows, that emerged out of the countryside. My friend Karl built a balsa wood outhouse as his contribution, so David and I assessed it and decided that Karl could also be in on our adventures. The only time my mother got upset with me was when we started hauling in bags of cement and plaster and then started drilling, sending clouds of dust billowing through the apartment. The town kept developing until we were into our midteens, at which time it was up on a coffee table that took up most of my bedroom.

That town was something that we created. It was its own world. It had its own logic and its own story. It reflected the world that we knew but it was something different. And I think I'm trying to do the same thing in my paintings. The more I get into a painting and the more I work on it, the more it develops its own logic and becomes its own world. And then my job is to try to make it enticing for others to enter that world in some way.

I went to Music and Art High School, but I dropped out after one year. I always hated school. Maybe it's my nature or maybe it was the influence and support of my older siblings. Maybe it was because it was the sixties and there was this kind of free vision of life. What I hated was people trying to control my behavior and my thinking and to what end? I didn't know. I just didn't take to discipline for its own sake or to being taught things that nobody had ever bothered to try to help me understand why we were learning all this stuff. Albert Shanker, head of the teachers' union, was my hero because we had all these days off from school, due to all the teacher strikes going on at the time. The thing was, when I had off, I would go to class at Cooper Union with my brother Eddie or to bookstores with my brother Jay. I was very excited about learning, but I wasn't excited about school. And I was excited about engaging with the world. So fast forward to tenth grade, where my parents were actually instrumental in helping me transition out of high school. They had me sign into a school down in South Jersey where my sister lived, just so the truant officer would have a harder time tracking me down.

All my friends were still sitting in classes when I got my GED. When I was eighteen, I was living in this apartment with my mother, father, grandmother, and then my sister moved in with her infant son. It was a no-brainer. I had to get a job and get out of there. By then I had already traveled to India and hitchhiked across America with my girlfriend. I moved in with Jimmy Boyle, my only friend who had his own place.

I had taken these civil service exams. I was very good at taking tests—or cheating at tests. For example, I had taken the post office test, but only got like an eighty or something. You're competing with veterans and disabled people who get ten to fifteen extra points so you have to get a very high score to get the job. One third of the test was memorization. There's a list of fifteen names and fifteen addresses connected with those names. You were supposed to stare at the lists for fifteen or twenty minutes, and then when the lists were taken away you were supposed to connect the dots. Well, if you spent a fraction of that twenty minutes copying the list . . . Needless to say, I aced that part of the test. I worked the graveyard shift at the Bronx General Post Office for one and a half years.

Luckily I was then invited to move into a commune in the Boston area with my brother Eddie and a bunch of people who were eight or nine years older than I. Living there I was able to focus on my art to a greater degree. What I found myself working on, in my first large painting, was the view from my parents' apartment in the Bronx. When I was seventeen, I had done a Magic Marker drawing of the view, so that became the starting point for that painting. I started it in Boston, but I finished it back here in this apartment in the Bronx. I moved back in with my parents when I was twenty-four and then went to the School of Visual Arts.

To attempt to capture the view from this apartment with this sprawling urban landscape and amazing sunsets is a daunting task. When I was younger I couldn't imagine drawing or painting such a thing because it's simply overwhelming. But I think that aspect of it was the thing that stuck with me. My early impressions of that vastness were very strong. How do you do it? How does one manage? How do we urban dwellers process all of the information, the myriad of sounds and sights that surround us and are constantly bombarding us? How do you bring order to the randomness and chaos? How do you create art that reflects all these things but that has its own logic, enough to draw the viewer in? That's the trick.

∾

Note: *Danny Hauben and his wife, Judy, told me about their conversation when they met for the first time at the Virginia Center for the Creative Arts.*

Danny: *"It's so much easier to meet people here in Virginia. New York, you know, it's like everybody is in their own world."*

Judy: *"Oh, you live in New York. Where do you live?"*

Danny: *"I live in the Bronx."*

Judy: *"Is that nice?"*

Danny: *I had no answer for that! I had never heard that response before. Who says such a thing?*

LOUISE SEDOTTO

Educator, principal of P.S. 76 in the Bronx

(1957–)

I GREW UP IN A SEMIDETACHED HOME WHERE THERE WERE ALWAYS
people coming and going—family, people from the block, people
from the neighborhood. My mother cooked these Italian feasts
so she was prepared for whoever stopped by. If it was dinnertime,
they'd just sit down to eat. There would be a three-course meal,
starting with the soup, and at the end my father's job would be
to cut the fruit. Then, of course, came the black coffee and lots of
conversation around the table.

My brother is eight years older than I am, so if he had friends come by after school they would eat. Whoever came would always sit down and join us, whether it was during the week or on the weekend. My grandmother also lived in the neighborhood, just a few blocks away from us. My father is one of ten kids, and my mother is one of seven, and each of their siblings had four to five children. It was a very large family, with extended family too. My childhood was a good one. You know, comfortable.

My mother had an uncle, Morris, who loved to entertain. He would come occasionally with his buddies and he'd play the harmonica. Even though he worked for the IRT he had a show with his friends who played with a band. They would set up in the backyard and the whole neighborhood would come by. They came for the music, and of course my mother put out food. It was a gathering with music and dancing and eating. It was a simple life, not complicated by too many distractions.

I went to a parochial grammar school and later to parochial high school. In the Catholic schools we still had nuns as teachers. My father owned a dry-cleaning business and we would always take home the habits the nuns wore. He dry cleaned them for the whole school. I always loved school even though it was very strict. I seem to have been very disciplined because I knew that I was in school to do my work. If there were a mischievous boy or someone like that, Sister Mary Eymard would stand him in front of the room. I'll never forget George Rogee. We were in third grade, and he was chewing gum. Sister made him stand in front of the room with the gum on his nose. That must've been about 1957. Sister would also walk around with a ruler and hit your hands. It was intimidating, oh yeah, and yet I had some wonderful nurturing lay teachers as well. And those were the ones I was very involved with.

There was Mrs. McGann, who wore perfume. I loved walking past her. She was also very well dressed, which made her so very different from my mom, who never even wore makeup. I was fascinated with those teachers who came well dressed to school, wore makeup, and smelled of perfume. I was just so amazed at the glamour of it all and it impressed me. And then again, I actually loved the work. I always wanted to be at my desk, I guess, to please them, but when I went home I played school for hours, especially since my father had bought me a school desk for my bedroom. I was always the teacher, and my imaginary playmates were the students. I knew even then that's what I wanted to be—a teacher.

I always felt that the people in the Bronx were so friendly and down to earth. I bought my first house there but when I moved up to Westchester it was very different. Playdates for the kids? Something we never had when we were growing up.

There's an old saying, "You can take the girl out of the Bronx, but you can't take the Bronx out of the girl." So here I am, back at a school in that borough. I'm home.

∽

Note: P.S. 76 was the neighborhood school that I attended as a kid. I don't think we had any particular academic distinctions at that time. It is definitely a better school now than when I was there in the late 1930s and '40s.

STEVE JORDAN

Drummer, musical director, composer, producer

(1957–)

MUSIC WAS ALWAYS IN MY HOUSE—ALWAYS IN THE FAMILY. MUSIC and baseball. Those were my two favorite things. My parents were big music fans. My mother used to sing classical music, actually. My father is an engineer/architect, but you could swear that he was a musician. I was sitting with him a couple of days ago, and he sang that great old Lionel Hampton tune "Flying Home." He sang the solo, the saxophone solo, verbatim. That's where I get that from, because I can sing a solo break too.

I was the class clown in school, so for a couple of years there my parents had to stay on me. But I wasn't like an evil kid. Nothing like that. Any time I got grounded, the one thing they didn't take away from me was studying music. So when I was sent to my room, I could listen to music and I could practice. So I was like, *Hey, this isn't too bad*. In fact, it kind of helped me focus.

From the age of two years, I played on pots and pans and, in fact, I was always also playing records for people. My parents were fascinated about how I knew, before I could read, how I knew which record was which. I had figured it out. I must've been able, because I have this photographic memory kind of thing, to just identify the labels and the print on the labels. I could remember which song was sung by which group by the look of the label.

When I was about eleven or so, if my aunt was having a party or somebody in the neighborhood was having a party, I was the deejay. If my class was having a party, I would deejay the party. I was on this AV—audiovisual—team in school. There was this record player that was made for schools, a big mono speaker, just one speaker, but it was heavy duty to withstand children. It always had a really big sound 'cause it was a bigger unit. It had a little bass happening. It was very sturdy. I always remembered that record player. So years later, I was producing a record—and they were still records in those days—in Milwaukee. I was going down the street and saw this AV repair shop, so I walked in and I saw all the stuff that I used to have in school. I bought all of it. So I have one of these record players in my home now. It sounds fantastic.

And of course I was a baseball fan. I played second base from the age of about seven years old through the clinic and then Little League. In the back of my head, my dream was to be the second baseman for the New York Yankees. To begin with, I wasn't very tall. In fact, I was always trying to figure out how to grow. *I gotta get taller here.* I'd try standing up straight. I loved milk, so I drank a lot of it. They had to lock up the fridge. One of my best friends, Steven Grant, was a guy who was almost like six feet when

I was five-four or something like that. Actually, he went on to play professional basketball. It kinda drove me nuts that he was so tall. My dad had to take me to a shrink because of it, to talk it out. To have this doctor explain to me that it was okay and that it doesn't mean that you're any less of a person or anything like that. You know, it got serious. The strange thing is that my father is six-one, so there was always hope. Hope springs eternal. I was gonna get there.

My mom started a neighborhood association. That was a big thing in the sixties and seventies—to try to get your communities back. The organization started a day camp, so the whole camp was able to get tickets to go to a Yankees game. It was the old Stadium, and of course we were sitting in the bleachers, where the seats were black. Those seats were about twenty degrees hotter because of that black paint. It was really a bizarre design, but the reason for it was because if you're hitting, if the bleachers were white, you wouldn't be able to see the ball, so there had to be a black background.

The Yankees did their best to try to help out the community. They teamed up with Con Ed and came up with a program called Con Ed Kids. They'd get a bunch of kids from different communities around the city and you'd get into a game for free. You'd also get a special gift, besides the seats from Con Ed. Some extra perk. There was this guy called the Answer Man. His name was Earl Battey. Now Earl Battey was a professional major league catcher who played for the Minnesota Twins. So he's sitting out there in the 900-degree heat and there's a field full of kids—just millions of them. Around the seventh-inning stretch, it's time for him to ask a question to one of the kids, and if you got the answer right you'd win two free tickets to sit in the mezzanine section at the Stadium and then get your picture taken with a Yankee. So we're out there—a sea of kids. And now it's time. He asks the question. And I, with all the other kids, I'm like—*Hey teacher*—and I raised my hand and I pinned on the Answer Man, and he looks right back at me, looks right into my eyes, and poses the question to me. So this is like incredible. The question is, "Who plays second base for the New York Yankees?" I'm like, *What?* I'm like, *This is crazy!* Or maybe the question was, "Who's number 20 for the Yankees?" Something ridiculously easy for me.

The second baseman for the Yankees at the time was a gentleman named Horace Clarke. It was a very tough position for him to fill because he was taking the place of the great Bobby Richardson, who had played second base for the Yankees. His number was number 1, and he was an all-star. I mean, he was a great Yankee and everybody wants to be like Bobby Richardson or Mickey Mantle or Roger Maris. And so these are the lean years for the Yankees, right after they won all the championships. Mickey Mantle's still on the team, but they're not doing so good. So it's like okay, *Who's number 20 for the Yankees?* Well, it's Horace Clarke. He's from the West Indies, I'm of West Indian descent, and to top it off my dad's name is Horace. So they ask me this question—it's like—*Is that the question? Don't you have a more difficult question?* So obviously I answered the question correctly and I won the two tickets.

My dad, Horace, took me to the game, which was the prize. I got on the field and I got my picture taken with Bobby Murcer, who was the guy who was supposed to be the next Mickey Mantle. It was amazing, of course. The Yankees. The Stadium. Earl Battey. Con Ed Kids. It was a Cinderella kind of thing.

NEIL DeGRASSE TYSON

Astrophysicist, author, science communicator, and
director of the Hayden Planetarium at the American
Museum of Natural History in New York

(1958–)

Kids have different profiles in school. Some are shy, some are sociable, some are purposely disruptive, and some are the class clowns. And I'll bet you that every successful comedian in the world today was a class clown in school, and that they would have been subjected to the ire of their teachers accusing them of disrupting the lesson plan.

At no time is anyone saying that maybe this person can become a world-famous comedian. Teachers generally don't think this way. They want to homogenize who and what you are so that you are quiet, that you get high grades, and that you're not disruptive. And your grades are their currency of judgment for your promise and performance later in life. In casual questioning that I've done, if you corralled the most influential people in the world—this could be attorneys or novelists or journalists, playwrights, poets, people who shape our culture—and put them all in a room and ask, "How many of you got straight A's in school?" I bet none of them would raise their hands. Include in that a list of CEOs and inventors. If hardly any of them got straight A's, then what is it that we're trying to breed in our students if you're after straight A's? Maybe there's something else that matters if school is to prep you for being a productive adult. Yes, you want to get as high a grade as you can. But if a student is left to feel inadequate, that's an unhealthy learning environment.

There was a teacher in the sixth grade who cut out an ad for me about taking classes at the Hayden Planetarium. But it's not like she said, *Oh, I recognize that this guy is brilliant.* That's not how it came across. It was *Look what he's doing. Maybe we can find some way for him to invest that energy differently.*

I was invited back to my elementary school to give a talk. They wanted me to talk about what a great education I had there. I said, "I can't do that. I became what I am in spite of the teacher attitudes about who I was, not because of those attitudes. If you want, I'll come back at another time and talk to your teaching staff."

We had a dentist friend who lived a few floors below the roof of our building, Skyview apartments. I went up to the rooftop with my telescope when I was about twelve. He allowed me to snake my hundred-foot electric cord through the window to his apartment. It's night, and so I'm not lit up. In New York, your sight line can land on so many different places. If you're looking out a window and you're looking up, there are thousands of windows. So why are they looking at your window? Except this one time I was noticed by people in this other building because they looked across.

And they called the police. Well, my telescope is a thick tube, and why would a police officer know or understand telescopes? Maybe binoculars, but not telescopes, and I have a cable going over the roof. This is the seventies, and it's Riverdale, and my skin color is substantially darker than that of anybody else in the community, and so suspicions were high. Since I was clearly a school-age kid, I think they felt a little better about it initially, but it wasn't until I showed them the craters of the moon through the telescope that they said, "Oh, that's great! Keep up the good work." So they were ultimately swayed by an actual observation of the universe.

My parents were born in the late twenties, and so they came of age in the forties. My father served in the segregated army. We were trained how to behave at any and all times if the police approached, or if we were in the presence of the police. *Don't make any sudden moves.* You want to minimize the occasions they would have to justify shooting you. And you address them as "Sir." And you don't run. It wasn't fear of the police that we were taught. It was simply that's what you had to do because the police are not your friends. If you have a question that you need answered or if you need help, go into a store, go to a merchant, a cabdriver, a medical doctor. Or, if you were crossing the street, a crossing guard.

Whereas my wife grew up in Alaska, where the police were friendly. They'd help you cross the street and give you a lift somewhere if you had a flat tire. Give you a lift? What kind of world is that?

As much as my head was in the stars, I was reminded that I was black every time I stepped into society. It was not an active awareness that I carried within me. It was how society defined me.

Another example of that didn't involve the police. It was just the conduct of strangers. I was into time-keeping devices. I liked timing the photographs through the telescope. I greatly value just the principle of measuring time. And so I had a watch that had too many knobs and dials on it, you know? It had a tachometer and time in six time zones. At one point the sweep second hand, if anyone remembers what that is, fell off. I went to the local jeweler to get it repaired.

"I have this watch that I need repaired."

So the guy looks at me, looks at the watch, and says, "I can't open this."

I said, "Why not?"

"It's stolen."

"Oh, I didn't know it was stolen."

Here I'm thinking that he knows something about it that I don't know, without realizing that he was accusing me of having stolen goods. And I'm too naive or innocent to imagine he was thinking that I was a criminal because I certainly knew I wasn't.

I tried to get the watch fixed in a variety of stores, and they said, "I'm sorry, I don't have the key to open this."

Well, necessity is the mother of invention. I found my own way to open the dial, and then I fixed it myself and put it back together. There's a little pry point in the back of the watch. So I got to learn how a precision watch is made.

We were residents of the Bronx my entire life while growing up. Later on, while in high school, I objected to what so many people around me were doing in Riverdale. They were not saying that they were from the Bronx. They said they were from Riverdale. In fact, even on the return addresses of envelopes it would say Riverdale, New York. I just thought that was wrong. I thought they were rejecting something important about the borough. My high school, Bronx High School of Science, had the word "Bronx" in the name as a fundamental part of its identity. The simple use of that word contributed to my association with the borough.

My earliest memories are of the East Bronx, in the Castle Hill housing projects. I went to P.S. 36 there, for kindergarten. At that time, my father finished school and started getting jobs in the city government. That's when his income level went above the level for the middle-income units of the housing project, and that's when we moved to Riverdale.

In Riverdale, we were high enough in the middle class for our building to have a doorman, an ice skating rink, a pool, and a parking garage. I enjoy swimming, and at one point became a lifeguard. These were opportunities that came about simply by proximity. I lament the absence of opportunities for so many other people who remained in whatever circumstances they were born into.

What richness of discoveries and what poetry have gone unwritten because of want of opportunity to express it? I really ask myself that question a lot.

MICHAEL R. KAY

Sports journalist and New York Yankees
play-by-play broadcaster

(1961–)

Wʜᴇɴ I ᴡᴀs ɪɴ ꜰɪʀsᴛ ɢʀᴀᴅᴇ, I ᴡᴀs ᴀʟʀᴇᴀᴅʏ ʀᴇᴀᴅɪɴɢ *Tᴏ Kɪʟʟ ᴀ*
Mockingbird. The principal called my parents and said they wanted
to skip me to fourth grade, but my parents didn't agree. They
said that I wouldn't be adjusted and maybe I'd even be malad-
justed if I were skipped. Since they didn't allow it, I remained
with my age group, which meant I was always one of the smartest kids in my class. My parents, especially since we weren't well
off, stressed education. I couldn't do anything unless I got good
grades. I mean, *really* good grades. It was tough for me because

my sister was brilliant and I had to be just as smart. I'd go to school, come home, do my homework, and then I could go down to play.

There were so many kids my age in my building on Evergreen Avenue, it was unbelievable. There was a little park outside, with monkey bars and stuff like that and this little dirt part, where we played baseball. That's where my love of baseball was first born.

I loved the Yankees. We didn't have the kind of money where I could go to a lot of games, but occasionally we'd scrape together a dollar fifty to sit in the upper deck. That was my seat. Right behind home plate in the upper deck, last row. I tell people that I now have the same seat, but a lot closer. But as a kid I'd watch every game on Channel 11. That would be the only time I wasn't outside. If the Yankees were on I'd be watching them. Who knows how many kids dream that stuff? I also knew that I couldn't play well, so I was practical and rational, even as a nine-year-old. *If I'm gonna be part of the Yankees, I'm gonna be that broadcaster!* So I'd interview my friends with a tape recorder. They'd make believe they were other athletes and I'd interview them. "What about that hit?" and stuff like that. I get people tweeting me now saying they remember me saying at that time that I was going to be the Yankees' announcer one day.

I was in P.S. 93, which was a block walk from our building. It became overcrowded, so the city converted a bowling alley four blocks up into a school—with no windows. It was such a weird school because of that, but I was in an accelerated class. The top class. We were like the outcasts that got thrown out of P.S. 93, because it was too crowded, so we were all in it together with unbelievable camaraderie. I still contend that those two years helped me become the person I am, more than any other two years of schooling, including Bronx High School of Science and Fordham University.

I had two teachers there who were phenomenal. One of them, in fifth grade, was Ken Wilkoff. My dad, who had emphysema and couldn't breathe well, really couldn't take me to ball games, so Mr. Wilkoff would take me and maybe two or three other kids to the games, 'cause he knew I loved the Yankees. In 1973, when I was in sixth grade, my teacher was Edward Baehr. I was in school when the Yankees were going to play the Red Sox with Ron Blomberg, the designated hitter, the first ever designated hitter in the history of baseball. Mr. Baehr had arranged something with Mr. Wilkoff because at two o'clock, when the game started, they wheeled in the TV, plugged it in, put it on, and said, "All right, Michael, you can see this." Blomberg walked with bases loaded, they unplugged the TV, and walked out. These two young teachers who were in their twenties knew what I loved, and they cared. Mr. Wilkoff even took three kids and me to Cooperstown to the Baseball Hall of Fame. I get goose bumps talking about what a great, great man he was. Both those teachers knew that I had an aptitude and they encouraged me. And my parents could see how special they were. They let those teachers mold me.

Although I was generally agreeable, I could also be an obstinate kid when it came to my fears. Our doctor was Dr. Loperfido and one time he chased me around his office to give me a shot. I was terrified. I picked up a shoe and I threw it at the doctor's head. I actually hit him in the head. He said to my mother, "He's got an anger management problem," even before that became a term. "He's going to be a problem." And every time I'd be angry about something, my mother would say, "You know, that doctor was right." I'm still terrified of blood. I knew that when they stuck that needle in, it hurt, and I didn't like pain. Pain drove me nuts. I would get into flop sweat when we'd drive up that road to the doctor because I thought that every trip to the doctor meant me getting a shot.

To this day, whenever I go in for an exam, the doctor knows

that they have to ignore the first blood pressure numbers they take because I have white coat fever. The doctor looks at me when I tell him that and he says, "Really?" and I say, "Let's just do the exam and take the blood pressure again." And at the end it'll be 120 over 80.

Because I was always one of the smartest kids in my class, I thought I was superbright. When I went to Bronx High School of Science that all went out the window. I started to be interested in girls, and all that brightness just drained out of my head. If I had it to do over again, I probably wouldn't go there, because I was definitely *not* the smartest kid there. I mean, I struggled to get a ninety-one or ninety-two. I think that was my average for three years, not four, because I had skipped one year from seventh to ninth grades. Ninety-two! And I busted my butt!

When I go to a reunion, I look at myself as a failure. They're doctors and engineers and I became a baseball broadcaster. *Why'd you go to Bronx Science to become a broadcaster?* Everyone in that high school was the smartest kid in their elementary or middle school. They were the cream of the crop. I almost look at it like this: in baseball, when you get drafted, you go to a minor league team. Every kid who's drafted is the best player in his city or town, and then all of a sudden he's in where *everybody* was the best baseball player in his town. So in Bronx Science, everybody was the smartest kid in their school—and it was tough. It was very, very difficult for me. You start to doubt yourself. You start to doubt that you're really smart.

I now give advice to kids. "Always work harder than everybody else, because you can control that. You can control effort but you can't control being the smartest person."

My struggles in high school actually made college easy. I went to Fordham and when I was done with Fordham I was done with school. I had had enough. If I weren't a sportscaster, I know that I would be involved in something where I could use my creativity.

I wasn't really built for being a doctor or anything like that. I mean, can you imagine me *giving* shots? Thank God I'm doing well, but I still think that it can go away. My mom to her last day said, "You have to watch out. People want your job."

My mom and dad got married in the Bronx County Courthouse. You could see that building from the broadcast booth in the old Yankee Stadium. I'd see that building all the time. In 2003, I was inducted into the Bronx Walk of Fame. The ceremony was in the Bronx County Courthouse, and my mom was there. And when my wife, Jodi, and I got our marriage license, we got it in the Bronx County Courthouse too.

MELVIN GLOVER
(GRANDMASTER MELLE MEL)

Award-winning rap artist

(1961–)

WHEN YOU'RE BROUGHT UP IN A DEPRESSED NEIGHBORHOOD, THE idea is that you want to leave the neighborhood when you are grown. Since there wasn't a lot going on, you had to work a little harder to actually get out of the Bronx or else you'd just be stuck there. Where I lived, even though it was a bad neighborhood, it had good people in it, and with a little bit of support from the school that I went to and the block that I grew up on I could think of life goals. There was a lot of encouragement to go to places outside of the Bronx, and I think that my generation, and maybe the generation after, we were probably the last generations that wanted to move on. Nowadays, they want to be on the street and it's more like they want to stay rather than be somewhere else.

At a certain point, I was still a good student. But instead of doing the curriculum, I was trying to be defiant against education and after a while, after I knew that I wasn't going to be able to educate my way out of the Bronx, I started getting into music and hanging out on the streets and seeing a lot of the break dancing and hip-hop. I was about seventeen when I realized that the education thing wasn't going to work for me 'cause I blew that, so I concentrated on doing the music thing. That's when my brother and me, we started writing rhymes, doing parties, doing routines, and things of that nature. I spent a lot of time doing those things. We have to specialize in something and my field of expertise was gonna be entertainment.

I had a mother and father at home, but my father was an alcoholic. My mother kept us stable because she was a housewife who stayed at home. She was like the voice of sanity for my father because he was very drunk and just a little weird. I had four siblings. Two brothers and two sisters. The older ones were the two girls and they kinda ran wild, so my mother would always say, "You're not messin' up my life because, you know, you're messin' up your life if you run wild." She was right. So I realized after a while that I was in charge of my life and I didn't want to mess it up.

Left to my own devices, though, I wouldn't have done the right thing, because I thought I had a certain amount of intelligence and I thought I was smarter than everybody. You know, I'm really not that smart because if I really was that smart, I wouldn't have gone around with that wrong crowd. We were a couple of young dudes, and we'd hang out, getting high, smoking weed. We'd go around and commit these little petty crimes. I remember there was a teacher who worked in the after-school center. His name was Mr. Torres and he also taught in the sixth grade. He was short. He was maybe five-foot-five or something like that. It wasn't like he was a big guy, but he was kind of husky. One of the gang guys really got to him so Mr. Torres said, If you don't come to my class, if you don't come to school, I'm gonna come and get you where you live. And I was in the fifth grade then, sniffing glue and picking pockets.

I remember it was a Sunday before the Monday when school started, and I was supposed to go and hang out with these guys, but figured that I had to stay in the house because on Monday, if I don't go to the class, Mr. Torres was gonna come to my house and get me. So that Sunday, these three guys kidnapped two girls, took 'em up to a roof, raped both the girls, and threw one of them off the roof. Everybody in the neighborhood knew that I used to hang out with these guys all the time, but I wasn't there. I had nothing to do with it. I had made up my mind that I was going to go to school because of Mr. Torres and deciding that basically saved my entire life, right there, because everything would've been totally different if I had been with those guys. Crazy!

When we were younger kids, we'd play basketball, softball, but we also played football. We didn't have a football so we'd take a milk container and a soda bottle and wrap the soda bottle in newspaper and stuff the soda bottle inside the milk container and shape it like a football. And we'd play football on the street. That's the way we'd pass a lot of time. That was before we got older and people started messin' with drugs. We didn't have football equipment, but we made our own football equipment, and we had fun doing things that regular kids were doing, but we just had to improvise a little bit.

And that same concept was basically what hip-hop was, because we had block parties and indoor parties. You'd make do. Between that and music, that's what basically kept me from going to jail. The one thing I'm not going to say was a great achievement was that I never went to prison. I've been arrested, but I don't have a criminal record. I was buying cars, but I didn't have a license. But I hung out with the good guys and I started doing music.

It's not like I'm the most talented guy, but I grew up in a black household where my father listened to country music, to Sinatra and to Dean Martin—we watched a lot of TV—and Mel Tormé. We listened to a lot of different types of music. Like Sammy Davis Jr., Dean Martin. The Temptations would've been more like the music we had, but format and the structure were more like the others. How they handled the mike. How they worked the crowd. Upscale entertainment. That's how I saw entertainment in my head. That was like what it was all about to me.

The hip-hop culture is music and entertainment. Hip-hop is a term that's used to describe it all. There was no such thing as hip-hop music. It came out of disco and all kinds of music, like jazz and anything that had that beat. It was jazz, it was rock 'n roll, it was reggae, it was R and B. It wasn't necessarily a dance, but they created moves, and a patchwork, like a quilt. All those different styles of music. Then the rhymes went onto that quilt and over time it was called hip-hop. That's how the whole thing started.

The main thing about the generation that I came up in, from the perspective of being a fan and the music we did, I think it's so commendable that the people all came from the same area. From a four- or five-block radius. We didn't just settle for what was brought to the table. Brooklyn. The kids call it Crooklyn, but we did music in the Bronx. That was our thing. We are able to go all over the world. By 1980, 1990, people all over the world were doing hip-hop. It's a certified music genre and it's all because we just wanted to have fun in our Bronx neighborhood. We just wanted to have a good time. And we knew that a lot of other people could have a good time, and I think that those people have a lot of enjoyment in their lives from what we started back then.

JAIME ("JIMMY")
RODRIGUEZ JR.

Restaurateur

(1962–)

I STARTED HELPING MY FATHER SELL FISH ON THE STREET NEAR Westchester Avenue and the Bronx River Parkway when I was about sixteen. He went to the market early in the morning and then we set up the outdoor fish stand where we sold shrimp and lobsters. We always bought a lot because my dad was saying, "Make the money on volume. You buy it and you make a couple of dollars, all on volume." After a couple of years we weren't allowed to sell there because we created congestions and didn't have a license for that corner. So we went to the Cross Bronx Expressway and

Webster Avenue underneath the highway. We created chaos there, too, with single parking, double parking. Neighbors complained. Other businesses complained. So then we moved to the side of the highway. We rented the property and built a shack that you could close. A typical wooden shack like you'd see in Puerto Rico on the side of the road. It was small, and they couldn't kick us out there because it was private property.

My dad taught me from an early age, *You buy, you sell. You make a couple of dollars, you don't hold on to what you buy. You sell.* Flipping. So my friend David's father, he had a used-car dealership license, which allowed us to go to car auctions at an early age. Between working with my dad with whatever money I would make, I'd buy a car and put a "for sale" sign on it. I would have two or three cars at home as well as at work. I'd buy a car for maybe a thousand and then sell it for fifteen hundred, seventeen hundred, so by the time I was nineteen I had about a hundred cars that I had bought and sold. It was about buying, selling, and a quick flip.

At one point, I would have five or six cars of my own. My own car went from being a thousand-dollar car to a two-thousand-dollar car so that eventually I was driving a sixteen-thousand-dollar car, a twenty-thousand-dollar car—my own personal car. I'd always have a "for sale" sign on it. It didn't matter if I sold it. I had a resale certificate and would just go to an auction and get another one. Between seventeen and twenty years old I was always driving something, advertising it, and selling it.

My earlier dreams were about baseball. About being a baseball player. My uncle was a Major League Baseball player. Ellie Rodríguez. He played for about twelve years in the major leagues. Actually, I went to Puerto Rico for a year to learn from him, but I wound up staying with my grandfather instead. The one bad part about baseball here is that it's seasonal, where everywhere else it's like ten, twelve months. When you're working and your job is six or seven days a week, Saturdays and Sundays, you can't really go to play baseball—so that changed my mind about it all.

I was lucky and more fortunate than a lot of guys because in the early eighties a lot of them were hustling and doing bad things. There were a lot of drugs. There were the empty buildings, the robberies, crack cocaine. And a lot of them went to jail and a lot of them got into a lot of trouble. I saw like the friends of the friends, while you only made a few hundred dollars a week and they were making thousands, but I'd still see them coming to our place to get lobster and shrimp. In the restaurant business, the greatest part is that *everyone* has to eat. Everyone has to eat and drink and socialize no matter what their walk of life. When it's dinnertime, you have to eat. You can't exclude yourself. Then a week later, I'd hear that this one went to jail and that one got killed, so the more stories I'd hear, and I heard more bad ones than good, it encouraged me to stay working. I realized that at any given moment what was really going on in the street was Russian roulette. I didn't want to be part of that.

My very first job in a restaurant was as a dishwasher. I thought that it was a lot of fun because you had to keep clean and organized. I also started working in a kitchen as a line cook/prep guy/expediter. I knew that whatever I did, I did with pride and that I was going to be good at it. No one was going to do a better job than I did. If I was going to make a delivery, I was going to be on time. I was going to be the best.

Some people have eyes, but they can't see. I built Jimmy's Bronx Café, which was a forty-eight-thousand-square-foot restaurant, which wound up probably being the largest Hispanic restaurant/lounge/bar in America. Before it was built I would tell people what my plans were. That I had a vision for what it would look like, but people—they all thought I was crazy. I couldn't borrow a dollar from my friends. I had used up every penny that I had and all the banks had turned me down. A former baseball player, Ruben Sierra, who was an investor, had pulled out of the deal. After Ruben pulled out and left me to hang and dry, I had no choice but to continue. *All the money I have is in this deal. I'm already building. I'm putting* forty guys to work every day. *I'm already in. All my money, all my cash and credit is in. If I quit, I sink. Either sink or swim.* So I kept building. I was looking to borrow money and I need a million one to buy the property and the broker Lenny Katz came to visit me. I was walking him through the space, showing him what I was building, and he said, "Let me see your family." So he went to my house and he met my wife and kids on Mosholu Parkway and he said, "I'll get back to you."

The next thing, his uncle Leon Katz, who used to be a councilman, came. I gave him a tour of the space, and he met my family too. He called me back and said, "I'm going to give you the money, at twenty-four percent. And the reason it's twenty-four percent is that you're building and improving someone else's property. It's not even yours, but I know that you're not going to quit. You're going to make this project win." I had told Leon, "I can't quit because this is all I have," so I kept building. Probably a year and a half later I was able to pay him back. You know twenty-four percent is a high interest. It was the highest you could charge, but it didn't matter because at the end of the day it was sink or swim. The restaurant was a big success and I paid him back everything that I owed him.

The saddest part is—and I'm so upset about this—that you send these kids to school and you spend thirty, forty, fifty, or two hundred thousand dollars on their education, and the first job they get out of college they get stuck with because they think, *What if I quit this job and I can't get another job?* The biggest fear in people that teach us, the educators, is that you'll be left without anything if you don't settle for what you now have. That's wrong. If you fail, it's okay. It's not failing. It's just a test. So you take another test. Your whole life is going to school. When you stop being educated by the educational system and you walk into life, you don't realize that that's part of another educational system and that you have to continue to grow and evolve on a daily basis.

I'm still learning and I'm never going to stop learning, because in the restaurant business I consider myself a freshman in college. After thirty-five years! I still have to earn my associate's or bachelor's degree. I haven't even gotten my master's yet. In the past, I failed three times. After the fish place on Webster Avenue I bought a restaurant in New Jersey and I failed. I had an auto shop on the Grand Concourse and that didn't work and then a car wash and that didn't work out. I didn't succeed in any of them. Each business, even though they didn't work out for me, I didn't quit. And when I started Jimmy's Café, that was even a bigger project than the first three, but I don't know how to spell fail. When I started the Café I said this is going to be great, and after the success of Jimmy's Bronx Café I started Jimmy's Downtown and Jimmy's in Harlem.

I've been to the White House, and I've met Bill Clinton. I had dinner with Fidel Castro from Cuba, and had a dinner party for Tito Puente's birthday. I never got my high school diploma and I didn't go to college, but I'm still learning in the college of hard knocks. You can achieve or attain anything you want, but believing is half the process. And you have to surround yourself with people who will help you move forward and not keep you back. I was fortunate as a young man to have met people who could guide me. It's very important to have people you look up to. To admire their work and learn from their hard work. You get out what you put in. If you put in apples, don't expect oranges. You're not going to fool anyone.

LUIS A. UBIÑAS

Businessman, former president of the Ford Foundation

(1963–)

THE THING ABOUT GROWING UP REALLY POOR IS THAT THERE AREN'T many carefree days. You don't have enough days in a row without knowing whether or not there's going to be enough food. You don't have a day when it's winter and it's snowing without knowing whether or not there's going to be heat the next day. It's not just the moment of not having that's challenging. It's knowing that the moment of not having will either continue or return. I think what's shocking is the permanence of the conditions of insufficiency we had. Of never having enough. Or even when we did have enough, knowing that not having enough would soon return.

We had a lot of housing insecurity. We were almost never in the same place two years in a row. Once we had an apartment that burned down. My mother had worked hard to buy a sofa, a bed, to buy things that you would need in an apartment, and then one day there was an electrical fire and our building burned to the ground. It was a wooden house of over a hundred years old. We lost everything.

Another time it was very hard to pay the Con Edison bill, so even if you can pay the rent you still need electricity. Once Con Ed cut off our lights there was no going back. We couldn't meet the monthly payment and certainly couldn't meet the back payments of three or four months, so we lost the apartment because we couldn't pay the electric bill. Many times we lost places because we couldn't pay the rent itself. Other times we lost places because they were condemned. Those were very hard times.

Unlike other great New York communities, the housing stock in the South Bronx was never good. There weren't beautiful brownstones, wide and made of stone, like in Bed-Stuy in Brooklyn. In the Bronx there were little wooden houses with little rooms, built almost like temporary housing about a hundred and twenty years ago. By the seventies they were way beyond their useful lives. They had never been upgraded for plumbing. They had never been upgraded for heating or electricity. In the sixties and seventies the city rules were different, and the enforcement of those rules was almost nonexistent. When you drove through parts of the Bronx in those years, the entire horizon as far as the eye could see was of entire blocks of rubble fields. And the rubble fields would end in abandoned buildings with birds living in them. That city with rubble—that place looked more like Dresden in World War Two than a part of New York City.

My mother was a seamstress. She sewed dresses in South Bronx sweatshops for thirty-five cents each. That somehow she managed to raise us is almost a heroic act, and it cost her her life. She had a form of colon cancer, but if she were middle class she'd probably be alive today. Health care wasn't available to her in any real way, and taking a break from work meant not making tomorrow's breakfast. My father died in his early thirties from drug and alcohol abuse. He grew up on the Lower East Side in the fifties and sixties. There was a business then, a business of addicting young people, mostly Hispanics, to create heroin addicts. They would actively take boys of fourteen or fifteen. Boys who weren't old enough to have their first kiss were encouraged and brought into the world of drugs.

One reason education mattered so much to my Hispanic family is much like it mattered to other immigrant families, whether the Jews in the 1890s or other Hispanics in the sixties or seventies. Education is the pathway to prosperity and prosperity is the pathway to safety. Safety means being able to wake up in the morning and having a place to eat, having hot water. Safety is knowing that when you wake up and you're hungry there's food. Safety is knowing that when you walk out the front door you'll be able to make it to the subway without being robbed.

By the time I was ready for first grade, we were living in my grandmother's apartment in a housing project. For us it was a safe haven. Every time we lost our own place, we knew we could go there. We also knew that my grandmother, with her limited resources, would feed us and make space for us. When we were there, we also knew we wouldn't be in a homeless shelter or in one of those homeless hotels, which were so horrible at that time.

I hadn't gone to kindergarten because we had moved so much, so I was put in a first grade with other kids who hadn't gone to kindergarten. Very quickly the teachers there realized that it wasn't the best environment for me. But I stayed in that school for the second and third grades, and in some way they gave me my own curriculum. At the end of third grade arrangements were made for me to go to a special school for gifted and talented children. In September, when I was supposed to go there, we found out that we hadn't received the paperwork because we had moved again. So I was put in a fourth grade in the only school that had space.

It was a bilingual school where instruction was in both English and Spanish. By then I was flat-out depressed. The chaos there! There was no teaching going on. Luckily, a guidance counselor–teacher looked at my record and realized that not only should I have been in the gifted program but that I scored among the highest in the city on the reading and math tests. I scored on a high school level in both those tests from third grade. So the initial solution was to put me in sixth grade. For many reasons, that solution had its own problems. First of all, I was a ten-year-old in a class of fourteen-year-olds, many of them having repeated a year or two. I think there was even one fifteen-year-old there. And many of them didn't speak Spanish, because they were either African American or non-Spanish-speaking Hispanics.

But this amazing teacher, who made such a difference in my life, who saw that I shouldn't be there, realized that my being in the sixth grade was not an ideal solution. So he then did something that I don't think would be possible now. He personally took me to the Bank Street School, Allen-Stevenson School, and St. Bernard's—all private schools in Manhattan. He took me out of school, took me by the hand, bought me subway tokens, bought me lunch. Where parental consent enters in all of this I have no idea. But he, thank God, took that step.

Miraculously, I was accepted in all three schools. He turned to me, in a way that would horrify helicopter parents in this day, and said, "Where would you like to go?" I said, "I'd like to go to the school where all the kids were wearing jackets and ties, where, when the kids ran through the hall, the teacher stopped them and where there was silence in the hallways." And he said okay. At the cost of twenty-five dollars a year, which was an enormous amount for my mother to come up with, I got to go to the Allen-Stevenson School on the East Side. That was a seminal moment in my life.

From Allen-Stevenson I went to Collegiate, and from there to Harvard and then to Harvard Business School.

At the Allen-Stevenson School I was with kids who were living a different kind of American reality. They lived on Park Avenue and West End Avenue and had things that were unimaginable to me. We would play soccer on Randall's Island. We would play baseball in Central Park. We would go on field trips to the art museums. A parent even donated a box at the Metropolitan Opera. Every chance I had, I'd go sit in that box, which seemed unfathomably and miraculously glamorous.

One of the least understood but perhaps one of the most important things about being in an environment where people come from different backgrounds is that they have different aspirations. It has to do with what the horizon looks like. The horizon from the South Bronx was limited to an everyday survival worry about clothing and shelter. The horizon when you're in a place like Harvard or a place like Collegiate is a distant horizon, and that one has things in it, like becoming a senator or even becoming president of the Ford Foundation. It is one of the gifts of a place like Allen-Stevenson or a place like Collegiate that they not only educate you, but they open up limitless horizons for you. My course was changed and set from that moment in fourth grade when a teacher decided to take matters into his own hands.

BOBBY BONILLA

Professional baseball player

(1963–)

As a kid, I knew that I excelled at playing certain sports, like baseball, but I had just as much fun playing basketball. I had just as much fun playing football in the snow and I had just as much fun playing roller hockey, which was my favorite. It was such a blast. My friends and I, we shared our interests in sports and played all year round. If it snowed, we put Baggies over our feet because otherwise our socks would get wet. My mother is a psychologist and wasn't big on sports. She just made sure that I was home before the streetlights came on. I never heard those words "Stay in the house." It was, "Be home before the lights come on." Now things are so different. Everything today is a playdate. Like, "What time should we meet on Thursday?" Really? Everything we did, we did on our own.

I never had the sense that we lived in small apartments. That's how everybody lived. I didn't have to worry about the "Joneses" because everybody in my neighborhood was the same as everyone else. We were all in the same situation. I had friends who had houses, and we had an apartment. I'm not going to say it was as luxurious as some of the apartments in the city, but it was home. This is something I can share with my kids now. "Why do you think you're cramped? Why are you complaining about being cramped?" We were four kids in our apartment. Two sisters and two boys. Fraternal twins and my little brother.

My dad was an electrician and would do little things to motivate me. For instance, I never really had jobs as a kid, but sometimes I would go to work with him and do odd jobs with him. We were somewhere in the South Bronx and the buildings needed an electrician because the wires were frayed. He'd diagnose a problem and try to find the live feeds and the negative feeds. So he's on the ladder, you know, and suddenly he gets shocked. He falls down from the ladder and doesn't say anything to me. He's okay and he climbs back up the ladder, finishes the job, and looks down at me and says, "Is this what you want to do for a living?"

He was telling me to go after what I believed I wanted for myself, but to also finish the job first. I couldn't ask for more than that, especially because my mom wanted me to go into the medical field. At the time I guess they were looking for male nurses and stuff like that. She was pushing me in that direction. They needed big guys to pull the gurneys around, and if anybody got unruly they needed someone stronger to hold them. But my dad would give me little words of encouragement, like he did on the ladder. I probably would've followed in his footsteps, but he wanted me to do my own thing. Me—*I like this baseball stuff.*

As I said, my friends and I, we were sports nuts. One time eight of us were gathered together at eight-thirty in the morning because we were going to another neighborhood for a basketball game in a gym there. There was this bizarre moment. *What the hell is going on?* This guy was chasing another guy with a pistol in his hand. It was a blur and we all just stood there in amazement. He was running after this guy and he missed on every shot. It was a shock to see something like that but it didn't deter us from our game.

Little League kept me busy. Which is not to say that other kids didn't have arts and music, but I didn't. Would it have been ideal if someone introduced me to art or something like that? Yeah, it would've been great. I play golf now, and say I wish that someone would've gotten that glove into my hand sooner. I just say that 'cause I'd be a better golfer, but I don't think it would've changed anything. Maybe one thing I wished I would've gotten into my hand—but it's more of a wish than something real—was an instrument. To play an instrument, that would've been a cool thing to do. To play the drums or a six-string guitar or something is a good way to unwind when you have a stressful day, instead of going to bars with your buddies. That can't lead to anything good. But would I change? Absolutely not.

I had such a love for my dad, it's indescribable. He died at sixty-three almost ten years ago. It was a big loss. My parents got divorced when I was very young but you'd never know that my parents were divorced because I saw my dad every day.

As things started to happen for me, he had an interesting take on fame. I was playing in a game in Boston, in Fenway Park, and he said after the game, "Listen, I don't want you taking this shit too seriously." "What's wrong, Dad?" He says, "They're all boo-ing you and everything"—I was not on the home team—"but you know what? I want to see you smiling a bit when you're out in the field. You're getting a chance to do what you wanna do, which is phenomenal. Not many people can say that. You're actually doing what you love to do. I wanna see you smiling. You should show people how much you appreciate what you have." He played such a big part in my life. He was truly a wonderful man with a great take on things.

SOTERO ("BG 183") ORTIZ
(1963–)
WILFREDO ("BIO") FELICIANO
(1966–)
HECTOR ("NICER") NAZARIO
(1967–)

Members of Tats Cru, graffiti artists

Nicer: In my family, I'm the first generation born here in the United States. That's how I'm from the Bronx. My family came over from Puerto Rico. My mother came over when she was fourteen in 1950-something. They didn't speak much English, so when I was learning English, like in kindergarten, first grade, second grade, my mother and other relatives hovered over my homework books. They were learning English as I was learning it. So it was, like, a group session.

We didn't think we were poor because we had everything we

needed right there on the block. You had your friends, you had your family. I also had grandparents who lived two blocks over. And I had great-aunts and great-uncles there too. Doors were never locked. I would go over to a neighbor's house and open the front door and say, "Is José here?" Every tenement building was like its own little community. A little city within a city.

My mother also went to school to learn English. You know, she always struggled with having that real strong accent. It was very funny. It took me many years to figure out that the Yankees didn't start with a J.

BG 183: I remember lunch hour when I was in second and third grade. Everybody was fighting. The teacher had no control over the kids. Kids just kicking and girls getting their hair pulled. It was like chaos. During that time you had the era of the karate movies so everyone's trying to kick, trying to imitate Bruce Lee. It was a real crazy time. But at the same time, you know, I enjoyed it. It was my exercise for the day.

Bio: We all grew up in different areas. I grew up in the Bronx River projects on 174th Street. We'd play mostly in the buildings. We'd go to the top of the elevators and jump from one elevator to the other elevator.

We were just kids. We're running free in the streets. So we would get creative, and these were our games. As one elevator was passing, we would jump from one to the other.

What you would do is, as soon as the elevator would pass a floor going down, you could see it through this little window on the door. You would jimmy the door and it would automatically stop, once that door was opened. And then you'd be able to get on top. When the door closes it begins to move again. Remember we had nothing but time, so we played in the building.

Nicer: We had to be more creative from having less available to us.

Bio: We'd get off the same way. As the elevator was passing by the door, there's a little latch you could push, and the door would open from the inside. But there were some of them where you would get shocked. Like if you touched the wrong spot, you'd get like a small shock. Those were part of our games.

I once also fell out of a window, playing in an abandoned building. I was on the second floor when I grabbed a window. The window gave way but the garbage below was piled up so high, when I landed, that's what saved me. That was just part of the day. Playing in abandoned buildings is what everyone did. I used to come home . . .

BG 183: With a nail through the sneakers!

Nicer: Yeah. Nail through your sneakers. 'Cause we had either PF Flyers or a pair of Pro-Keds, and the rubber soles would wear out. If you had a hole, you'd put a piece of cardboard in there. But the thing was, everyone always stepped on nails. There were always these abandoned buildings, so you'd step on pieces of wood with nails that were rusted.

Bio: We never went to get any tetanus shots. We had the ghetto treatment. Your mother would put some purple stuff on you, and she'd be like, "You'll be okay. if you just stop jumping in the buildings."

Nicer: Or she'd wash it and put alcohol on it.

BG 183: My mom had this remedy from Puerto Rico. After stabbing myself a couple of times with rusty nails, I already knew what to do. My mom said the first thing to do is to take out the blood. Start squeezing the blood out. Then I'd go home and my mom would put garlic on the wound and then a Band-Aid. That was the only remedy she had.

Abandoned buildings were like our playgrounds. You got to remember, this is what it boils down to. You're born with this creative energy of wanting to play. We used creativity back then as opposed to the kids nowadays. We would find stuff and make things.

Nicer: You'd find a round rock that was smooth enough that you can create a game with it. You get as creative as you can because of the things that are set around. That's why they were able to invent, like, jumping up on the elevators.

We saw a lot of families displaced during the times when the buildings burned. All of a sudden when the building went they were gone.

BG 183: There was a time that the building I was living in actually started burning. But a lot of people didn't move out because we still had lights that worked. The only thing, in the winter, you didn't have oil. There was no landlord to take care of things, so because there were lights you could live there for a while. Just in the wintertime you suffered. My mom would put up the stove every night. We slept in one room because it was much warmer to stay together as one unit. But for me, it was like, "Hey, it's cold!"

But at night I would see these abandoned buildings burning, burning, burning. That was my entertainment of the night. Then, the next day, you'd hear like five firefighters got hurt and two got killed, but I didn't know what was really going on. For me, it was like, "Look at this fire."

Nicer: Probably it was the late seventies, we would be moving a lot. A few years later, I asked my mother, once I became an adult, "Why did we move so much?" She said, "Because after a while once the landlords would disappear and no one was putting heat in the building and there was no one for us to pay rent to, then there was panic in the building." We had family in the neighborhood and they would be like, listen, come over here and we'll get you an apartment.

When there weren't landlords, there was panic. Like, since the landlord stopped coming around to get the rent, that means this building might be next to burn. So let's prepare ourselves. Let's get out of here. There was a lot going on, but as kids we didn't worry. As a parent you always make it safe for your kids, provide the best shelter you can for them.

We lived in the Bronx all our lives, except for probably about eight months. My mother finally got a nice gig in some office downtown, big raise, starting to manage an office. "I'm going to move out of the Bronx and bring my kids to a safer neighborhood. I'm moving to Jamaica, Queens." So we move out of the Bronx. I'm like, "Out of the Bronx? Are you crazy?! Our grandmother's here. Our other relatives are here."

We were going to move to a better neighborhood, where there were trees. It was like what you see on TV, nice little houses with trees. So I finished out that first year in the Queens junior high school, like in seventh grade or something, and six months into living there they break into our apartment. They rob all the money we had for our rent, our bills, like the television. They rob us! I come home from school and I see my door in half, 'cause they kicked our door in. Right after that, around eight months after we got there, we were back on the train moving back to the Bronx. Coming back to where it was safer. It was funny, 'cause I remember going to school in Queens and people were like, "Where you guys from before?"

"Yeah, I grew up in the Bronx."

"Oh, the Bronx is dangerous."

You hear all this stuff. Oh, get out of here. And we move to this so-called fancy neighborhood and we get robbed.

In all that traveling on the subway from Queens to the Bronx on weekends to be with our family, and back again from the Bronx to Queens, I started realizing that a lot of stuff was being painted on the trains. My curiosity was piqued. As a kid, I was always interested in art. I was always sketching and drawing and tracing. So all those train rides really opened me up to a lot of stuff that was going on, which started me asking around: "Who's doing that? How do you do that? Who does this?"

Bio: We all met in art classes when we were in high school. As a kid, I would always try to re-create the *Beetle Bailey* comics, the Sunday comics. And I was, like, playing with letters. In the fourth grade, a teacher gives us an assignment to do a project with our initials, to create a logo with our initials. I did it and kind of enjoyed that exercise with my letters. From then on, I always had a notebook where I would sketch my name and sketch comics.

BG 183: When I fell into art, I was really young, like four years old. I remember seeing my sister drawing, so I went to my room and started sketching. When she noticed me, I tried to hide it. She saw what I was doing. "It looks good. I like it. Keep it up." When she said that to me, from then on I just kept drawing. For Christmas, instead of getting a toy, my mom would bring like a painting set or crayon books. So that was my introduction to art. And I just kept on from there. I learned what I could: drawing, finger painting, charcoal, anything that was related to art I got into. The one thing I was never taught in school was graffiti. That was something you had to learn from the outside.

Bio: Once when I was coming from downtown and getting off the subway car, when the doors closed, I saw these huge top-to-bottom cartoon characters on the outside of the train. So I was like, "Whoa! I like this. I want to do that." I went back to my neighborhood and started asking questions: "I saw this stuff on the train. What was it? Oh, that's graffiti?" You got to learn. You got to get up. I didn't know about any of that. When you first start out, you are considered a "toy." So nobody really deals with a toy. So you hang out with other toys who are maybe a little more than you, or maybe nothing at all. Then you continue, you start learning how to go to the trains, where they laid up at night, the schedules. And then you realize, "All right, I don't have paint." So then you got to go stealing paint. And it's been thirty-one years since.

We would travel to get our paint because in our neighborhoods we were already coming in late in the game. Writers from the seventies, they had already "killed"—what they called "burnt"—all the spots where you could steal paint. "Burnt" means you couldn't go in and steal. The stuff was either in cages or locked up. So you'd have to travel far. You'd have to go to Queens or Jersey or different areas that weren't as hip to the graffiti game where they would still leave the spray paint out right on the shelf.

Nicer: Most of that was done in the winter, when we had these huge down jackets. You'd get the bubble jackets from Alexander's department store. Then you'd set up a system. You'd learn it from other graffiti artists. Asking around.

Bio: Wear a long shirt tucked into your pants and leave an opening so you could then push the cans in.

Nicer: There were so many different ways. But you start getting creative here. Remember, we didn't come from families that kind of embraced this art form. Or any art form, or had any extra money to buy you supplies. We believed in it and wanted to participate in it so much that we would risk even being incarcerated.

BG 183: And for us, we didn't even see it as being like shoplifters. It was just part of that culture.

Nicer: That's what you had to do.

Bio: Obviously paint is expensive. We needed hundreds of cans. So you'd spend the whole day doing that. And hopefully by the end of the day you'd have twenty, thirty cans. Same thing with markers, to draw. We would go to Pearl Paint, which was like one of the biggest contributors to graffiti art.

Nicer: You'd go in and steal the markers, the designer markers.

BG 183: It was like getting out. You had drugs going on. You had the gangs during that time. Everyone was doing their thing. So you became a graffiti artist. People were going to clubs, like hanging out on a Friday, dressing up, going to jams, but we dressed all dirty on Fridays going into the subway. That was our mission. Our thing was subways. We didn't notice that people didn't like it. It got our name out there for other people to see it.

Nicer: When you got your name out there you became a ghetto superstar. It's a very competitive art form, so you're always trying to outdo what someone else did. We basically did it for the attention of each other. But the way a person takes a tag, it's a form of calligraphy, but brought into modern times, two or three hundred times forward. It's a stylized writing and it has a certain movement and certain flow that someone that's into the art of calligraphy can appreciate. Like even the name we painted and the colors we used, they gave birth to a lot of the culture of design nowadays. It's kind of like the guideline or introduction to a lot of designs.

The best part since we're from the Bronx? So the thing was, we would paint this train, a number 6 train in Pelham Bay Park in the Bronx. And our paintings would roll through the Bronx into Manhattan, all the way through Manhattan and end up in Brooklyn. And then all through Brooklyn graffiti artists there would see it. And all through Manhattan graffiti writers would see it. So, in a way, it was our communication to other graffiti artists, throughout the city. It was like how Indians used to use smoke signals to kind of send a signal to say they were existing. It was our way of having this rolling gallery of our work go to the other boroughs. Then we'd also see what others were doing on their end. It was competitive.

BG 183: That's why I think that people born and raised in the Bronx come out, you know, being good. Because there's always a competition going on. That's why I think we became real good artists after a while. Because of the competition, we wanted to be good.

Nicer: Those creative juices we have are like the eight-year-olds running around playing street games and being creative. That carried into our teenage years where still, though you didn't have much, the energy came out in music, in fashion, and in what we were painting.

A lot of people see graffiti as a crime, but considering where we come from and what we were around? A lot of friends are sitting in jail right now, doing thirty years, life. A lot of them went on to become armed robbers, murderers, contract killers, stuff like that.

Bio: We were doing graffiti and although it was a crime we didn't see it as a crime, and it kind of kept us away from what was going on. Like, this guy's going to rob a bank. I'm going to go steal spray paint to go paint a train.

MAJORA CARTER

Urban environmentalist, strategist, MacArthur
"Genius" grant recipient

(1966–)

My parents were both from down South. Neither of them finished high school, or even went, to tell you the truth. There was always this understanding, though, mostly from my mother, that I would get a good education. I was the youngest of ten kids, and I think she saw something in me. It's not clear to me what that was, but I had a level of creativity that she nurtured as best she could.

When I was little, there weren't that many educational TV shows, but there were some. They would repeat them during the day. It didn't matter what time of day it was. If Majora wanted to watch, if it was *Sesame Street* or *Mr. Rogers'* or *ZOOM* or any of those shows, everything stopped and Channel 13 was turned on for me. My siblings hated me for it. It was like maybe there was a lesson I didn't get so I had to watch again. My mother's like, *Majora's got to watch* Sesame Street—*sorry!* To this day, my brothers and sisters talk about it and this was nearly forty years ago. *So you're going to watch* Sesame Street? *You know how much we hated you?*

At the age of seven, I knew that I wanted to get out of the neighborhood and school was the way out. I was reading on a twelfth-grade level when I was in the third or fourth grade. I knew I was smart. *Well, I'm smart enough to get out of here. I know I can go to a good high school and I'm gonna go to a good college and I'm never gonna look back.* And my goal at that time was to be a neurosurgeon.

My parents had each been married twice before. There were six kids at home, including me. That's a lot of kids! In junior high school, I knew that I wanted to go to Bronx High School of Science. My teachers at Intermediate School 74 worked with a bunch of us, tutoring us. We weren't at all prepared otherwise. Our school was definitely not up to par, so there were about ten or twelve of us who got tutored. Two of us got in. Eric Nuñoz and I.

There were drugs in the neighborhood. I didn't do drugs because my mother would've killed me. Actually, this is what people don't quite understand. I didn't really try pot until I had gone out with white people. They were like, "Really?" I mean, I totally faked it. We pretended, but we didn't really inhale. It also didn't occur to me to have sex early. Again, that was something that more of my white friends were doing than almost any of my black and Latino friends in high school. And the drinking? It never occurred to me to drink like that before high school.

So I'm in Bronx High School of Science, and I've never seen so many white people in my life. *Wow, they're everywhere!* We had only one white kid in my junior high. All the rest were either

Hispanics or African Americans. So there I was in a school with about three thousand kids, and everything about it was miserable for me. At the time there were three kids from the neighborhood in addition to me who were going there. It was hard because it was really intimidating. I was smart, but I was in with kids—not even kids who went to private school—but kids who went to decent public schools in the city, and I was so far behind in my first year that I almost failed everything. Like, I was really bad at grammar. I actually said "aks," A-K-S, instead of "ask." I was shocked when finally someone told me that's not how you say it. I was like, *Really?* Am I saying everything else completely backward too? I made it clear to my teachers that I didn't want to fail. I was like, *Okay—let's make it happen.* I got back on track.

I also found out about a program run by this amazing, very wealthy woman named Alice Miller. She lived on Park Avenue and she basically paid for this program for inner-city kids interested in science to learn about medicine, by spending Saturdays at either Albert Einstein or Mount Sinai Hospitals.

I took a bunch of classes. That's how I spent Saturdays for the first two years of Bronx Science. I got a chance to examine babies' hearts for different kinds of heart disease. We dissected everything on the planet and we literally got to sit in on autopsies with cadavers. I am so grateful for that experience in a big way. And then something happened. I don't know exactly when it switched, but I realized that I didn't want to do that anymore. I actually wanted to be an actress. Which was really bizarre, considering I was shy.

I just fell in love with movies and I said, *I can do that,* and I *want* to do that. So I went to see Alice Miller at her Park Avenue apartment. We sat and had a wonderful lunch, or maybe it was tea. I told her that I didn't want to be part of the program anymore. She asked, "So what do you want to do?" "I want to act." She said, "Okay. Do you still want to go to college?" Of course I still wanted to go to college. She asked me which one. I didn't know, although

I was thinking about Carnegie Mellon and Purchase. She said, "How about Wesleyan? I know the financial aid officer. Maybe you should think about Wesleyan. You'd love it and it's not too far away."

So I applied early decision. I got a call from the financial officer at Wesleyan, saying that they got my application, my essays, but that they didn't have any of the records from my school. I'm like, "What do you mean you don't have anything from my school? They knew I was applying." "We don't have it." They had nothing from Bronx High School of Science. I had this guidance counselor who was a hateful woman. I would hand her all my stuff and she would kinda sneer. So my father and my sister went to school to see her. *What's goin' on?* She basically said that of course she had submitted everything. "We've spoken to the financial officer. He said that Wesleyan had everything except what you were responsible for." The counselor looked around, the papers appeared, and then my father and sister got them to Wesleyan. That's where I ended up going.

CARLOS J. SERRANO

Playwright, poet, and theatrical producer

(1970–)

My GRANDPARENTS LIVED DOWNSTAIRS FROM US IN OUR APART-
ment building. Whenever they needed something or we wanted
to communicate with them, instead of us calling each other, we'd
hit the radiator—a steam pipe—with a spoon. The steam pipe went
from the top of the building all the way down, so my grandparents,
who were directly under us, would answer, *Ding-ding-ding. Ding-
ding-ding.* We might just be asking them, *Are you downstairs?*
Then we basically just invited ourselves there.

My mom worked at the Woolworth's store on 163rd Street on

Southern Boulevard for at least the first five or six years of my life, so my grandparents were our babysitters during that time. They were also the people we went to if we wanted to get away from our parents. We were individually happy, but you had to deal with a lot of domestic arguments, like, *Oh, no. Dad's drunk. It's the weekend.* Or *Dad's drunk again so let's go downstairs and get away from that.* Or, you know, when my mother was in the middle of a personal hurricane, *Let's get away. Let's just go downstairs and hide.*

My dad would get hired on the weekends to deejay a party or to go to some party, but he'd also drink and get really drunk. So my mother had to go out there, find him, and bring him back to the house safely. That led to another set of arguments, which weren't out of the ordinary, 'cause you heard arguments in the neighborhood in one way or another. I mean, the arguments in our house weren't violent, but they were screaming matches with my mother always threatening to leave. That's the thing, at least in a Puerto Rican household. "You know, one day I'm not going to be here." And that's what she would tell everybody. "I'm not going to be here. You guys take me for granted, I'm going to go. I'm going to go to Puerto Rico and you'll never find me." Once when I was a teenager, when it was just me and her alone with her screaming that, and I said, "Why don't you leave?" She had no answer. No one had ever asked her that before. She had absolutely no answer.

People say that I look a little bit like my father, which kind of takes me aback. I don't see myself that way, but then I see pictures of him and I see pictures of myself, and I do. Or I hear my voice. I hear how my voice is when I'm yelling. It's the pattern, the voice pattern when he's yelling in Spanish about why everyone is taking money from him. Money was always the basis of the arguments. *Why do you need money for that? Why is everybody taking from me?* That's always the thing about Latino parents, or maybe just Puerto Rican parents. They're always wondering why someone needs this or that. *Why they need money, why they need* me? *They're taking me for granted.*

We weren't poor, or maybe we were as about middle class as a blue-collar family can be with one working parent. I guess when I look back, we took whatever we could ask for, and they did provide. For me, when I was growing up, a lot of examples of what a domestic family should be like I got from watching reruns of *The Brady Bunch* and *The Dick Van Dyke Show*. These shows got me wanting something better.

In the South Bronx, where we lived, there were gangs and there was a drug situation. My mom used to hate it when I would go downstairs to play with friends. I felt like I was never in any danger until I was a teenager and understood what those dangers were. But even then, it was like I knew how to take care of myself. But my mom would catch me downstairs and then hit me all the way up. So I tried to figure out how to get out without her knowing. I never had keys to the apartment, so I would just lock the door, go down through the fire escape, and come back up through the fire escape.

My mother was afraid that I'd be recruited for a gang or something. What I did downstairs was play stickball and stoopball. Nothing dangerous. But she never really understood. When I was a teenager she never liked my friends. To me, they were just the neighborhood friends. Everybody had a particular role and characteristic. There was the guy who was the womanizer and would just joke around. And then there was this guy, Julio, who was probably the guy who would get into trouble because he looked like he would joke way too far. It would pass that boundary, and then he'd end up being in a fight. One day the boundary that he crossed was with me and I kind of fought him, but the next day it was like, "Hey, how ya doin'?" That was also the time when there were still those vacant lots and burned-down buildings, so we played in the rubble. As I said, my mother never really understood.

I think I always had a moral compass. I understood right away what was bad and what was good. I saw people being beat up by gangs or getting hurt, and I heard stories of this person who got shot or that person who got thrown in jail. And I could see what people looked like when they were high on cocaine or other stuff. I also had a view of the neighborhood characters through my window and could see how they could get, and I saw my father when he was drunk, in his wobbly stupor. It just never appealed to me.

My mother took us to church as kids. I was baptized late . . . when I was four . . . but I never did like church. My mom used to beat me to go to church when beating was the in thing to do. Nowadays, it's like, "How can you treat your child like that?" But she'd say to me, "The reason I'm doing this is because I don't want you ending up like them," meaning the guys on the streets. And I always felt, like, *I'm not!*

My mom was also into Santeria and she took me to her Santeria groups. There's always this one leader of the group who would sit in the center and preach to everybody. I think at some point he would hold people's heads and just shake them, I guess to get the bad spirits away from them. And people would go, "Viva Chango." The God, Chango, is the head guy in Santeria. There are also a bunch of saints. There's a learning thing there. Chango was just a flawed guy and when he became a God he took advantage of his position, so he had to learn the lesson that responsibility comes with power. I think that's the whole learning thing about that God and the whole Santeria, that mistakes happen when you're younger and that there are consequences to your actions. That Spider-Man credo. *What comes with great power comes with great responsibility.*

I always felt myself different from everybody else. I think I was drawn into theater and the arts very early. I was the quietest of my three siblings, so I observed a lot and I watched a lot and I saw a lot. I'm fascinated with how people act and what people do. There was a PBS presentation of *The Elephant Man*. It was a stage presentation that was on TV and the actor that played the Elephant Man didn't have makeup on. I remember asking why that was, and my sister explained to me, "I think it's because everybody has a different perception of what ugly is." So to have a fixed idea of what ugly is would give you only one point of view, but to have to imagine . . . For some reason, that stuck with me. So I started writing when I was thirteen because on those days that I couldn't get away from my mom, or couldn't figure out that escape, I wrote. I imagined stories. I imagined these adventures that I wanted to have, but couldn't, or imagined adventures that I thought adults had, like looking for treasure or fighting a bad enemy. In seventh grade, one of my teachers said about something I had written, "We should produce it in front of the whole school," and that was a big deal for me, you know, to have people laugh and enjoying themselves, and to have teachers saying, "You really did a good job." Writing was an arena I felt really comfortable in. One where I thrived.

After high school I ended up at Brooklyn College because they had just begun a new creative writing program there. The professor there, Saul Galen, said to me, "Carlos, I know that you're a writer. You should apply to this program." So I did it, just on a whim. Meanwhile, I had gotten a scholarship to Rockford College in Illinois. Then I got a call from Professor Galen. He said that they got my application and that they would like me to come down for an interview. So I went there to see him—he's one of those close talkers, so he's right in your face—"You know, Carlos, I understand that you got accepted to Illinois, and you'd probably be close to Chicago, but for theater, New York is where it's at." I said, "Really?" He said, "Yeah, you should stay here. You should do this program." And that pretty much convinced me because that was the first time that I was seriously encouraged to write. My teachers before that had said to me that I did a good job, or that I should continue because it was a fun thing to do, but this was the first time that it really felt serious. I wanted to write and there was a program for that. And at that same time, I wrote a play about my senior year in high school and it won honorable mention in a citywide contest for young playwrights. It was a sign that I was headed in the right direction, with both the recognition and the encouragement.

RENEE HERNANDEZ

Physician, founder and owner of Tirado Distilleries
in the Bronx

(1973–)

BECOMING A DOCTOR HAS BEEN MY PASSION SINCE THE AGE OF fourteen. Initially, since I loved animals, I wanted to be a vet. Then at a certain point I think it just was easier to learn about one animal than a lot of different animals, so it boiled down to learning about humans. That's how I became an MD. And then it evolved further into serving the people, serving the community, serving the area in which we live. I wanted to create an environment that was very different from what my mother used to go to, which was more like a Medicaid mill. They were just pumping out patients and not really giving them the attention they deserved. I love what I do as a doctor. I would do it for free. It's what I dreamt of since I was young so I'm blessed that I'm living my dream.

As a kid, we lived on Beech Terrace, with relatives living in the same building. I had a couple of aunts living floors above us and a couple of uncles living below us. My father was a chef who worked at the Mary Manning Walsh nursing home on Sixty-Eighth and York Avenue in Manhattan. My mom was a stay-at-home mom until we were a little bit older. Then she worked as a home health aide.

I had been in the gifted program at I.S. 149, the same program as Ruben Diaz Jr. Where I was in the South Bronx, buildings were burning, and there was the crack epidemic, HIV. That was all around me, but basically as a kid in the gifted program I escaped that. One of the things they did in that program was to separate the top ten percent of the students and make them compete with one another so that they pushed one another to their limits. You challenged each other as to who was going to be the best. With that as your background, you knew you could pretty much handle whatever situation was presented out there.

I would say that coming from a loving family that's supportive, that's constantly pushing you to achieve, was especially important. And the church was very important in my life too. You can't do this job of doctoring without being spiritual. You can't do this job without dedicating your work to God—dedicating your work to serving others. If you don't have that foundation it's hard. It's really hard. You can get corrupted. You realize as you get older that money is nice to have but it's not everything.

I went from the junior high school in the Bronx to being a scholarship boarding student at Suffield Academy in Connecticut. Although I was lonely there, I realized how blessed I was. A lot of students there were from privileged homes economically, but their families were really in disarray. I had my very strong family background with a lot of love within the family. And then I got to have that education opportunity at Suffield. It was awesome. Just thirteen students to one teacher. And in Spanish class, there were three students to a teacher. We also had advanced math courses. Suffield gave me the preparation and foundation for college.

In the sixties and seventies, there was a shift in the Hispanic population in New York. That's when a lot of Dominicans came in. It was a new culture for us as Puerto Ricans. There was initially a clash between the two cultures, which I think stems back to the island and the exploitation of each other in Puerto Rico and then continuing in the United States. The Dominican view, which is interesting, is you gotta work. We're gonna work and we're gonna do whatever it takes to make it here. The first generation wants to go back, but by the second and third generations they've already created enough networking to stay here.

I married a Dominican. The cultures are similar in the food that they eat and the music that they hear. The difference is in their identities. For example, Dominicans are very proud of who they are, because they have their own country. Puerto Rico is in between. We really don't know what we are. As an unincorporated territory, we're really part of the United States. That limbo creates a different uncertainty. But the United States is a beautiful country. I love it here. It's the only country that a son of a cook could actually become a doctor. I would die for the United States at any given moment.

I went to visit Puerto Rico with my wife and her father, my Dominican father-in-law. It was his first visit to Puerto Rico. On that trip we ended up going from San Juan to the West Coast. The Mayaguez area, where my parents are from. When we were in San Juan we went to the Bacardi rum factory. I was amazed to see what they did there that transformed the rum industry. It was so simple. They charred the oak barrels. When you do this, you get a charcoal formation along the barrel. The charcoal acts as a filtering agent and it also acts as a coloring agent. Just in doing that, they made the rum a little bit smoother and cleaner. Charcoal is what you get in a Brita water filter. It acts as a filtering agent, so it smoothes it and takes out the impurities. That's when I got the idea for opening up my own distillery.

My background was in organic chemistry at Fordham University and I did a lot of research there. In that research, we used a distillation apparatus. Basically, it's heating up the chemicals, allowing water to cool down the vapors, and collecting the materials at specific boiling points and temperatures. And that's what alcohol distillation is.

Once I saw what Bacardi was doing, I knew that I could do it too. I knew that I could manipulate some of the properties to create my unique flavor and that if everything went well I could probably leave a mark behind in the world that I actually existed. For me, to standardize the process, the process has to start and finish the same time every time. At some point, there are different people that taste it, but I don't. I'm the type of person who does things excessively when I like something, so I prefer to not even place myself in the kind of situation where I may lose control. Therefore I've never touched alcohol. My father likes drinking, so he's one of the tasters and part of the process.

I love what I do as a doctor. I'm serving others. I'm blessed that I'm living my dream, but the distillery is different. Which one do I value more? Definitely saving someone's life. There's nothing better in life than doing that.

RUBEN DIAZ JR.

Politician, Bronx borough president

(1973–)

WHEN I WAS TWO YEARS OLD WE MOVED FROM JACKSON AVENUE in the South Bronx to the Soundview section in the East Bronx. We got out of the projects. My father bought a house that was burned down and literally fixed the house from the ground on up. That's why he got a good price when he bought and that's why we were raised in a one-family house with a backyard sitting on two lots. We were the only guys, my brother and I, who grew up with their biological father. For us there was structure. There was discipline. There were expectations. There was fear! Fear of Dad, right?

Although we moved from the South Bronx to the East Bronx, we still had a strong connection to the South Bronx. My brother and my sister and I were still going to school at P.S. 5, which was on 149th Street in our old neighborhood. Then I was identified as a gifted and talented student, which meant that I went to a special program at P.S. 31, which is on the Grand Concourse. It was almost as if I had two lives. I had my neighborhood friends that I grew up with in the East Bronx, and then the kids I went to school with out of the neighborhood.

At school, there were a bunch of important teachers for me— Mr. Coletti and Mrs. Beckham. Mr. Peloso was my sixth-grade teacher and he's the reason I know:

> *"When shall we three meet again?*
> *In thunder, lightning, or in rain?*
> *When the hurlyburly's done.*
> *When the fight is lost and won . . .*
> *Where the place?*
> *Upon the heath.*
> *There to meet with Macbeth."*

Those are the opening lines of *Macbeth* and I still remember them.

Mr. Coletti is the reason why, although I'm not much of a writer, when I write I don't use the word "but." I use "however" or "on the other hand." Not "but."

And then Mrs. Beckham in middle school—she was the person in social studies class who put American history in chronological order for me. A lot of times, kids study different wars and other historic events and the dates are all chaotic. It's because of her that the chronological order of events is neat in my mind.

I was that normal Bronx kid who sometimes got into trouble. I played a lot of sports, so there were broken windows from hitting baseballs, or throwing baseballs and cracking car windows. We also played in empty lots. Those were our playgrounds. Remember,

I'm speaking from the late seventies all the way to the late eighties. There were people who burned down their buildings for insurance purposes, insurance scams. There was flight. And then you had rubble. The bouncing gym for me was a bunch of mattresses stacked up in an old dirty lot. If you look at movies like *Fort Apache, the Bronx*—if you look at those visuals, those are the lots.

Today on Commonwealth Avenue between Gleason and Watson, there are a bunch of houses. But prior to that it was just a whole street of empty lots. And it was like a jungle. We used to play "manhunt" there. And we got into trouble because our parents didn't know where we were. We would bring canned foods, put on our fatigues and camouflage gear with combat boots. We would take Chef Boyardee and Campbell's soup and we would camp out there and make a fire, put the food in a pot and warm it up as if we were in the military.

I've only lived in five different places in my whole life. All within two-point-eight miles of one another in the Bronx. For me, that's everything. It's the good and the bad. I grew up with a good home life. You know, Mom was the stay-at-home mom. We had good meals. We had the dogs, the yard, everything. But I also grew up, you know, in the late eighties, early nineties, with the crack epidemic. Traveling back and forth to school, having guys I loved—I saw their sensitive and emotional side, but they were not the nicest boys to the rest of the world. Some of them suffered from drug abuse. Some of them suffered from fantasizing about being rich and then took the wrong route to making that money. So you sort of had to come together for protection from everybody else, right? These days we call them gangs. Back in the days, it was "crews" and "blocks." I remember being chased by crews of two, three, or four hundred, without exaggeration. So nowadays, if you see a group of, let's say, twenty guys, that's a lot.

We used to get chased by a few hundred. Hundreds from Bronxdale houses. And let's say, we then teamed up with Bronxdale. But now if you team up with Bronxdale, you've inherited beef with Castle Hill, or you've inherited beef with Bronx River. That was when I was a teenager. And when they chased you, you ran.

Individuals like my father and the world of politics influenced me in a positive way. Being around senior citizens' centers and the programs that my father started influenced me. My mother became an assistant teacher involved with day care. And hanging out with the guys on the block—that influenced me as well. And everything in between. Everything I didn't want to be part of and everything that I wanted to—they all influenced me.

When we hung out in the neighborhood, the store was mecca. There's this sentiment that there's a bad element there. But what people don't realize is that in our communities in the Bronx, the store was a communal place in addition to where you did your grocery shopping.

In the summertime when your parents worked, they had an agreement with the store owner. In Spanish we call it *fiao*. So my parents had a tab going with the store owner. We would get pastrami sandwiches and would get all the drinks, you know, cookies and the quarter order—we'd always call them the quarter order potato chips—and you'd go there and they'd put it on the tab. You get a *fiao*. And at the end of the week, my father would come into the store and say, "Okay, what do I owe you for my kids?" If you went too far, they'd tell you to slow down. You guys are getting too much *fiao* from the corner store.

There was Dona Clara, who used to live on the fifth floor. If she needed help with her groceries, we'd all help her. There came a time when she couldn't come out of her apartment, so whenever she needed something she used a long rope with a big basket. She would tell you what she needed and then put the money in the basket and would lower it. Think of the level of trust there. We were the guys on the corner. There were bad guys there, along with everyone else, so instead of taking the money and running,

Dona Clara, whoever she sees, and I mean, these guys were tough guys but even if she saw Crazy Hector, or whoever, she'd say, "Hey, I need you to . . ." "Okay, lower the thing." If something was a gallon of milk, something she couldn't haul up, then you brought it up to her apartment. It was a good deed, you know. It wasn't done for a tip. Nowadays you get kids who hang out in front of a building. If someone comes in a cab with groceries, you'd be lucky if they even make way for you to go through the door. But not only did we make way, like the whole crew would take all the grocery bags up in one trip. 'Cause there would be six, seven, eight, ten of us. So everybody gets two grocery bags, two other guys open up the doors. Here we go.

I struggle every day with that difference between the kids then and now. All I can say is that something happened in the eighties and nineties and even in the turn of the century where the relationship between parents and their children changed. I mean parents have always been young, but parents weren't always your friend. And then it went from parents trying to be your friend to parents not being around and then just a level of disrespect. That translates to the grandparents too. I don't know if I'm making sense here, but it was like, my mother was not my friend. My father was not my friend. My mother was the police. My father was the police. Not just for me but for all my friends. You know, their mothers were the police. There was a respect that you had. And for the grandparents too. It's almost like young kids now view themselves as equal to adults. The boundaries are blurred. The young folks feel like they don't have to go the extra mile for you. You don't do it for me. If you're talking down on me, I'm going to talk down on you. In my day, Dona Clara could talk down on us all she wanted. That didn't mean that the guys from up the block could talk down on us without having a problem. You know what I mean. But Dona Clara could talk down on us all she wanted.

I think it's all about memories. My first kiss at Rosedale Park, that's where I kissed Krystal. I remember Krystal. You know, when you like somebody, maybe you didn't kiss them but now you're playing freeze tag, now you're teasing them. These are all memories. This is what helps formulate who you are as an adult. This is what I'm trying to provide. Chances for good memories, concerts for young teenagers out in the street. And what I want is for that thirteen- or fourteen-year-old to go to the concert and not to start a fight with another group of guys but maybe even to meet a girl there. To hopefully start a relationship that lasts. My wife, Hilda, and I have been together since we were sixteen. We met each other when we were fourteen. You know, to say, I met your mother when that guy Ruben Diaz used to do concerts—that's a good memory. We met at the concert or we met at a salsa fest at Orchard Beach. Those are good memories.

We fought in my generation, but when you talk to those guys now and you speak of growing up, fighting is not what they talk about. Sure you can pull it out of them if you're around them enough and if you're asking the questions, but that's not who they are now. That's not the first thing they want to put out there.

No matter where you grew up, no matter how bad it was for you, whether it was in the Bronx in the seventies or eighties, or wherever it was, the good memories can overcome the negativity.

JEMINA R. BERNARD

Educator, CEO of ROADS Charter High Schools

(1975–)

I'VE BEEN LIVING IN HARLEM FOR ALMOST FIFTEEN YEARS. I purposely chose the place where I live, 145th Street in the Sugar Hill area, because I can look out my window and see the 145th Street Bridge and, across it, the Bronx.

From my window I can see the building where I grew up, which happens to be the same building where my grandmother and aunt still live. That's at 142nd Street and Brook Avenue, in the heart of the South Bronx. I can even see the public school that I went to, which was P.S. 31. I can also see Lincoln Hospital from my window. I was born there, although I was born in the old building. And then if I turn my head, I can see the new Yankee Stadium and the courthouse. Even though I now live in Harlem, I will never let go of being a Bronx girl—of being a Bronx native.

My memories have been, and still are, of family. My grandparents on my mom's side are both from Puerto Rico. They moved here in the 1950s. My mom went off to boarding school in the ninth grade, but she got pregnant with me at fourteen, and ended up coming home in her junior year. It's tough for me to say that I was a mistake since she gave birth to me, for which I'm so grateful. But I don't think that my mom would be where she is, or I would be where I am, if it weren't for the fact that my grandparents understood the value of family and of being there for you, no matter what. They clearly played a big role in raising me along with continuing to raise her. After coming back home she graduated from Morris High School.

I grew up in a setting where, frankly, I didn't know what the terms "extended" and "immediate" family meant. I grew up with my mom, my grandparents, my mother's brother, and my aunt, who was thirteen when I was born. At various times we also had other family members living with us, family from Puerto Rico or my uncle who came back to New York after being in the marines. He and his wife and kids also lived with us. I grew up thinking that's what family meant. Wasn't everyone's family that way?

We lived in a HUD-owned building. It was low-income housing for sure. It had a lot of bedrooms—maybe five? I could be rewriting history here. It felt like we had a lot of space. Maybe it was closer to three or four bedrooms.

My godmother and her two kids lived on the third floor of the same building. My oldest aunt and her daughter lived on the twelfth floor. Another aunt and cousin lived on the fourteenth floor. My mother and I moved to the sixteenth floor. So while I didn't at that point in my life have any siblings, our family ruled the building.

On any given weekend, you would find me with my cousins Jasmine and Vanessa in one of our apartments. This concept of a lot of family being around was the norm for me. It wasn't until seventh grade, when I was in private school, that this concept of "extended" versus "immediate" family came into play. My classmates at that point lived with their moms, their dads, and their siblings. They referred to their aunts, uncles, and grandparents as extended family. I was like—what are you talking about?

I would not be the person I am today if it weren't for the love and nonstop constant support of my whole family. And frankly, you couldn't even get away with stuff, right? There was this concept of everyone watching you for your own good. But you know what's funny? I was a good girl in a lot of ways. I was the kind of girl who would say to my cousin, "You might want to think twice," or "You know you're gonna get caught."

I'm blessed to know and love my father. He's always been in my life. I love my dad, his wife, and my siblings on that side of my family just as much as I love my South Bronx family. But my grandfather, on my mother's side, was the person who was in my life on a daily basis as I was growing up. He held my hand when Jasmine and I walked to school. Jasmine and I were the same age and so we were in the same classes because we were cousins and not siblings. My grandfather walked us to school every day. He was one of the very few parents who came to school at lunchtime to bring us our own lunch because we were picky eaters and he was afraid that we wouldn't eat the school lunch. He would also pick us up after school. When I started taking the bus to school, he was the one who walked me to the bus stop every morning because my mom had to go to work. She was working in Manhattan at the time. And Pop (grandpa), at that point, wasn't. When I think about eyes watching you—you couldn't get away with a thing.

In second grade it became clear that I was on a different path than the other kids in the class. Mrs. Schwartz was my teacher.

I'll praise her day and night. Mrs. Schwartz put me in my own reading group. I didn't understand it at the time, but over time I began to appreciate what she did because I was reading way above grade level. She had me in my own corner reading books, pushing my own ability to read, while she spent most of her time with everyone else. Everyone saw it, but no one said anything about it. At the end of the day, whether we were in the lunchroom or the library or back in the building where we lived, I was just Jemina. I was just another girl who sometimes was funny and wore funny things the way all kids do or said silly things, so at that point until second grade I definitely didn't feel like an outsider. When I left to go to the Gifted Program in P.S. 31, I started going on a school bus to 149th Street and the Grand Concourse. It was then that I began to realize that even though the kids in my new school were not from my immediate neighborhood, they were all from the Bronx. I began to understand that the Bronx was bigger than just my neighborhood.

By contrast, the kids from where I lived were all black and Latino. My street was largely Puerto Rican. I happen to be half black and half Puerto Rican. My dad is African American, but I grew up in a very Puerto Rican household in a very Puerto Rican neighborhood. I wouldn't even say Latino, because at that point Dominicans lived in Washington Heights.

But when I got to P.S. 31, there was more of a mix, even though it was largely black and Latino. In fifth or sixth grade, a Chinese family moved into the district. It was a big deal in our school because they were the only Chinese there. There was Lee, who was in my class, who also had a younger brother and a sister, Shirley, who I've since connected with, because she ended up going to boarding school with one of my very good friends from Yale. The sixth grade was the first time I got to know people other than those who were black or brown. Also, that was my first time getting to know kids who had to learn how to navigate the system because they didn't know English. In our neighborhood, you could get away with not speaking English, because of the majority of Latinos in the area, but if you were a Chinese immigrant in the South Bronx at that point, it was much harder. It was fascinating to watch the teachers having to figure out how to help the kids learn, even if they didn't speak their language. That was my first experience with real diversity, and it helped shape my life path, I think.

I had no idea until I started working at the Department of Education, years later, that I had grown up in the lowest-performing district in the whole city. You know how that saying goes, "You don't know you're poor until you've seen rich," right? I had no idea. No idea.

I'm looking out the window in my Harlem apartment again. When I think about home and I think about the Bronx, it means so much to me to meet other people who grew up in the Bronx. We have this affinity. I appreciate it.

AMAR RAMASAR

Principal dancer, New York City Ballet

(1981–)

Wʜᴇɴ I ᴡᴀs ᴛᴡᴇʟᴠᴇ, ᴍʏ ᴜɴᴄʟᴇ Dᴀɴɴʏ sʜᴏᴡᴇᴅ ᴍᴇ ᴛᴀᴘᴇs ᴏꜰ ballet dancers and asked if I'd like to do ballet. When I watched the tapes I saw them handling the women and I was like, *Huh? You get to touch them there?* It was quite a shocker. My uncle took me on the subway to the American Ballet School for an audition. They literally put me at the barre, lifted up my leg, played some music, told me to step in time to the music, and they accepted me. When I got in, I was extremely surprised because I had never done a ballet step before that audition. In class, I found out that it wasn't easy. I really struggled, but that struggle fueled my love for dance because I took it on as a challenge.

After starting ballet, I felt different than the other boys on my block and so I actually kept it a secret for a while. When I'd come home and play baseball outside with the kids they'd ask, "Where've you been for the past four hours?" "I've been in Manhattan doing this and that." When I finally told them I was doin' ballet, oh what I got from those guys. They were like, "What? You're wearin' tutus and all that stuff?" "You don't understand. It's the opposite. I get to dance with these women and hold them and touch them and lift them." When I danced in an eighth-grade talent show then they were like, *Wow*. The immediate respect I got was incredible.

Before my lessons, I was just a Bronx kid having a great time enjoying my childhood, an ordinary kid going to P.S. 67, playing on the baseball team and having block parties with everybody. In school, I loved science and was also the citywide champion of the storytelling contest.

I first competed in those contests when I was in fifth grade. I had to memorize a story of not more than three hundred words from any children's book or story that had a message. I won the boroughwide the first year, lost the citywide, but wound up winning the all-citywide in my third year, which was seventh grade. I won with *Why the Sky Is Far Away*. It was a good story with a great message about not being wasteful. That was the beginning of performing for me, to have an audience intrigued with a story by how you communicate. I had no idea it would be so important in my current life.

In our neighborhood there was a definite ethnic mix. There were a lot of Puerto Ricans, a lot of Spanish influences, and a lot of Jamaicans. My mother is Puerto Rican and my father is Indian from Tobago. Our neighborhood was multicultural. The minorities were the majority and I got along with everyone. I always felt at home because I had an even bigger family. My nickname was

Kool-Aid, because I was always smiling. I had the Kool-Aid smile, like in the ads. *Hey, Kool-Aid.*

My parents divorced when I was around twelve or thirteen. My mother was supportive of whatever I wanted to do but my father, on the other hand . . . It was quite difficult for him to accept my choices, because he was a marine, and he himself was brought up in a strict way. I think the crucial issue was that when I applied for high school, my ballet was just starting its fire. I was accepted into Bronx High School of Science and also LaGuardia School for Performing Arts. When I chose LaGuardia, it was a big blow to my father. *What are you doing?* He didn't realize what I could achieve with ballet and he didn't realize how important the arts were either. He backed himself out of my life for a while. There were years when I didn't speak to him, not even on holidays. I basically created my own life without him for several years, working hard on my own without his influence.

While I was dancing as a principal in the New York City Ballet, my father and I got together again and now we can talk as gentlemen. He explained that he was so brokenhearted with the decision about ballet and school that I made, but realized that his actions didn't help in any way.

My mom is so fantastic. Without having any knowledge of the arts at all she just allowed me to follow my path. When I got into the ballet, I called my mother and said, "Mom, I got my contract for the New York City Ballet corps." She said, "Baby, that's fantastic. What does that mean?" She had no idea what it all meant.

There are so few people of color dancing. The roles I've danced, I would never have guessed that I would ever have danced. It may be because I've taken my race out of it. I approached it as an artist, totally believing that a boy from the Bronx could play a prince in the *Nutcracker*—could do the Cavalier and be a classical ballet dancer. That's what I focused on. My background was a plus when I played Bernardo in *West Side Story* with the mambo and salsa, because that's what I grew up with. *Okay!* It was like being in the living room with my momma. I also did *Fancy Free* by Jerome Robbins. It takes place in 1945 in New York City but who would've seen an Indian sailor walking down the street at that time? The New York City Ballet allowed that to happen. You have the style and the character, and you portray him the way you see, from the inside.

I guess I had a lot of confidence growing up. I had great teachers. Great family. I had support. The world was my oyster. I didn't realize that, but I lived it. I felt like I could do anything. Anything and everything.

When I was at the School of American Ballet, though, from the ages of twelve to nineteen, I had a lot of growing up to do. You're given a lot of responsibility on the one hand, but you're given a lot of freedom on the other. They treat you as an adult. So I broke rules by going out and drinking and being with a lot of ladies. Living a free young college life at the age of sixteen. But I learned that if you play hard, you have to work hard. I got married two years ago and I've settled down now.

It makes me feel great to have these memories. Manhattan wasn't home until recently, when I moved there. It was always associated with work and studying, but the Bronx is different. It was, and I think always will be, home, comfort, love.

GABRIELLE SALVATTO

Principal dancer, Dance Theatre of Harlem

(1989–)

I DANCED IN MY FIRST *NUTCRACKER* AT THE BRONX DANCE THE-
atre when I was around six. I was cast as a Brat. The Brats were
the two little girls and one boy in the house who basically tried
to wreck the Nutcracker by throwing things around. It was a
good fit for me since in my own family I was the younger child
who wanted the things that my sister had. As a Brat, I could be
onstage and turn that into something beautiful.

Since the *Nutcracker* was something done in the holiday season, I associated dancing with beauty and magic.

At that same dancing school we also had a teacher with curly hair and a thick accent from the Islands. I thought she was like my secret mom because I thought we looked alike. We did this wild dance with masks on and our hair standing out. It was crazy! I loved the intensity of it—that freedom of movement while running around.

I went to school in Riverdale but our home was near Arthur Avenue in Little Italy of the Bronx. My mother was a teacher in Tarrytown, so I think she found out where the best school district was in the Bronx and that's where my sister and I went.

I got to be part of Eliot Feld's Ballet Tech program from third grade to fifth grade. They would pick up two children from public schools in each borough and bus them to downtown Manhattan. That was the beginning of my formal training, so the dynamic of academic work and going to dance after school—of going into the city from Riverdale—was always very exciting to me. That started the dedication and the serious training for me.

My mother encouraged me to be independent by teaching me how to use the subway. She took me once, showed me where to get off, and said, "You got it." I was just about eleven. She instilled that independence in me but was also cautious. "Stand in the first car. Don't wear your nice headphones on. Don't talk to strangers. Come right home." I was very excited because no one else I knew took the train alone. And then the devastation of 9/11 happened.

It seems so long ago now. I had no fear until then. I was at the Professional Performing Arts School where I had started middle school, on West Forty-Eighth Street in Manhattan. My sister was at Hunter College, which is on East Sixty-Eighth Street. I didn't have a cell phone, but my mother paged me on my beeper to tell me what had happened and what to do. I called my mom from a pay phone and she told me that Tiana, my older sister, would pick me up. There was no way for my parents to get me since they were both working outside the city. My mother insisted that we not go to a subway, not only because most of the trains weren't running but also because she had a fear that the subways might be blown up. So my sister and I started walking home to the Bronx. We walked for about five hours, stopping for food at a Spanish restaurant somewhere in the Nineties, but by the time we got to 125th Street we took the A train to 207th Street and then the bus from there to Fordham Road. I sat on the floor of the bus, because I was exhausted, not only from the walking but also from all the textbooks I had with me since it was the beginning of the school year.

There's a terrible stereotype that the Bronx is not safe. I felt more unsafe in the Lincoln Center area where I went to LaGuardia High School than I did when I went home to the Bronx. Right across the street from our school was the Martin Luther King School, where they had to install metal detectors at the entrance. At LaGuardia there were kids from all the boroughs, kids with pink hair and kids in general who may have looked different. We weren't allowed out for lunch because the school officials thought that the Martin Luther King kids would beat us up.

I also never felt totally at home in Manhattan because there was a contrast of wealth that I wasn't aware of in the Bronx. You would have a beautiful brownstone and then a public housing project. And in the Lincoln Center neighborhood, west of the theaters, it wasn't particularly residential. I was not aware of a sense of community. I went back home to the Bronx on the train and I always felt safe going home.

From the ages of ten to eighteen, I trained at the School of American Ballet, which was a classical ballet company, but not very diverse at all. At the time I think I was the only ethnic dancer in the program. It didn't really affect me particularly until I went to college when people questioned me about how it felt being the only African American there. During that time, I had no idea that being a role model was important because I thought of myself as just a dancer, like everyone else. But later on, going back and forth to the Dance Theatre of Harlem, where I trained in the summer, I met a lot of African American kids. There's a lot more diversity in contemporary dance than there is in ballet. It was then I began realizing that there were very few female African American dancers in ballet and that these dancers didn't have serious role models.

Dance is a great activity and a fun thing for kids to do, but to go further with it you have to be very serious and you have to have someone to look up to. Someone similar to you so that you can see yourself achieving like they have. Aesha Ash was an African American dancer in the New York City Ballet and was the only African American dancer there. She is so beautiful, both physically and mentally, so she was a huge role model for me.

The battle I had between wanting to continue to dance or study academics more seriously was something that I dealt with my whole life, it seems. I honestly wasn't sure if I had the stomach to try to be a professional dancer, so I went to Juilliard, which I thought was the best combination of academics and dance. I continued to dance at Juilliard and proved to myself that I could do it.

I'm biracial, but I was brought up Italian. I loved the food—and the bread. My grandma always made her own sauce. She'd probably not be happy if she were still alive and knew that we've started using jar sauce. I grew up with the importance of cooking and of having meals together. A lot of kids my age at that time didn't eat with their families, but we ate together every night, no matter what. We had home-cooked meals. A lot of pasta. Sausage. The best. Amazing that I didn't get fat.

My grandmother was one of six girls in her family and grew up very Italian, even though she was brought up in America. She both understood Italian and cursed in Italian. She instilled in me a sense of pride because growing up she herself had little but worked very hard her whole life and was proud of that.

My mother's and grandmother's work ethic influenced my sister and me a lot. As soon as we were sixteen both my sister and I were told to get jobs. And we did. My sister worked at the Bronx Zoo and I worked at Darryl's, a clothing boutique on the Upper West Side. Darryl is still a great friend of mine.

I have a strong sense of my Italian heritage, extending even to the Italians not liking the Albanians. In the early 2000s, when my grandmother was still alive, the Albanians started owning and staffing some of the shops in our neighborhood. There was DeLillo's Italian bakery and Palumbo's bakery across the street, which began hiring Albanians as staff. She'd say, "I don't think the pastries are as good. Very Albanian. Go get me a cannoli. Don't go to Palumbo's."

The whole of it, even with the conflict involved, was still very comforting to me. I knew the food. I knew the shops. We had our own public library. Everything I needed was basically in one place and I felt safe. It's also so much cheaper than the city.

I'm in the same private house I grew up in, but now I've taken over the second floor and my mom lives on the first floor. Living there is affordable, even though our neighborhood is changing a little because of Fordham University, which means the cost of housing is going up. Down the block from my house Fordham has taken an entire complex and turned it into dorms. We now have, like, smoothie shops in our neighborhood. We never had smoothie shops in the Bronx. You know, frozen yogurt. Parts of the borough are becoming more trendy—and maybe that's a good thing.

ERIK ZEIDLER

Naturalist, businessman

(1991–)

When I was in middle school I was seen as a bit of a trou-blemaker, doing things against the rules, like finding ways to go outside to look for snakes, and talking when I shouldn't have been. Maybe teachers picked on me a little because of that. My father worked for the Parks Department and there was one teacher who he helped out when a tree fell on her house in a storm. From that point on, things in school changed for me, for the better. I could see that someone was looking out for me. Someone was there smil-ing, saying, "Hey . . ." There was a changed attitude. That teacher would tell others, "Oh, that's Erik. He's okay. You can leave him alone." My father's job not only helped me out in school, it also sparked my early interests.

From the time I was three or four years old, I was interested in snakes and animals and nature in general, so I read books and watched as many movies on those subjects as I could. I was very passionate about them. I didn't have friends that shared my interests but I had friends I'd kind of bring along when I looked for things like giant snakes or snapping turtles or lizards. When I was nine years old, I started going to Pelham Bay Park, which is a surprisingly good place to look for things in the wild. My father would take me there because his coworkers told him about snakes in the area. It's not easy finding them. Where are the nooks and crannies where snakes would hide? It's never a dull moment and always gets your brain going. When there are woods and fields, they're usually teeming with animals if you know how to look for them. My biggest awakening was seeing that a very urban community still had these possibilities.

A few times, my father had mentioned that there were snapping turtles in the Bronx River. I had heard a lot of stories, like, *Oh, we saw a six-foot snake down the street* and this and that, so I was skeptical but I had to go look for myself. In Bronx Park, in the river, I'd go in the water, sometimes wading up to my chest or going under entirely. But I actually did find these snapping turtles. I'm talking about fifty pounds. Three feet from head to tail. Turtles you might find in Africa and South America. What also amazed me about the Bronx River was that it was crystal clear. Unless it had just recently rained, which would muddy it up, it was crystal clear. So beautiful. It was like a secret I had discovered. The whole experience there was like opening presents when you're not sure what the present will be, whether it's going to be something you really want or nothing. Seeing and finding these giant turtles in the river is a present I'll never forget.

When I was at Bronx Science, I did a research project about the turtles, so during that time I actually caught about three hundred and twenty-five individual snapping turtles. I was able to trap each turtle where it lived and give every turtle a number on its shell. I measured them and weighed them and I discovered that there were about seven hundred snapping turtles living in the Bronx. Some discoveries I made were very surprising. The turtles in the Bronx grow larger than the ones upstate. Usually when a pond gets too crowded, turtles leave and go find another pond. Here, in the river, they can't do that. After decades of being in that situation, only the biggest survive. I'd commonly find turtles that were just a few inches shy of the world record. I found some of the densest populations of snapping turtles that were ever recorded anywhere in the world—in the Bronx. I also found that there was a disease that they were getting, that hadn't been recorded anywhere else. Part of their faces were being eaten away by bacteria or very serious diseases. Some of the snapping turtles were able to live to between thirty and fifty years old, which shows how tough these animals are.

After high school, I went to the University of Kansas because that's the place to study reptiles. I only went there for one year, but while I was in Kansas, the Bronx accent stood out tremendously, of course. It was really funny, because I kind of got celebrity status there. Like, people would call their friends. *We got a kid from the Bronx over here.* People wouldn't believe it. I had some call me and put their little brother on the line. *I just want to hear your accent.*

In the final few weeks of being there, I was doing a research project with a professor, who oddly enough also came from the Bronx. During that time, I was bitten in an artery by a rattlesnake, and it turned out that I had developed an allergy to them. There was no antivenom in the local hospital, so they flew me by helicopter to the next biggest hospital, in Kansas City. My heart stopped. I had no pulse. No blood pressure. I had stopped breathing. My professor was there with me, and when I was partially gone I thought I heard his voice saying, *Listen, kids from the Bronx don't die in Kansas.* That brought me back to life. By the time I got to Kansas City, I was in rough shape, but got through it.

In the hospital, I was a celebrity too. Not because I had a rattlesnake bite, but again because I was from the Bronx. Their image was of *Fort Apache.* Their reactions were mixed. Fifty percent trembled and with the other fifty percent there was the *wow* factor. When I got through that experience, it all came together for me. When I was younger, I had thoughts like: "Could I work and live in Australia? Or in Africa?" Everything happens for a reason. I thought of all the natural, unspoiled areas of the Bronx, and I knew that was the most important place for me to be. So I came back.

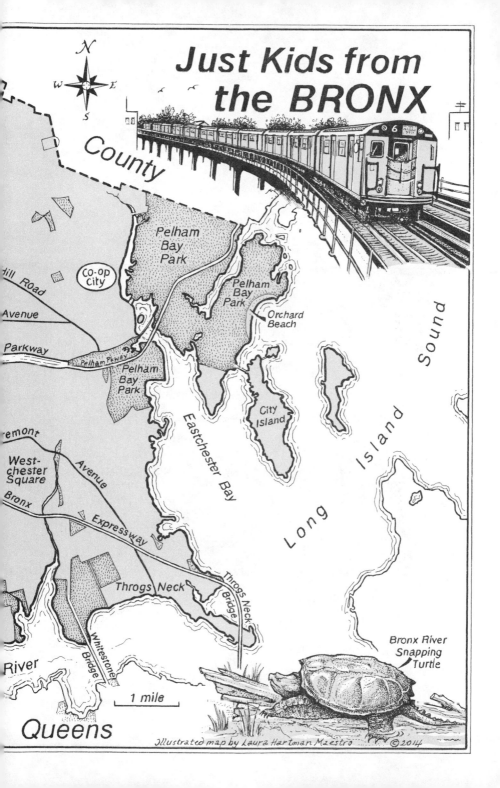

BIOGRAPHIES

Arlene Alda graduated Phi Beta Kappa from Hunter College, received a Fulbright Scholarship, and realized her dream of becoming a professional clarinetist, playing in the Houston Symphony under the baton of Leopold Stokowski. She switched careers when her children were young and became an award-winning photographer and author who has written nineteen books, including *Just Kids from the Bronx*. She is the mother of three daughters and the grandmother of eight. She and her husband, actor Alan Alda, live in New York City and Long Island.

Anonymous found her place in the world of advertising on Madison Avenue. She is now retired, spending time with her beloved dogs, her writing, and work in her community.

Emanuel ("Manny") Azenberg is a theatrical producer who has had seventy-one productions on Broadway. His first producing credit was *The Lion in Winter*, in 1968. He became the producer of Neil Simon's plays in 1972, which include *The Odd Couple*, *The Sunshine Boys*, *Brighton Beach Memoirs*, and *Biloxi Blues*. Additional credits include *Mark Twain Tonight!* and Baz Luhrmann's adaptation of *La Bohème*.

Mr. Azenberg has won twenty Tony and Drama Desk Awards combined. He was elected to the American Theater Hall of Fame in 2009. He received a Lifetime Achievement Tony Award in 2012. He has also taught theater at Duke University for over two decades.

Jemina R. Bernard graduated from Yale University and Columbia Business School, where she received a master's degree in business administration. She was an officer of the Upper Manhattan Empowerment Zone, worked as an adviser to Chancellors Joel Klein and Dennis Wolcott at the New York City Board of Education, and was senior vice president of regional operations for Teach for America.

Since September 2013 she has been the chief executive officer of ROADS Charter High Schools. Ms. Bernard has dedicated her career to having an impact on low-income communities and young people of color.

Roberto Martin Antonio ("Bobby") Bonilla played major league baseball from 1986 to 2001. His teams included the Pittsburgh Pirates, the White Sox, the Mets, the Baltimore Orioles, the Florida Marlins, and the Los Angeles Dodgers. As a free agent and because of a favorable deferred payment contract with the New York Mets, Bonilla became the highest-paid player per year in the history of baseball and the three other major professional sports in the United States.

Martin Bregman is one of the leading producers in the entertainment business. Among the more than two dozen films he's produced are *Serpico* and *Dog Day Afternoon*, which was nominated for six Academy Awards and won an Oscar for Best Original Screenplay. His other films include *The Seduction of Joe Tynan*, *The Four Seasons*, *Scarface*, and *Carlito's Way*.

He currently lives in Manhattan with his wife, the actress Cornelia Sharpe.

Dr. Michael Brescia received his bachelor's degree from Fordham University in 1954 and his medical degree from Georgetown University in 1958. He is cofounder and executive medical director of Calvary Hospital in the Bronx, the only fully accredited acute care specialty hospital providing care for adult advanced cancer patients. He is the coinventor of the Cimino-Brescia fistula, an internationally renowned hemodialysis method that represents a milestone in the field of kidney disease. It is used almost exclusively for artificial kidney therapy. Dr. Brescia has received many awards for his professional work and his service to the community.

Majora Carter is an urban environmentalist and strategist. She graduated from Wesleyan University with a bachelor of arts degree and in 1997 received a master of fine arts degree from New York University.

Ms. Carter served as project director (1997–98) and associate director of community development (1998–2001) for the Point Community Development Corporation, working on youth development and community revitalization in Hunts Point. She founded Sustainable South Bronx in 2001. Ms. Carter received a MacArthur "genius" Grant in 2005, and since 2008 has been president of Majora Carter Group, LLC, a private consulting firm. She was responsible for bringing the Hunts Point Riverside Park into existence. It is the first open waterfront park in the South Bronx in sixty years.

Mark Cash graduated from New York University in 1952, went into the army in 1953, and returned to New York University for his bachelor of law degree, which he received in 1957. He received his master's of law in taxation from NYU in 1963. He practices in New York City, where he does tax law, estate law, and commercial litigation.

Mary Higgins Clark is a worldwide bestselling author, having written thirty suspense novels, one historical novel, a memoir, and two children's books, in addition to being coauthor with her daughter Carol of five holiday suspense novels. Her books have sold more than one hundred million copies in the United States alone. In her memoir, *Kitchen Privileges*, Ms. Clark quotes an old saying, "If you want to be happy for a year, win the lottery. If you want to be happy for life, love what you do. I love being a storyteller."

Ms. Clark has also won many awards for her writing, as well as having received twenty-one honorary doctorates, including one from her alma mater, Fordham University, where she graduated summa cum laude as a philosophy major in 1979.

In 1996 Ms. Clark married John Conheeney, former Merrill Lynch Futures CEO.

Avery Corman is a writer and the author of the novels *Kramer vs. Kramer, Oh, God!, The Old Neighborhood, 50, Prized Possessions*, and *A Perfect Divorce*, among others. The first two were made into movies that have become classics. In line with his passion for basketball and his ties to his old neighborhood, Mr. Corman gifted to the City of New York a restored basketball court in his childhood school yard, which became a catalyst for the creation of the City Parks Foundation, for which he has served as a board member since its inception in 1989.

Kenneth S. Davidson graduated from Colgate University in 1966 and a year later taught ninth-grade English in the New Rochelle public school system.

In 1968 he got his first job on Wall Street at Cowen and Co. and five years later founded Davidson Capital Management Corporation, managing hedge funds for wealthy individuals, endowments, foundations, and retirement funds.

Kenneth Davidson is a founding partner of Aquiline Holdings, LLC, and in 2012 started Balestra Advisors, an investment advisory business.

Mr. Davidson has been a member of both corporate and not-for-profit boards, including the Juilliard School, Bridgehampton Chamber Music Festival, Carnegie Hall, and from 1997 to the present American Friends of the National Gallery/London.

Ruben Diaz Jr., the Bronx borough president, graduated from Lehman College with a degree in political theory. When he was twenty-three, he became the youngest member in the New York State Assembly, where he served seven terms. He is known as a champion for working families in the Bronx, a leading voice against environmental racism and injustice, and an advocate for justice and equality for all.

Dion DiMucci, singer, songwriter, and guitarist, a founding member of Dion and the Belmonts in his early vocal career, is a multiplatinum recording artist, Grammy nominee, and inductee into the Rock 'n Roll Hall of Fame. His hits include "Abraham, Martin and John," "Runaround Sue," and "The Wanderer."

Dr. Mildred S. Dresselhaus, a physicist, graduated from Hunter College with a degree in science, got her master's degree at Radcliffe College, and received her doctorate from the University of Chicago. She became the head of the Materials Science and Engineering department at the Massachusetts Institute of Technology in 1977, a physics professor at MIT in 1983, and institute professor in 1985.

In 2012 Dr. Dresselhaus was awarded the prestigious Kavli Prize for her original work in nanotechnology and carbon molecules. She is also the recipient of the United States National Medal of Science and a corecipient of the Fermi Award.

She still practices the violin and plays chamber music as often as she can.

Millard ("Mickey") S. Drexler attended the City College of New York, got his bachelor's degree from the University of Buffalo, and a master's in business administration from Boston University. He worked for twelve years in New York City department stores before moving on to Ann Taylor, where he was president and CEO from 1980 to 1983. He worked for the Gap, Inc., for eighteen years, serving as president and then CEO. He is currently the chairman and CEO of J.Crew and is often called the "Merchant Prince" and "the man who dressed America."

He is married to Peggy Drexler, a research psychologist and author. They have two children.

Jules Feiffer is a cartoonist, playwright, screenwriter, and children's book author and illustrator who has created more than thirty-five books, plays, and screenplays. He is well known for his long-running editorial cartoons for the *Village Voice*. He was also the first cartoonist commissioned by the *New York Times* to create comic strips for its op-ed page. Mr. Feiffer has won a Pulitzer Prize and a George Polk Award for his cartoons; Obies for his plays; an Academy Award for the animation of his cartoon satire *Munro*; and lifetime achievement awards from the Writers Guild of America and the National Cartoonist Society. He has been honored with major retrospectives at the New-York Historical Society, the Library of Congress, and the School of Visual Arts.

Wilfredo Feliciano ("Bio"): See **Tats Cru**

Leon Fleisher, who lived in the Bronx for a short time, is a renowned pianist and conductor. He made his public debut as a pianist at the age of eight and played with the New York Philharmonic under Pierre Monteux at the age of sixteen. Mr. Fleisher studied with Artur Schnabel and is linked via Schnabel to a teaching tradition that descended directly from Beethoven. Mr. Fleisher received a 2007 Kennedy Center Honors Award and continues to concertize and record. He teaches at the Peabody Conservatory of Music, the Curtis Institute of Music, and the Royal Conservatory of Music in Toronto.

Milton Glaser graduated from Cooper Union and received a Fulbright Scholarship to study at the Academy of Fine Arts in Bologna. He founded Push Pin Studios in 1954 and was a cofounder of *New York* magazine with Clay Felker in 1968. He teamed with Walter Bernard in 1983 to form the publication design firm WBMG.

He has had one-man shows at the Museum of Modern Art in New York and the Georges Pompidou Center in Paris. He designed the "I ♥ NY" logo in 1976, perhaps the most reproduced logo of our time.

In 2004 Mr. Glaser received a National Design Award for Lifetime Achievement from the Cooper Hewitt National Design Museum and, in 2010, the National Medal of the Arts from President Barack Obama. In 1974 he opened Milton Glaser, Inc., and continues his work in the many fields of design.

Grandmaster Melle Mel, born Melvin Glover, is an American hip-hop musician, one of the pioneers of rap, and the leader of the Furious Five. The group produced the song "White Lines (Don't Don't Do It)." The 1983 music video of that song starred the young actor Laurence Fishburne and was directed by then unknown film student Spike Lee. Grandmaster Melle Mel became the first rap artist ever to win a Grammy for Record of the Year after performing a rap on Chaka Khan's hit song "I Feel for You," which introduced hip-hop to the mainstream R&B audience.

Sam Goodman graduated from Kenyon College in 1975 with a bachelor's degree in political science. He received his master's degree in urban-suburban administration in 1995. His master's thesis was on his Grand Concourse community.

When he graduated from Kenyon, Mr. Goodman became a Westport, Connecticut, school bus driver and served on the Westport Democratic Town Committee. From 1981 to 1993 he served as executive director of the Westport Transit District. In 1993 he relocated to the Bronx full-time. Sam Goodman has worked as an urban planner for the Bronx borough president's office since 1995. His family has had ties to the Grand

Concourse since the 1920s. Mr. Goodman conducts tours of his neighborhood. "What I really enjoy is sharing perspectives on my home community in order to inform, enlighten, and inspire those who want to learn about this place and its people."

Joyce Hansen is a writer of children's books that explore African American themes. She has been writing books and stories for more than twenty years. Her first children's book, *The Gift-Giver*, was inspired by her students and her own Bronx childhood. Six of her fifteen books were named Notable Children's Trade Books in the Field of Social Studies and four of her books received the Coretta Scott King Honor Book Award.

Ms. Hansen lives in South Carolina with her husband, Matthew Nelson, and writes full-time.

Daniel ("Danny") Hauben received his degree in fine arts from the School of Visual Arts. Born, raised, and still living in the apartment in the Bronx that his family moved to when he was nine years old, Hauben's focus has been the urban landscape. For more than thirty years he's been painting on location in streets and parks, from windows and rooftops. He is an eight-time recipient of the BRIO Award for Excellence in the Arts from the Bronx Council on the Arts. He recently completed a twenty-two-painting commission for the new North Hall and Library, designed by Robert A.M. Stern, for the Bronx Community College. These panels represent the largest public arts commission since the era of the WPA. His paintings are in public and corporate collections, including the White House, the Library of Congress, the New-York Historical Society, and Harvard University. He currently teaches at the Spitzer School of Architecture at City College and the Riverdale YM/YWHA. He can be seen painting on his show *Art and About* on Bronx.net.

Dr. Renee Hernandez received his premed degree in organic chemistry from Fordham University and his medical degree at the State University of New York at Buffalo. He did his residency with Albert Einstein College of Medicine of Yeshiva University and is board certified in internal medicine. He went back to the Bronx to serve his community, where he has his office and medical practice.

In 2012 Dr. Hernandez created the first legal rum and whiskey distillery in the Bronx since Prohibition.

Steve Janowitz is a retired math teacher who taught at Middle School 118 in the Bronx for thirty-two years. The last ten years of that time he was the school's math staff developer, where he held workshops on new teaching methods.

His second career became that of comedy writer for and with his wife, the actress and comedian Joy Behar. He modestly says, "My comedy writing was not by design. It just evolved. I always tried to make Joy laugh out loud at least once a day. Often I would say things that she thought were funny and they would end up in her act. I never thought of myself as a writer, only someone who liked to make wisecracks. It took a real comedian to pick out what was worth repeating on the stage."

Steve Jordan is a musician, composer, a multiple Grammy Award-winning record producer, and the Emmy Award-winning musical director for the CBS television special *Movies Rock*. In his early career, he played drums for the Saturday Night Live Band and for the Blues Brothers. From 1982 to 1986 he was the founding drummer in The World's Most Dangerous Band on *Late Night with David Letterman*. Mr. Jordan has also worked with Keith Richards and the X-pensive Winos as a composer, producer, and player. Currently, he is a member of the John Mayer Trio, and records and tours with Meegan Voss, his wife, under the band name The Verbs.

Maira Kalman is an artist, illustrator, author, and designer. She is the author and illustrator of thirteen children's books, including those of Max Stravinsky, the poet-dog. She's done covers for *The New Yorker* and created sets for the Mark Morris Dance Group production of *Four Saints in Three Acts*. She has illustrated several books for adults, including *The Principles of Uncertainty*, *And the Pursuit of Happiness*, and *Food Rules*. Ms. Kalman has had shows of her art in the Jewish Museum in New York City and the Skirball Museum in Los Angeles. She is represented by the Julie Saul Gallery in New York.

Michael R. Kay received a bachelor of arts degree in communications from Fordham University but began reporting while still at

Bronx High School of Science and then at Fordham University for WFUV.

He started his professional career with the *New York Post* as a general assignment writer, with sports-specific assignments to basketball, and later received the Yankees beat writing assignment.

Mr. Kay left the *Post* for the *Daily News*, in 1989, still primarily reporting on the Yankees. At that time, Kay also served as the Madison Square Garden Network Yankee reporter and the television play-by-play broadcaster of the New York Yankees.

Dr. Arthur Klein, pediatric cardiologist, is a leader in pediatric medicine. His many appointments, positions, and honors include being a Fellow of the American Academy of Pediatrics and a Fellow in the American College of Cardiology. He has served as the senior vice president of children's services and chief of staff at the Children's Medical Center of the North Shore Long Island Jewish Hospital health care system and is now president of the Mount Sinai Health Network.

Robert Klein is an actor, singer, and stand-up comic. One of his first jobs was as an improviser in the Second City theatrical group in the 1960s. He made his Broadway debut in *The Apple Tree* in 1967. His first comedy album, in 1973, *Child of the Fifties*, was nominated for a Grammy and his second Grammy nomination came for his album *Mind Over Matter*. Robert Klein returned to Broadway in the Neil Simon comedy *They're Playing Our Song*, for which he earned a Tony nomination. Mr. Klein has appeared in such films as *The Owl and the Pussycat* and *The Back-up Plan*. He is the author of *The Amorous Busboy of Decatur Avenue* and has done eight comedy specials for HBO.

Robert F. Levine graduated cum laude from Harvard Law School in 1963. He has practiced law for more than forty years, representing clients in all major areas of the media and entertainment industries. Mr. Levine has a particular expertise in the publishing industry, where he acts as attorney and literary agent for many celebrated authors. He also produced the motion picture *That Championship Season*, based on the Pulitzer Prize–winning play.

Suzanne Braun Levine, writer, editor, and nationally recognized authority on women, families, and the media, was the first editor of *Ms.* magazine (1972–88) and the first woman editor of the *Columbia Journalism Review*. Suzanne Levine was named a *Ms.* "Woman of the Year" in 2004.

She developed and produced the documentary *She's Nobody's Baby: American Women in the 20th Century*, which won a Peabody Award. Ms. Levine reports on the continuing changes in women's lives in her books, on television and radio, at lectures, and on her website. She is the author and editor of numerous books, including *Inventing the Rest of Our Lives*, *Fifty Is the New Fifty*, and *How We Love Now*.

She is married to attorney Robert F. Levine and has two children.

Born in Poland, **Daniel Libeskind** became a U.S. citizen in 1964. His firm Studio Daniel Libeskind has designed cultural, commercial, and residential projects around the world. They include the master plan for the World Trade Center in New York City and the Jewish Museum Berlin. Current projects include Zlota 44, a residential high-rise in Warsaw, and Haeundae Udong Hyundai l'Park, a mixed-use development in Busan, South Korea, which when completed will include the tallest residential building in Asia. Mr. Libeskind has received numerous awards, including the 2001 Hiroshima Art Prize, given to an artist whose work promotes international understanding and peace. It had never before been given to an architect.

Rick Meyerowitz is an artist/illustrator and writer, who over the course of his career has done thousands of illustrations for advertising agencies and magazines. He is also the author of eight books, at last count. He and his friend Maira Kalman created the much talked about *New Yorker* cover "NewYorkistan," which was published in December of 2011. Later that week, the *New York Times* magazine wrote, "When their cover came out, a dark cloud lifted."

Hector Nazario ("Nicer"): See **Tats Cru**

After graduating from Pratt Institute in 1960, **Barbara Nessim** entered the New York Society of Illustrators show, which marked her becoming a professional artist, her childhood ambition. Ms. Nessim was one of the few full-time professional women illustrators working in the United States in the 1960s. She carved a niche for herself in the competitive field of graphic design, doing illustrations for publications such as *Rolling Stone, Time, Ms.,* and *New York.* Her work has been exhibited in museums worldwide, including the Louvre in Paris. Her most recent major show was a fifty-year retrospective at the Victoria and Albert Museum in London in 2013.

Margaret M. O'Brien, S.C., attended the College of Mount St. Vincent during and after her novitiate period, where she majored in English and education. She later earned her master's degree from Columbia University in library science. She has been a teacher, a library media specialist, and a school principal and has overseen the Sisters of Charity mission in hospital care, nursing homes, and hospice. Sister O'Brien's work has taken her from Staten Island to Guatemala, culminating in her current position as treasurer of the Sisters of Charity, New York, where she has helped maintain the focus on the religious and human values in the midst of difficult financial circumstances.

Sotero Ortiz ("BG 183"): See **Tats Cru**

Al Pacino's acting career has spanned more than fifty years and has included plays such as *Does a Tiger Wear a Necktie?* for which he won a Tony Award in 1969. He has starred in many movies, including *The Godfather, Serpico, Dog Day Afternoon,* and *Scent of a Woman.* Mr. Pacino has won all of the major acting awards—Tony, Oscar, Emmy, British Academy Award, and Golden Globe, as well as having been elected the best actor of all time by the British television audience for Channel 4. He has also directed, produced, and starred in *Looking for Richard,* a documentary about William Shakespeare's *Richard III,* and has performed as Shylock in Shakespeare's *The Merchant of Venice* both on Broadway and on film.

Chazz Palminteri is an actor, writer, and director. He wrote and performed in his one-man play *A Bronx Tale,* which led to his acting in the movie of the same name, directed by and costarring Robert De Niro. Mr. Palminteri has appeared in more than fifty films, including *The Usual Suspects* and *Analyze This.* He was nominated for an Academy Award for his portrayal of Cheech in Woody Allen's *Bullets Over Broadway*. He also directed the movie *The Perez Family*, starring Susan Sarandon and Robin Williams. Chazz Palminteri is a member of the Actors Studio in New York City.

Regis Philbin graduated from the University of Notre Dame in 1953, earning a degree in sociology. He is a media personality, actor, and singer, known for hosting talk and game shows since the 1960s. He is most widely known for *Live! with Regis and Kelly* as well as *Who Wants to Be a Millionaire* and *Million Dollar Password*.

Regis has been in front of the camera for some fifty years and is considered a cultural icon in TV broadcasting. He has beaten his own record in the *Guinness Book of World Records* for most hours on camera . . . 16,548.5 hours over the span of his career.

Regis Philbin has recorded four albums of songs. His latest CD is *Regis and Joy, Just You, Just Me*, which was made with his wife, Joy.

Colin Powell graduated from City College of New York (CCNY), earning a bachelor's degree in geology, but found his real calling in the Reserve Officers' Training Corps (ROTC) during that time. He graduated from CCNY with a commission as a second lieutenant in the army. Powell served two tours in Vietnam, earning a total of eleven military decorations, including a Purple Heart, a Bronze Star, and the Legion of Merit.

General Powell earned a master's in business administration from George Washington University in Washington, D.C., in 1972. He is a retired four-star general, former United States secretary of state, national security adviser, commander of the United States Army Forces Command, and chairman of the Joint Chiefs of Staff. He has advised Presidents Ronald Reagan, George H. W. Bush, Bill Clinton, and George W. Bush. He is the founding chairman of America's Promise Alliance, dedicated to improving the lives of children and youth. His many accomplishments also include that of bestselling author of his autobiography, *My American Journey*.

Amar Ramasar, a principal dancer with the New York City Ballet, got his performing start at TADA! Youth Theater, in the musicals *Prop Shop* and *Sleepover*. In 1993 he studied at the School of American Ballet (SAB) as well as the American Ballet Theatre Summer Program and the Rock School of the Pennsylvania Ballet.

Mr. Ramasar became part of the New York City Ballet as an apprentice in 2000 and joined the corps de ballet in 2001. He became a soloist in March 2006, and in October 2009 he was promoted to principal dancer.

I. C. ("Chuck") Rapoport is known for his work as a photojournalist in the 1960s and more recently as a television and film screenwriter. Mr. Rapoport's photography career is notable for his *Life* magazine photo essay on the aftermath of the tragic Aberfan, Wales, mining disaster and for his exclusive photos of the fitness master Joseph Pilates. From 1970 to 2004 he wrote a dozen Movies of the Week for television and worked as a staff writer and producer for *Law & Order*.

Carl Reiner is a writer, actor, director, producer, and comedian. He has performed and written for stage, television, and movies and has also written novels, autobiographies, and children's books. He created *The Dick Van Dyke Show*, in which he was also an actor. He appeared on television with Sid Caesar in the *Admiral Broadway Revue*, which ultimately became *Your Show of Shows*.

His album, with Mel Brooks, *The 2000 Year Old Man*, was a hit comedy record in 1961. In addition to having received many Emmys, he is in the Television Hall of Fame and has won the Mark Twain Prize for American Humor. Most recently he has acted in the movies *Ocean's Eleven*, *Ocean's Twelve*, and *Ocean's Thirteen* and is currently busy writing another memoir.

Jaime ("Jimmy") Rodriguez Jr. is a restaurateur. His Jimmy's Bronx Café (1993–2003) included a three-hundred-seat dining room with an outdoor deck that seated another four hundred people. The Café hosted New York Yankees ballplayers and other celebrities. In 2003, Jimmy was listed in *Crain's New York Business* as one of the Top 100 Minority Business Leaders. He currently owns Jimmy's Don Coqui, in New Rochelle, which he runs with his two daughters, Jaleene and Jewelle. It specializes in authentic Puerto Rican cuisine.

A. M. ("Abe") Rosenthal had a distinguished career of almost sixty years in journalism. He was a Pulitzer Prize–winning foreign correspondent, an associate managing editor, managing editor, and executive editor of the *New York Times*. Of his many achievements, he was most proud of the Presidential Medal of Freedom, the highest civilian award of the United States, which was bestowed on him in 2002 by President George W. Bush.

Joel Arthur Rosenthal, known professionally as **JAR**, graduated from Harvard as an art history and philosophy major in 1966 and soon after moved to Paris, the city he loved. There he wrote scripts for movies, designed tapestries, and worked in the couture world, which he realized was not for him. His interest in jewelry design led to opening his company, JAR, with partner Pierre Jeannet. JAR's designs are known worldwide for their unusual stones, vibrant colors, and remarkable workmanship. His exhibit at New York's Metropolitan Museum of Art, "Jewels by JAR," is the museum's first retrospective of the work of a living designer of jewelry.

Andy Rosenzweig has been a policeman, a detective, and a chief investigator for the Manhattan district attorney. As chief investigator, he solved a double murder that had previously remained unsolved for twenty-five years. That case was the subject of an article for *The New Yorker* and a subsequent book, called *The Cold Case*, written by *New Yorker* staff writer Philip Gourevitch.

Since his retirement from the police force, Andy Rosenzweig has gone on to earn a master's degree in writing. He is currently working on his first novel.

Gabrielle Salvatto began her ballet training at the Dance Theatre of Harlem at age eight. She continued her studies at the School of American Ballet and received her high school diploma from Fiorello H. LaGuardia High School of Music & Art and Performing Arts. She graduated from the Juilliard School with a bachelor of fine arts in dance, where she performed repertoire by Ohad Naharin, Jerome Robbins, Nacho Duato, Eliot Feld, and José Limón. Ms. Salvatto has since danced for Austin McCormick's Company XIV and Sarah Berges Dance. After a year dancing and performing with the Professional Training Program at the Dance Theatre of Harlem, Gabrielle proudly joined the newly formed company in August 2011.

Lawrence Saper is an inventor as well as an entrepreneur. He graduated from the City College of New York in 1949 with a bachelor's degree in electronic engineering. He had worked in that field for fifteen years when he invented the first synchronized heart monitor and founded Datascope. He is the former chairman of the board of directors and chief executive officer at Datascope, where he served in those capacities from 1969 until January 2009. Datascope makes high-tech medical diagnostic equipment. The company went public in 1972. By the mid-1980s it was the market leader in both patient-monitoring equipment and cardiac-assist devices. Its two principal products were intra-aortic balloon pumps and patient monitors. Mr. Saper also started Genisphere, which is a subsidiary of Datascope Corporation.

Julian Schlossberg, movie, theater, and television producer, is also a distributor and teacher of film. During his tenure at the Walter Reade organization, he hosted the radio program *Movie Talk*, which was on the air for nine years.

His stage productions include *Sly Fox*, *The Beauty Queen of Leenane*, and *It Had to Be You*. He was the producer of PBS's American Masters special *Nichols and May: Take Two*, about the comedy team of Mike Nichols and Elaine May. In 1978 Schlossberg left Paramount and went on to establish Castle Hill Productions, a film production and distribution company. Castle Hill has distributed more than five hundred first-run and classic movies to theaters, pay TV, basic cable, home video, TV syndication, and all other motion picture outlets worldwide. It has become one of the largest independent film distribution companies in the world.

Mr. Schlossberg is also a producer's representative for prominent figures such as Dustin Hoffman, Robert Duvall, and Elaine May.

His work in progress *Witnesses to the 20th Century*, a documentary series, examines the major historical events of the twentieth century from the perspectives of some of the prominent people of the time.

Louise Sedotto is currently the principal of P.S. 76, the Bennington School, in the Bronx. She received her undergraduate degree from Iona College and her master's degree from the College of New Rochelle and holds administrative and supervisors degrees from Mercy College.

Ms. Sedotto began her teaching career at Saint Frances de Chantal School in the Throgs Neck section of the Bronx and five years later began teaching at P.S. 26, part of the New York public school system. In 2001 she became the assistant principal in P.S. 76 and in January 2003 she was appointed principal.

P.S. 76 was cited by President George W. Bush as one of the highest-performing schools in the city. A photograph of President Bush, some students, and Principal Sedotto hangs in her office at school.

Carlos J. Serrano, playwright, director, poet, and theatrical producer, graduated with a bachelor of fine arts in creative writing from Brooklyn College in 1993. While there, he won the Irwin Shaw Award in Playwriting and the Grabanier Drama Award. He is a member of the People's Theatre Project's resident playwrights unit and its literary manager. Mr. Serrano's play *The Ortiz Sisters of Mott Haven* was produced at the Puerto Rican Traveling Theatre in 2005 and was featured as the inaugural play for the forty-seventh annual Puerto Rican Theatre Festival in San Juan and Arecibo in 2006. His other playwriting credits include *24 Hours at Tiempo*, *The Day a Mariachi Band Followed Charlie Home*, *Charlie Needs a Shrink*, *The Blues of Daisy Peña*, and *Alter Ego*. He is currently working on the *Nuyorican Circus and Medicine Show*.

George Shapiro graduated from New York University and became an agent at the William Morris Agency in New York, after which he became a personal manager and producer with his partner and friend Howard West. They formed their production company and executive produced the Peabody, Emmy, and Golden Globe award-winning series *Seinfeld*. George Shapiro is the personal manager of Jerry Seinfeld. He has also packaged hit programs such as *The Steve Allen Show*, *That Girl*, starring Marlo Thomas, and *Gomer Pyle*, starring his client Jim Nabors. He also packaged a number of specials for Dick Van Dyke, Mary Tyler Moore, and Carol Channing.

Robert F. X. Sillerman is an entrepreneur whose company, in the past, owned seventy-one radio stations. He is the founder and serves as the chairman and chief executive officer of SFX Entertainment Inc., concert promoters. He was the owner of Elvis Presley's estate and the TV hit

American Idol and was also the major producer of the hit Broadway show *The Producers*. Mr. Sillerman has been the CEO of Viggle Inc., his new company, since June 2012.

Valerie Simpson, songwriter, pianist, and producer, formed the legendary songwriting duo Ashford and Simpson with her husband, Nick Ashford. Together they received ASCAP's highest honor, the Founders Award, in 1996 and were inducted into the Songwriters Hall of Fame in 2002. In January 2007 they accompanied Oprah Winfrey when she opened her Leadership Academy for Girls in South Africa.

At President Barack Obama's 2009 inauguration, Ashford and Simpson rewrote their song "Solid as a Rock" as "Solid as Barack." They dedicated it to the president at his inaugural festivities. Nick Ashford died in a New York City hospital on August 22, 2011, of complications from throat cancer.

Ms. Simpson released a new solo album in June 2012, *Dinosaurs Are Coming Back Again*, that features the last recorded performance of Nina Simone, a second duet with Roberta Flack, and an instrumental version of "Ain't No Mountain High Enough." Ms. Simpson is especially proud of her induction into the Bronx Walk of Fame.

Dava Sobel, a former *New York Times* science reporter, is the author of four highly acclaimed books, including *Galileo's Daughter* and *Longitude*. She is also the coauthor of six books, including *Is Anyone Out There?*, with astronomer Frank Drake. She has received many awards for her contributions to the public awareness of science. Ms. Sobel is currently the Joan Leiman Jacobson Visiting Nonfiction Writer at Smith College in Northampton, Massachusetts.

Sotero ("BG 183") Ortiz, Wilfredo ("Bio") Feliciano, and Hector ("Nicer") Nazario are dedicated graffiti artists and professional muralists. They are three of the original members of their company **Tats Cru: the Mural Kings**. They are known individually and collectively for their many letter styles, complex designs, and explosive use of color. Their work has been featured in many publications, music videos, and documentaries.

They are also known for their memorial murals, dedicated to young victims of violence.

Tats Cru has been part of the artists-in-residence program at MIT and has traveled and lectured all over the world, including England, France, China, Ireland, Italy, and Germany.

Their studio is in the Hunts Point section of the South Bronx.

Neil deGrasse Tyson is an astrophysicist, science communicator, director of the Hayden Planetarium at the Rose Center for Earth and Space in New York City, and a research associate in the department of astrophysics at the American Museum of Natural History. He also has hosted the PBS television series *Nova* and the current Fox series *Cosmos*.

Dr. Tyson majored in physics at Harvard University but was active in wrestling and rowing as well as various dance styles, including jazz, ballet, Afro-Caribbean, and ballroom. He did his graduate work at the University of Texas at Austin, getting a master of arts in astronomy in 1983. Dr. Tyson attended Columbia University and earned a master of philosophy degree in astrophysics in 1989 and a doctor of philosophy degree in astrophysics in 1991. He collaborated with Brian Schmidt, a winner of the 2011 Nobel Prize in Physics, in the study of the measurement of distances to Type II supernovae and the Hubble constant.

Dr. Tyson lives in New York City with his wife, Alice, a physicist, and their two children.

Luis A. Ubiñas graduated magna cum laude from Harvard College, where he was a Truman Scholar. In 1989 he graduated from Harvard Business School with highest honors.

Mr. Ubiñas spent eighteen years at McKinsey and Co. and led McKinsey's media practice on the West Coast, and in 2007 became the president of the Ford Foundation. He stepped down from the Ford Foundation in September 2013.

He serves on the board of trustees of the Collegiate School and the New York Public Library. Luis Ubiñas is also the northwest regional chair for White House Fellows.

He is married to Deborah Tolman and they have two sons, Max and Ben.

Lloyd Ultan is a historian, author, and educator. In 1966 he was named the official Bronx Historian by the Bronx borough president and has served in that position under five consecutive borough presidents. He teaches history at Fairleigh Dickinson University in Teaneck, New Jersey, and at Lehman College in the Bronx.

Mr. Ultan has written ten books, including *The Beautiful Bronx: 1920–1950*, *The Bronx in the Innocent Years: 1890–1925*, and *Bronx Accent*. His latest book is *Blacks in the Colonial Bronx*. He also writes some fifty articles a year for newspapers, magazines, journals, and Internet sites.

Mr. Ultan has lived in the Bronx his whole life and is a devoted advocate, giving walking tours regularly. He is a cofounder of the Bronx County Historical Society journal.

Howard West graduated from Long Island University with a degree in business administration. After serving in the army he joined the William Morris Agency and eventually moved to the Los Angeles office of the agency, where he represented writers, performers, and directors as well as actors. Mr. West specialized in television packaging, bringing together the creative talent and selling the project to the network. The television shows he packaged included *The Glen Campbell Goodtime Hour* and *The Bobby Darin Show*. Howard West is partnered with George Shapiro in the management firm Shapiro/West Productions.

David Yarnell became a lawyer, practiced law for two years, hated it, and ultimately landed a job at radio station WNEW and loved it. He became program director of Channel 5 in New York, and then vice president of RKO General, where he formed a network of independent television stations carrying sports events emanating from Madison Square Garden. Mr. Yarnell later became an independent producer of television shows and documentaries. He lives in Los Angeles with his wife, Toni Howard, a talent agent for ICM.

In June of 2010, while a senior at Bronx High School of Science, **Erik Zeidler** won the American Museum of Natural History Young Naturalist Award for his survey of the snapping turtle population of the Bronx.

After leaving the University of Kansas, Mr. Zeidler formed his own educational company, New York World, which brings exotic animals to schools, camps, fairs, and special events. His mission is to provide creative and innovative ways of exposing the urban children of New York City to nature.

ACKNOWLEDGMENTS

Without the generosity and trust of all the interviewees, *Just Kids from the Bronx* would not exist. My heartfelt, deepest gratitude to them, and especially to Millard ("Mickey") Drexler, whose trip back to our Bronx building inspired my thoughts and ideas. A special thanks to Shirley Lord Rosenthal, for her abiding friendship and generous donation of A. M. ("Abe") Rosenthal's chapter to the book.

Sincerest thanks to Jason Epstein, and to Andrew Blauner, my always receptive, incredibly supportive agent, who brought the book to Steve Rubin at Henry Holt and Co. I couldn't ask for any better publisher than Steve for *Just Kids from the Bronx*. His support has been steadfast and vigorous. And how fortunate I was to have Barbara Jones as my editor at Holt. Her intelligence, understanding, and warmth made her a total joy to work with. And thanks, too, to Joanna Levine, Stella Tan, Maggie Richards, Pat Eisemann, Leslie Brandon, Richard Pracher, Meryl Levavi, and the whole team at Holt; an extraordinary group of dedicated people.

I owe an enormous debt of gratitude and deepest thanks to Jean Chemay, my ever-helpful, smart, willing, and therefore overworked assistant, who always makes my work not only easier, but possible. And thanks to Nico and Grace, who assisted Jean.

Special thanks to dear friends Henry Schleiff, Roger and Ginny Rosenblatt, Carol Kitman, Marlo Thomas, Letty Cottin Pogrebin, and Abigail Pogrebin, who gave of their time with encouragement, professional advice, expertise, and smiles of approval.

And to Holly Block and her always helpful staff at the Bronx Museum of the Arts. Thanks, too, to Nikki Gonzalez, who willingly gave me a teenager's perspective of her current life in the Bronx. And to the wonderful Connie Rosenblum, whose positive comments were unwavering. Her remarks, right on.

Special thanks, too, to Michael Bregman, a friend in need, and to Toni Howard for her personal friendship, caring, and help in locating some of the interviewees.

Thanks to my sister Shirley Rubman, and my niece Beverly and nephew, David, who knew the Bronx intimately for many years after I had left, and whose stories awakened my own. And to my wonderful daughters, Eve, Elizabeth, and Beatrice, always interested in, and encouraging of, my work. And to Jennifer, Bea's partner, an avid listener and questioner.

And deepest gratitude to dear Alan, my spouse, best friend, and confidant, never wavering from his willingness to break the routine by going out for a walk and lunch.

ARLENE ALDA

ABOUT THE AUTHOR

Arlene Alda graduated Phi Beta Kappa from Hunter College, received a Fulbright Scholarship, and realized her dream of becoming a professional clarinetist, playing in the Houston Symphony under the baton of Leopold Stokowski. She switched careers when her children were young and became an award-winning photographer and author who has written nineteen books, including *Just Kids from the Bronx*. She is the mother of three daughters and the grandmother of eight. She and her husband, actor Alan Alda, live in New York City and Long Island.